THE
TEXAS GARDEN RESOURCE
A Guide to Garden Resources Across the State   BOOK

THE
TEXAS GARDEN RESOURCE
A Guide to Garden Resources Across the State BOOK

by

NAN BOOTH SIMPSON
& PATRICIA SCOTT McHARGUE

bright sky press
Houston, TX

bright sky press

2365 Rice Blvd., Suite 202, Houston, Texas 77005
www.brightskypress.com

ISBN 978-1-933979-67-0

10 9 8 7 6 5 4 3 2 1

Library of Congress information on file with publisher.

Book and cover design by Isabel Hernandez and Hina Hussein
Illustrations by Bobbie Beal
Cover photography by Scott Hill

This book is dedicated to the memory of Lady Bird Johnson. More than any other person in the country, she opened our eyes to the inherent beauty of Texas. Her Wildflower Center, now part of The University of Texas, has brought worldwide acclaim to this state. Her untiring efforts will change the way people garden for centuries to come.

Table of Contents

Acknowledgements

We want to especially thank Hilary Smith of Houston, Ann Moore of McAllen and Tim McCloskey of Abilene who helped us locate resources in their respective areas of the state. We are also very grateful to Rue Judd, President of Bright Sky Press, who liked our first book enough to publish our next two books, offering support and encouragement throughout the writing process! We also appreciate the efforts of Big Red Sun, an extraordinary nursery and design firm in Austin, for providing the site and "styling" the furnishings for the cover photo. Another big "thank-you" to photographer Scot Hill, who brought his patience and expertise to the cover photograph and to Bobbie Beal, whose illustrations add immeasurably to the book's charm. We also thank the many friends and family members (including Nan's husband, Gary Harlow), who visited nurseries and offered their own observations.

The Twelve Gardening States of Texas

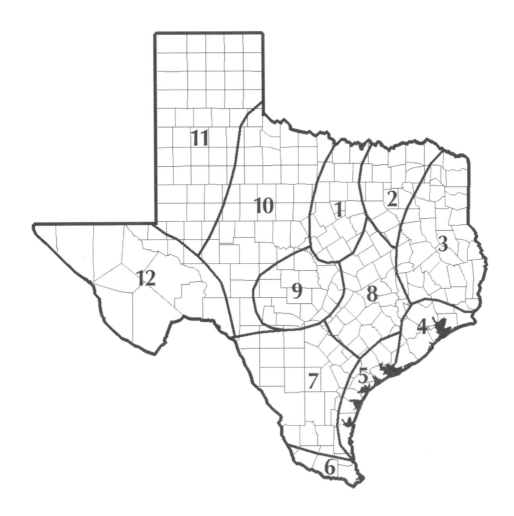

The Twelve Gardening States of Texas

1. Cross Timbers & Grand Prairie
2. Trinity Blacklands
3. Piney Woods
4. Coastal Prairies & Marshes
5. Coastal Bend
6. Valley
7. Rio Grande Plain
8. Central Blacklands & Savannas
9. Hill Country
10. Red Rolling Plains
11. High Plains
12. Trans-Pecos

Introduction

"It is our hope that *Great Garden Sources for Texans* will serve the inexperienced gardener as well as the connoisseur." So began our first book, self-published in 1999, and while our mission has not changed, this edition, published by Bright Sky Press, has been expanded to two books. *The Texas Garden Resource Book*, will introduce you to all of the state's best nurseries and garden furnishings retailers. A companion to this volume, *Texas Gardening for the 21st Century*, will cover sustainable design and maintenance. In it, Nan will share everything she has learned (often the hard way) during her 25 years as a landscape architect specializing in residential design. Its pages contain a wealth of information about designing new gardens, improving existing landscapes and methods for maintaining the finished garden with the least impact on the environment and on the gardener's time and money.

One of the most difficult tasks we faced in writing the original book was deciding how to divide the state into gardening regions. After much deliberation, we based our decision on a combination of factors including major market areas, USDA growing zones, physiographic characteristics, soil types, typical native vegetation and similar ranges of average annual rainfall. Given these factors, we believe that, for the purpose of gardening, there are twelve distinct regions in this vast state.

In organizing this book, Pat and I decided to begin with the Northeast quadrant of the state. Next, we work our way (clockwise) through the regions that border the Gulf Coast. Then we go up through Central Texas and, finally, cover vast West Texas. Within each of these 12 regions there are state parks and nature preserves that provide clues to the plants that "belong" in the area.

A Sense of Place

The state's diversity makes it impossible to simplify a book about Texas gardens. The average annual rainfall ranges from 56 inches in Port Arthur to a mere eight inches in El Paso. Mean minimum January temperatures range from 24° in Amarillo to a mild 51° in Brownsville. When it's time to plant lettuce in Lubbock, it's time to harvest in Houston. A prescription for amending the soil in El Paso would be poor advice for gardeners in Tyler. Considering the different climate zones, vegetation patterns and soil types, we believe that the state can be divided into no less than 12 regions. Even within these regions, you'll find striking variety. The city of San Antonio, for example, occurs at the junction of three regions, so gardeners in its suburban areas must understand their property's soil type before their choosing plant materials.

The one thing all Texas gardens share is intense summer heat. Only the eastern part of the state has an annual average rainfall that exceeds the evaporation caused by heat and drying winds, and even the forested region is subject to occasional droughts. After the months of heat and drought, a "blue norther" may send balmy temperatures plummeting forty degrees in a matter of hours. Then throw in hail, hurricanes and tornados…Gardening here has always required a sense of humor.

GEOLOGICAL HISTORY

Geologically, Texas is fascinating. Its history in rock explains the wide variety of soil types that are found within its borders. Precambrian rocks more than 600 million years old underlie the entire state. These ancient rocks are exposed only in the Llano uplift of the Central Texas Hill Country and in the Davis Mountains. Shallow seas repeatedly covered the state over the eons, depositing sediments that hardened into limestone (the fossil remains of sea creatures), sandstone or shale. Ancient mountains and volcanoes arose only to be weathered and worn down by rivers and streams.

Dinosaurs inhabited Texas during the era between 225 and 130 million years ago. Approximately 140 million years ago, the state was inundated again by shallow seas that deposited the limestone one can see in the eroded canyon walls of the Big Bend National Park and along the Balcones Escarpment. Volcanic eruptions in the Trans-Pecos area ejected volcanic ash and lava, which can still be found in this arid landscape.

About 65 million years ago, huge amounts of sand and gravel washed into the Texas panhandle as the Rocky Mountains were forming. Meanwhile, the thick, sandy and clayey soils of East Texas and the Coastal Plains began developing. Deposits in broad, river-fed deltas and marshy lagoons gave rise to luxuriant vegetation. The grasslands began forming some 55 million years ago.

During the past three million years, successive periods of worldwide glaciation caused sea levels to rise and fall. While glaciers never extended as far south as Texas, the Ice Age created a colder, more humid climate. The Caprock was formed about two million years ago as the Panhandle area became isolated from Rocky Mountain streams and the heavy flow of alluvial material began to recede. From the lower sections of Texas, rivers carried extensive sand and gravel deposits into the Gulf Coastal Plain. The present day sea level was established only in the past 3,000 years. All of our beaches and barrier islands have formed since that time.

TOPOGRAPHY

Elevations in the eastern portion of the state rise almost imperceptibly from sea level along the Gulf Coast to no more than 700 feet along present-day I-Hwy 35. Just west of this freeway, Texas rises to a level above 1,000 feet. The most dramatic rise occurs along the Balcones Escarpment. This series of fault lines is imperceptible in places, and in other places the escarpment reminded Spanish explorers of balconies, hence its name. The Escarpment runs from Del Rio on the Rio Grande River through Central Texas between Dallas and Fort Worth to the Red River. As one drives from east to west through the Hill Country and Red Rolling Plains of western Texas, the land gradually rises another 2,000 feet.

Toward the Panhandle, the striking Caprock Escarpment marks another sharp rise. In some places it is a 1000 feet high wall, but in its southern reaches, the boundary between the High Plains and Red Rolling Plains is less well defined. The virtually treeless High Plains region appears to be flat, but it actually rises another 1,000 feet to an elevation of 4,000 feet at the extreme northwest corner of the Panhandle. The area west of the Pecos River Valley is known as the Basin and Range area. It is punctuated by the Chisos Mountains in the Big Bend, Davis Mountains and the Guadalupe Range, which boasts the state's highest spot, Guadalupe Peak (8,749 feet), near the New Mexico border.

WATER RESOURCES

The rivers in Texas basically flow from northwest to southeast. The Canadian River crosses the Panhandle north of Amarillo. The Red River forms the northern border of most of the state. (One of its forks created Palo Duro Canyon.) Both the Canadian and the Red Rivers end up in the Mississippi River system. The Sabine River forms the lower half of the state's eastern boundary line, and the Rio Grande marks the boundary between Texas and Mexico. The Pecos River runs 900 miles from New Mexico through Texas before it empties into the Rio Grande near Del Rio. Between the "border rivers," nine other rivers (Neches, Trinity, San Jacinto, Brazos, Colorado, Lavaca, Guadalupe, San Antonio and Nueces) rise within the state and funnel into the Gulf of Mexico.

Texas rivers and their numerous tributaries have been impounded into 203 reservoirs that provide about half of the water we drink and use for irrigation. Our only other source for water is underground. Aquifers underlie 81% of Texas. Unfortunately, pumping already exceeds recharge from rain in most years. Texas *will* continually face water shortages as demand increases.

LAND USE

Of the state's 170.7 million acres, only about 1.6 million are covered with water. Dry ranchland used primarily for grazing accounts for 100 million acres; 36 million acres are utilized as cropland. Forests cover 23 million acres. Texas is rapidly becoming urbanized. According to the 2008 *Texas Almanac*, post-2000 population growth has become increasingly concentrated in the central cities and suburbs while many rural areas are losing population. More than 80% of Texans now live in cities of more than 100,000 people. Urban development has increased to more than 5-million acres. Additionally, the state has 69,000 miles of highway, including 3,000 miles of Interstate Highways. (Highways require between ten and thirty-five acres per mile.) Parks and recreational land account for the remaining land within the state.

VEGETATION

Environmentally speaking, Texas is a transition zone between the humid eastern and arid western portions of the United States. Moreover, the state spans four USDA Hardiness Zones (based on average lowest winter temperatures) from Zone 9 in the sub-tropical Rio Grande Valley to Zone 6 in the Panhandle where the winter thermometer readings more closely resemble those of Pennsylvania or western Idaho. In this one big state, the national regions designated as Southern Coastal Prairies, Southeastern Pine Forests, Central Hardwoods and Tallgrass Prairies, Great Plains and Southwestern Deserts all merge. These overlapping zones produce 5,000 species of wildflowers and a wealth of grasses, shrubs and trees we can proudly call "Texas natives."

Nature Maintains a Fragile Hold

Why is it important to understand our cultural and geological history? Without such knowledge, we are likely to continue practices that degrade the larger environment. We are stewards not only of our personal properties, but also of the land we own in common with others — parks, roadsides and wilderness. Most of us are indignant when we read about the destruction of tropical rain forests. Few of us realize just how profoundly agricultural activities and urban growth have impacted our Texas landscape in just two centuries of settlement.

First, the tall grass prairies in the eastern half of the state were plowed under for cotton farming. Then ranching, as it was practiced in the nineteenth century, profoundly degraded the shortgrass prairies of West Texas. When ranchers overstocked the land, cattle quickly ate the most nutritious grasses to the ground. Then less desirable grasses took over. Bare spots eroded, topsoil blew or washed away, and finally the land produced even weaker grass. Overgrazing was profitable for a few years, but eventually the land supported fewer and fewer cattle.

The soil that underlies the shortgrass prairies is thin and fragile. Geologists tell us that it takes nature about 100,000 years to weather one inch of limestone into topsoil. With both grass and soil gone from the shortgrass prairies, much of the beef production in Texas has moved to regions of the state where cotton was once the primary crop. To produce cattle feed on farms depleted of nutrients by cotton crops, however, ranchers must heavily fertilize the soil, which in turn contributes to the pollution of our waterways. The irony is that the native tallgrasses of Central Texas, which were plowed-up for farming in the nineteenth century, would have been better suited to cattle ranching at the time!

Just as farmer's plows and free-roaming cattle stripped away the lush prairie grasses that once covered the western three-quarters of the state, the richly layered hardwood and pine forests of eastern Texas were cut down and have been largely replaced by single-species, same-age pine plantations. Coastal wetlands have been systematically drained to make way for industry and agriculture. Texas now ranks third in the country for number of endangered plants. While plant extinction is not a new phenomenon, there is cause for alarm when rare plants face extinction before botanists can fully explore their potential use in the fields of medicine, industry, horticulture and agriculture.

Homeowners have played a role in the degradation of the landscape as well. By the mid-1850s, several mail order nurseries had been established here, and the fruit trees, roses, iris and other ornamental plants they introduced set new standards for domestic gardening. But Texans' eagerness to obtain nursery stock from other places has continued unabated. Austin's soil too alkaline for Japanese maples? No problem. Dig a crater and backfill with a few cubic yards of Canadian peat moss. Houston's summer too humid for Oregon-bred hybrid roses? Spray fungicides twice weekly to prevent powdery mildew. Too little water to run the automatic sprinkler systems needed to keep these landscapes green? Dam every running stream in the state...

As Richard Phelan wrote in his beautiful book, *Texas Wild*, "We are poor compared with the wealth that might have been ours if we hadn't plundered the land." Noting that the first rule of business is conserve capital, he continues, "we Texans have not just dipped into our natural capital, we have squandered it — forests, grass, water, soil, oil. Not only is Texas poor compared with what might have been, it is getting poorer all the time. — being used up, worn out...Mistreated land wears out gradually, unnoticed, the way clock hands move, the way men grow old," he concludes. "And because we don't see it happening, we let it happen."

Please believe that we are not condemning growth and development. Our concern here is to encourage a new appreciation of our natural botanical heritage. Mankind has taken for granted that plant life, which is necessary to our survival, will continue to flourish no matter how poorly we treat the land. We now know differently. As citizens, property owners and gardeners, we can help repair the damage done by previous generations. We hope to show that by doing so, we can reap rewards in terms of both environmental quality *and* economics.

Causes for Optimism

The 21st century has ushered in a new sense of urgency about how we should manage the land. Many of our generation (those of us who grew up in the mid-20th century unconcerned about environmental issues) are now supporting the public and private organizations working to protect the Texas we will leave for our grandchildren. A younger, environmentally educated generation will undoubtedly spend the time and capital necessary to bring nature back into harmony before it is too late.

Already there is widespread acknowledgement that water is a precious resource. In spite of above-average rainfall in 2007, we Texans have come to terms with the fact that our water demands will soon exceed the capacity of our reservoirs. We're beginning to appreciate plants that can survive on scant rainfall. In every region of Texas there are new water-wise demonstration gardens and nature centers that extol Xeriscape™ gardening. (The word xeriscape was coined in 1978 from a combination of two other words: "xeri" derived from the Greek word "xeros" for dry; and "scape," from landscape.) Xeriscape™ and the xeriscape logo are registered trademarks of the Water Department of Denver, Colorado, but the word has come into such common usage that it will probably appear in dictionaries, just as we use kleenex to describe all soft tissue paper. In practice, xeriscaping means landscaping drought-tolerant plants to conserve water.

The landscape every homeowner in Texas should visit for inspiration is the **Lady Bird Johnson Wildflower Center** in Austin. One of the most striking of the complex's ten buildings is a tall limestone-clad cylindrical cistern for collecting roof runoff, which is used for drip irrigation watering throughout the site. The central theme of the entry court is water, which is played out in charming little ponds, a simple waterfall and a bubbling pool that mimics a spring. Not a drop is wastefully sprayed into the air. A transition area between the courtyard and demonstration gardens features freeform paths of decomposed granite. These paths recall dry streambeds ambling through pastel ribbons of grasses and native flowers. Storm water filtration ponds surround the parking areas.

Even the attractively composed native plantings in the courtyard beds are arranged according to water requirements. The Center uses neither pesticides nor chemical fertilizers to grow its collection of Texas trees, shrubs and wildflowers, and the natural landscape around the center is largely undisturbed. The few trees that had to be removed were ground and recycled for mulch on the trails. All stone excavated for the construction was incorporated into the site design. Of course, many of the plants that grow here are indigenous to the Austin area. Some would not be ideal for the soils or climates of Dallas, Houston, Tyler or El Paso, each of which has its own store of underutilized native plant materials.

Until quite recently few native plants were available in any part of the state. Texas growers resisted experimentation with natives because "the designers were not demanding them." Landscape designers, on the other hand, were hesitant to specify plants that were difficult to obtain. This "Catch-22" has been resolved, thanks in large part to the Wildflower Center's efforts to educate the public. Now aware of the advantages of natives over imported plants, homeowners are finding a wide array of hardy indigenous species in their local garden centers.

We're also seeing new enthusiasm for gardening without the chemical fertilizers and pesticides that pollute rivers and groundwater supplies. More and more gardeners are switching to organic products. In the face of an exploding population and dwindling resources, it is becoming clear that working in harmony with the environment makes good sense economically.

The Texas Department of Transportation's wildflower program has not only helped our highways look nicer, but has also proven to reduce the cost of maintenance. Cities have begun to value "urban forests" as major resources. Ordinary citizens are influencing new ways of development within their own cities that preserve larger tracts of open space. We've come to realize that a healthy mature shade tree is worth up to $10,000, and we have begun to look for builders and developers who cater to an environmentally friendly ethic. While it may be cheaper (for the builder) to strip the lot clean, homeowners have learned that they will save a great deal of money in landscaping costs, maintenance and water consumption by finding a builder who is willing to retain as much of the native vegetation as possible.

Another exciting development is that the Texas Department of Agriculture is widely promoting Texas-grown plants. While this is an era of global thinking, there is much to be said for buying locally. There are many advantages to buying plants grown in Texas. First, it's good for the economy. In 2006, the most recent year available, Texas ranked third in greenhouse and nursery cash receipts, behind California and Florida. The estimated figure for Texas-grown landscape plants is a whopping $1.5 billion (about 9 percent of the US total), which puts nursery crop production almost on a par with cotton or cattle!

More importantly for Texas gardeners, buying Texas-grown means that the plants are acclimated to our climate. Most of the species grown here are also better adapted to our generally alkaline soils than those grown in California or on the East Coast. Large wholesale growers in Central and East Texas are now producing many of the trees, shrubs and bedding plants we see in Texas-owned retail nurseries. New drought-tolerant turf grasses are being developed by growers in the High Plains, and the Valley is actively employed in the production of palms and tropical houseplants sold around the country. A significant number of these growers have joined the Texas Department of Agriculture's program that allows them to display a GO TEXAN label on their wares. Look for it whenever you visit a garden center!

Making the Most of Texas Garden Resources

Texas gardeners have developed sophisticated tastes from travel and exposure to books and magazines that picture well-designed gardens from all over the world. Our garden centers have kept pace by offering a wider variety of plants and new hybrids of old, familiar shrubs and trees. While there is now a wealth of plants from which to choose, the plants you'll find in the marketplace are not all equally easy to grow. Make friends with the personnel at your local garden center. Take a note pad. Jot down the names of the plants you like best. Browse the book section. Peruse the tools.

BE PREPARED TO ASK INTELLIGENT QUESTIONS

If the salesperson doesn't seem knowledgeable about plants you are considering for your landscape, ask to speak to the owner or manager. Unlike minimum-wage clerks in the big home improvement stores, the personnel at most Texas-owned garden centers are trained Nursery Professionals. These people will know about local soil and climate conditions. They'll be qualified to answer your questions and willing to spend time helping you find native and hardy adapted species for your specific site. They'll direct you to the varieties that are most resistant to pest and disease problems. They can explain the proper cultural practices that will mean the difference between poor and good performance once the plant is in the ground.

Establishing a relationship with a garden center is not unlike finding the right medical care for your family. We know from personal experience how important it is to find a local nurseryman we can trust. This returns us the subject of big box stores; we found a particularly delicate variety of Japanese maple for sale in a home improvement store in West Austin. Knowing that its chance for longtime survival in the Hill Country's rocky, alkaline soil was akin to "a snowball in hell," Nan asked to speak to the manager. "Well, you're right," the manager said when we observed that this species is inappropriate for most Austin gardens, "but we have to take what's sent to us by the central purchasing office in [another state]."

Do we ever go to the home improvement stores to pick up a package of bone meal or a flat of petunias (which may or may not have been grown in Texas)? Sure. We've also found some handsome pots and good soaker hoses at "big box" retailers. Would we shop there for our garden's important trees and shrubbery? No way. Not only do we want a garden center that supplies top-quality, locally grown plants, but also we want to establish a relationship with a firm where we feel comfortable taking a diseased leaf for diagnosis. The home improvement stores have brought garden supplies into markets where there was little in the way of resources, especially some of our smaller cities and new suburbs. Because these companies buy in volume, the prices are often low. Sometimes the merchandise is excellent, and the manager is actually a trained Nursery Professional, but don't count on the sales clerks for expert garden advice. And, don't be afraid to ask a chain store manager where they get their plants.

It makes us sad that these stores have put a lot of "mom and pop" nurseries out of business. When a fine old neighborhood nursery closes, we lose more than just convenience. We lose the years of practical gardening experience the owners and staff members have to share.

WHY IT'S IMPORTANT TO CONSULT A NURSERY PROFESSIONAL

The Texas Nursery and Landscape Association (TNLA) represents all segments of the "green industry" in this state — wholesale nursery-stock growers, garden center retailers, landscape contractors and designers, maintenance contractors and allied suppliers. The Association certifies nursery personnel through training programs, apprenticeships and examinations. To become a Texas Certified Nursery Professional a person must pass a four-part examination that covers basic principles of plant identification, plant growth, plant disease and insect control, weed control, fertilization and proper use of chemicals. To become a Texas Master Certified Nursery Professional, one must attend classroom training and pass an examination that requires an advanced level of knowledge in these subjects.

Most garden centers listed in this book employ Texas Certified Nursery Professionals to give advice on plant selection and answer gardening questions. Some also provide design and landscape installation services. You'll find a number of nurseries that offer free classes and send out newsletters not only to promote products, but also to keep their customers informed about new developments in the field of horticulture. Explore the garden centers, specialty nurseries and garden furnishings shops in your area. Ask to be added to the mailing list of every place where you regularly trade!

In writing this book, we visited garden centers, specialty nurseries and garden furnishings shops throughout Texas. We found that the people who run the independent nurseries in this state are the most generous, passionate, hard-working folks you can ever hope to meet. They spent hours showing us around, freely shared their expertise and offered us unmitigated encouragement. They will be willing to share information and offer advice to you, as well. Take a look at "out-of-the-way" suppliers in your region. Some are one-person operations in residential neighborhoods. Others may be large wholesalers who, although they are not set up to meet the public, will sell to homeowners under certain circumstances.

Within each region's chapter, the reader will find our commentary on local retail resources — the look and feel of the place, the staff's credentials, products offered, hours of operation, directions, special events and seasonal sales. Some readers may only be interested in the resources for their own region, but we hope that everyone will read (or at least skim) the chapters on the resources of other regions. We suggest that you tuck a copy of this book into the glove compartment of your car when you travel around Texas! This book tells you about all the wonderful public gardens and nature preserves you'll find and will introduce you to nurseries and shops you'll want to visit. You wouldn't believe how many plants, garden tools and accessories we piled into the back of Nan's car as we returned to our homes after weeklong research trips!

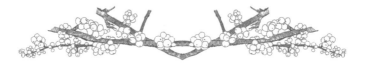

Invitation to Readers

Let us know if you are familiar with other resources that should
be included in the next edition of this book. (Send information to
ruejudd@brightskypress.com) We were unable to visit every town in this
huge state, and we're certain that we have missed a few good places
in the cities and towns we did visit. We respected the wishes of those
who asked not to be listed because the owners are getting up
in age or they have more business than they can serve.

We've tried diligently to avoid mistakes like the one Nan found
in a respected garden book on the subject of manure:

"For the same expenditure,
far better results may be obtained
from the use of domestic humans
or commercial fertilizers."

To err is humus.

1

Cross Timbers &
Grand Prairie

Cross Timbers & Grand Prairie

Between the Red Rolling Plains of West Texas and the Blackland Prairies of Central Texas, two long bands of woodlands once jutted down like fingers through North Texas. A long narrow swath of grassland, the Grand Prairie, cut through these western and eastern Cross Timbers. Fort Worth, the region's major market center, stands on that prairie's western edge. In terms of climate, Fort Worth quite correctly bills itself as "Where the West Begins."

The alternating bands of woodlands and grassland prairie run more or less north-south from the Red River down through Lampasas County and west almost halfway to Abilene. The region includes Gainesville and Denton to the north and the towns of Brownwood, Cisco, Cleburne, Gatesville, Glen Rose, Goldthwaite, Hamilton, Lampasas, Mineral Wells, Stephenville and Weatherford to the south and west of Fort Worth. The Grand Prairie and Eastern Cross Timbers region of Texas funnel between Dallas and Fort Worth, incorporating suburban areas as far east as Arlington and the city of Grand Prairie.

The millions of acres of blackjack and post oak that were the Cross Timbers have long since been cut down and converted to farmland. Originally these were very significant physiographic features, forming a natural barrier beyond which the forest fires that roared through the Great Plains could never penetrate. In 1852, Army Captain Randolph Marcy wrote, "At six different points I have found the Cross Timbers with the same peculiarities — the trees standing at such intervals that wagons can pass between them. The soil is thin, sandy and poorly watered. This forms a boundary line between the country suited to agriculture and the great prairies, which for the most part are arid and destitute of timber."

These forests can still be enjoyed in a number of public places, including the 3,000-acre **Lake Mineral Wells State Park**, east of Mineral Wells in Parker County. Here, the forest covers a ridge east of the lake — a rugged setting that was never heavily used. Some of this park's venerable post oaks may be more than 250 years old (although usually less than thirty feet tall, with trunks not more than two feet in diameter). Most of the trees that remain are small and scrubby, commercially useful mainly for firewood and fence posts. Shinnery, blackjack, post and live oaks predominate. Where the oaks are thin, thickets of mesquite and cedars have invaded. Sandy loam soils generally underlie these wooded areas.

The Grand Prairie is of a different character from the Cross Timbers. Its thin, limestone-based soils are rocky and clayey. Here, white chalk hills and dark green cedar breaks stand in bold contrast with the verdant fields that now cover the gently rolling landscape. Before it was put to agricultural uses, such mid-size grasses as big and little bluestem, sideoats grama, indiangrass, Canada wildrye, Texas wintergrass and buffalo grass predominated on the gently rolling prairie. Interspersed among the grasses, such prairie wildflowers as purple coneflower, butterfly weed and Englemann's daisy bloomed in profusion.

Nature trails at **Cedar Hill State Park** and **Cedar Ridge Preserve** in southwestern Dallas County showcase the beauty of this unique area of Texas. Its scenic, rugged hills are covered with cedar elm, honey locust, mesquite, and juniper (cedar) trees, and there are several pockets where you'll find remnants of tall-grass prairie replete with wildflowers. Botanists have found species of 80 different plant families within this 1,810-acre preserve.

Stands of native trees still occur along the numerous streambeds that run east-west throughout the region. The Grand Prairie widens out south of Fort Worth. One of the best places to experience the prairie's distinct environment is at **Cleburne State Park**, ten miles southwest of Cleburne off Hwy 67. Here, oak, elm, mesquite, cedar and redbud clothe the chalk hills, and bluebonnets bloom around a spring-fed 116-acre lake. Because the dense woods and plains included several clearwater springs, this region was once a favorite hunting ground for Native Americans, and later it provided campsites for cowboys on the Chisholm Trail.

Rare golden-cheeked warblers nest in the thick stands of cedar at **Meridian State Park** in Bosque County, where western Cross Timbers and Grand Prairie merge in an area called the Comanche Plateau. This Cross Timbers landscape (about three miles southwest of Meridian off State Hwy 22) remains heavily wooded with ashe juniper and oak, as well as abundant woody plants and wildflowers.

A locale where you can observe plant communities of three different North Texas ecosystems (Cross Timber forest, Grand Prairie and Trinity River marshland) is the **Fort Worth Nature Center and Refuge** (ten miles northwest of the city). Along the western edge of the region between Abilene and Fort Worth, a small, scenic formation of hills called the Palo Pintos forms a gentle transition between Cross Timbers and West Texas prairieland. North of these hills, the landscape dissolves into short-grass prairie more typical of the Red Rolling Plains.

Average annual rainfall in the region ranges from about 28 to 33 inches per year. The terrain is primarily adapted to raising livestock and growing grain crops. Farmers produce pecans, peanuts and a variety of fruits and vegetables in the southern reaches of the area. The soils around Stephenville, Graham and Denton have proven to be suitable for prosperous greenhouse and nursery industries. Gardeners in the region must regularly irrigate all but the hardiest native plants.

The encyclopedic **Fort Worth Botanic Garden** is the best possible place to visit for inspiration if you garden within the Cross Timbers region. Here you will see just about every plant that can (or should) be grown. If you wonder what the sound of water might add to your garden, go downtown to visit the **Fort Worth Water Gardens**. Searching for inspiration for an Asian garden? The **Japanese Garden** at the Fort Worth Botanical Garden and the Chinese-inspired **Chandor Gardens** in Weatherford will point the way. Both combine Texas native plants with adapted species imported from the respective countries whose garden traditions they celebrate. Between Weatherford and Mineral Wells is another important place for ideas, **Clark Gardens Botanical Park**.

Public Gardens and Nature Preserves to Visit

Fort Worth Metropolitan Area (Tarrant County)

Fort Worth Botanic Garden and Japanese Garden
3220 Botanic Garden Dr
Fort Worth, Texas 76107
817.871.7689 (general info), 817.871.7685 (Japanese Garden)
www.fwbg.org
Hours: Gardens: Daily (year-round) Mon–Fri 8–10, Sat 8–7, Sun 1–7 (closes at 5 on weekends Standard Time). Conservatory: Mon–Sat 10–6, Sun 1–5 (closes at 4 on weekends Central Standard Time). Japanese Garden: Mon–Sun 9–7 (closes at 5 daily Central Standard Time). Check website for restaurant and gift shop hours.
Admission: Gardens: $1 (adults); $.50 (seniors & children); free (children under age 4). One adult may sponsor up to 5 children; Japanese Garden: $3 weekdays, $3.50 weekends and holidays (adults), $.50 off regular admission (seniors), $2 (children 4–12 yrs.), free (children under 4). Portions of the grounds have limited stroller/wheelchair access.

More than a half-million people visit this garden every year! For locals, this is the single best place to see the region's wide range of gardening possibilities, and for gardeners from other parts of the state, it offers a world of design ideas. The Fort Worth Botanic Garden began as a rose display in 1933. Now, the oldest public garden in Texas has grown into an impressive collection of specialty gardens tucked into a 110-acre park-like site. Within the planted areas and surrounding woodlands, more than 2,500 native and exotic species are waiting to be explored. The main building houses a large conservatory, and behind the building is the Adelaide Polk Fuller Garden with its curving paths and attractive stone garden structures. A path through the courtyard south of the Conservatory leads to the Texas Native Forest Boardwalk. From the south end of the Boardwalk, across the road, the landscape opens into extensive formal European-style rose gardens and a naturalistic Perennial Garden set in dappled shade alongside a fern-lined brook. Tucked behind the Garden Restaurant along the Old Garden Rd is a Fragrance Garden designed especially for the visually impaired.

The garden's hidden treasure is a 7.5-acre Japanese Garden that features water cascading down a bluff, gurgling over rapids, shimmering in large reflecting pools and swirling symbolically in raked gravel. Schools of brightly colored koi can be seen darting through interconnected ponds from the several bridges that crisscross the garden. Each of the many pathways leads to yet another undiscovered pleasure: an island where ducks reside, a teahouse, Kyoto's Ryoan-ji temple complex, a moon-viewing deck or a five-tiered pagoda.

Labyrinthine paths guide the journey. Choose one path and you happen upon a recreation of a garden where rocks rise out of the sea of swirling patterns of gravel. A different fork leads to a spot where you can rest and ponder an island "inhabited" by graceful bronze cranes. On the distant shore, water cascading down a dark, rugged limestone escarpment calls to mind a mountain spring. The path will disappear enticingly around a corner, then a stone lantern half-hidden in the foliage will mark the beginning of yet another sensory experience. *Directions: Take I-30 W from downtown; exit at University Dr. Travel north on University Dr to the main garden entrance.*

Fort Worth Nature Center and Refuge
9601 Fossil Ridge Rd
Fort Worth, Texas 76135
817.237.1111
www.fwnaturecenter.org

Hours: Mon–Fri 8–7, Sat & Sun 7–7 (May–Sept.); Daily 8–5 (Oct.–April); closed Thanksgiving & Christmas Day. Interpretive Center Mon–Sat 9–4:30, Sun 12–4:30

Admission: $4 (adults); $3 (seniors); $2 (children 3–17); free (children under 3)

This 3,600-acre refuge preserves richly diverse habitats much as they existed before European settlement. Twenty miles of trails provide an opportunity to observe plant communities of three different North Texas ecosystems: Cross Timber forest, Grand Prairie and Trinity River marshland. People from all over the world come to see the birds, buffalo herd and prairie dog town here. These and other animals couldn't exist here without the plants that are described in this organization's field guide. A variety of educational programs for children and adults are held at the Hardwicke Interpretative Center, and staff naturalists facilitate guided hikes and canoe trips to explore the world of nature. There is a regular Saturday morning hike with no reservations required, plus numerous other special tours (some with reservations required and some requiring fees for non-members). Memberships are available, and the facilities include a natural history library and Nature Center Gift Shop.

Directions: Take Hwy 199 (Jacksboro Hwy) northwest of the city. The entrance is 4.0 miles outside of Loop I-820. At the gate you'll pay entrance fees and receive a day pass and map.

Fort Worth Water Gardens
1501 Commerce St
Fort Worth, Texas

Hours: Daily (during daylight)

Admission: free

"Water does all kinds of funny things — it jumps, it's quiet, it makes noise, it makes films, it goes high, it goes low, it falls down," observed the late architect Phillip Johnson, who thoroughly explored the capabilities of water here. Although it's set in the city center, the only sounds you'll hear once you enter the Water Gardens are those of children laughing, birds chirping and the music of the water. Much of this park is inaccessible to people in wheelchairs or babes in strollers, but the views from street level are spectacular. While the water features here are too large in scale to replicate in a residential landscape design, the relaxing sights and sounds will make you yearn for a fountain, pool or pond in your own garden. It's is an enchanted landscape!

Weatherford (Parker County)

Chandor Gardens
711 West Lee St
Weatherford, Texas 76086
817.613.1700
www.chandorgardens.com
Hours: Sat 9–3, Sun 1–5 (April–Nov.) or by appointment
Admission: $5 (adults and teens); free (children 12 and under). Must be accompanied by an adult). Private tours of the home and gardens available by appointment.

White Shadows, as it was originally named, was carved out of four rocky acres of a former cow pasture. When English portrait artist Douglas Chandor married Weatherford native Ina Kuteman in 1935, she convinced him to build his home and studio on property behind her parents' house. Here the painter discovered his real passion as an artist. Between 1936 and his death in 1953 (when Ina renamed it after her husband), this barren site evolved into a world-class landscape. With picks, shovels, dynamite and mule-drawn plows, Chandor painstakingly sculpted a series of outdoor spaces combining Chinese and English landscape styles. Truck-loads of topsoil and tons of boulders were required to assemble the individual gardens, each with its own character, all connected by meandering paths and bridges.

Prominent visitors from all over the world traveled to Weatherford for elegant parties in this work of "living art." After Douglas died, Ina struggled to keep the gardens open to the public (she charged a $1 fee to help defray the high maintenance costs) until her death in 1978. The exquisite place was left to deteriorate until 1994 when local residents Charles and Melody Bradford purchased the property and assumed the enormous task of restoring the home and gardens. While the large old trees, Douglas' original wisteria and boxwood plantings, and his inspired hardscapes remained, the Bradfords painstakingly clearing debris and replanted much of what had been lost by neglect. The City of Weatherford purchased and reopened Chandor Gardens in 2002. The website gives but a glimpse of the serene beauty visitors will discover there today. You'll enter from the back of the property, but make your way around to the front of the house and stand at the green front door to experience the garden as Douglas and Ina viewed it every day.
Directions: From I-20 take Exit 408 (Main St) north into town toward the courthouse. Turn left on Lee St at the stoplight before reaching the city center.

Clark Gardens Botanical Park
567 Maddux Rd
Weatherford, Texas 76088
940.682.4856
www.clarkgardens.com
Hours: Mon–Sat 7:30–6, Sun 10–5
Admission: $7 (adults); $5 (seniors); $5 (children 5–12); free (children under 4). Motorized cart tours and guided tours extra ($10 for the first person and $6 for each additional person, with a maximum of 5 people per cart).

Between Weatherford and Mineral Wells lies another of this region's hidden treasures. The small private gardens that Max and Billie Clark began developing in 1972 have grown into a 35-acre botanical park that was opened to the public in 2000. It is now maintained as a non-profit organization. The gardens serve as an educational and scientific facility, as well as a working model of beautiful, yet sustainable, landscapes with numerous native Texas and hardy drought-tolerant plants. Although the topography is less than dramatic, the Clarks effectively used the gentle changes in grade to create a series of color gardens, three lakes graced by trumpeter swans and a natural woodland filled with hundreds of azaleas in pots. It has been featured in many magazines and on HGTV.

Stroller/wheelchair accessible pathways lead through such appealingly named areas as Oxbow Overlook, Hummingbird Island and the White Garden. Spring is especially beautiful with wisteria-covered pergolas shading the paths and arbors laden with cascading Lady Banks roses. More than 2,200 varieties of iris are interspersed with coral-colored poppies. During the summer and into fall, roses become the star attraction. This is a National Earth-Kind™ Rose test site and ARS test garden, where the rose bushes are pampered the first year and then left to fend for themselves. Especially charming trellises support hundreds of climbing roses. All of the plantings are well labeled, and there are plant sales daily year-round.

Directions: Located between Weatherford and Mineral Wells off US 180. Turn north Maddux Rd. The garden entrance is about 1.0 mile.

Cross Timbers & Grand Prairie Resources

Argyle/Bartonville/Flower Mound/Lewisville (southern Denton County)

Garden Centers

Calloway's Nursery Inc.
423 East FM 3040
Lewisville, Texas 75067
972.315.3133

2901 Long Prairie
Flower Mound, Texas 75022
972.691.2650
www.calloways.com
Hours: Daily 9–6; generally open until 8 in spring and during Christmas holidays

Calloway's is synonymous with color — it's where these nurseries really shine — in a profusion of flowering trees and shrubs, herbs, annuals and perennials. The company operates 18 stores in the Dallas/Fort Worth Metroplex and three Houston stores (dba Cornelius Nurseries). The company uses its great buying power to contract with mostly local specialty growers, who may, for example, supply Calloway's with 200,000 pansies in a single weekend! The buyers use published data and research from Arboretums and University trial gardens to select the best performing varieties of plants. New introductions, as well as old-time favorites, are included in the diverse product mix, and the buyers profess

(LISTING CONTINUED ON THE NEXT PAGE)

to be on a continual search for the new or unusual plant to offer to their customers. Containers of hard-fired ceramic pottery are imported monthly. "We guarantee everything, so it must be the finest available," explains Jim Estill, Calloway's Nursery president.

"Calloway's own fertilizers, soil amendments and mulches are manufactured to rigid specifications to ensure our customers have the very best. For example Landscapers Mix (composed of Canadian sphagnum peat moss, expanded shale and composted bark) is one of the company's most popular products." There are more than 80 Texas Certified Nursery Professionals and Texas Master Certified Nursery Professionals among the personnel you'll meet when you visit one of Calloway's garden centers. "We strongly believe in continuing education and regularly send our employees to classes and seminars sponsored by the Texas Association of Nurserymen. Our basic philosophy is that we want gardeners to succeed. We do everything we can to ensure success by offering high quality and knowledgeable service." Ask to be on the mailing list to receive the Garden Club Newsletter when you visit one of the Calloway's stores or sign up on the website under the "Specials" section.

Huggins Nursery
1616 Arrowhead Dr
Flower Mound, Texas 75028
972.539.4011
www.huggins-nursery.com
Hours: Mon–Sat 8–6, Sun 10–5

Bob Huggins Sr. began a nursery in Carrolton in 1950 and moved it a couple of times as the Metroplex rapidly expanded. He's retired now, but his son Bob, Jr. who runs the landscaping division, and granddaughter Christine, who has run the nursery for the past 8 years, are carrying on his traditions across from Parker Square. Realizing that a younger generation has begun shopping almost exclusively on the internet, the younger Huggins' are taking a new, untraditional look at the nursery industry. By the spring of 2009, they plan to have all the wares available in the nursery listed on their website so that customers can order items at 11 o'clock on a Tuesday night for delivery at their home the following weekend. What a great idea! Thankfully they are not planning for the virtual nursery to replace the real one where people can bring a diseased leaf for diagnosis or come to ask for landscaping advice. "We are here to help gardeners with their problems. As landscape and maintenance contractors, we are out in the field every day, so we know what solutions actually work," says Bob. "That makes a big difference."

Lantana Gardens
3229 East FM 407
Bartonville, Texas 76226
817.961.0400
Hours: Mon–Sat 9–6, Sun 12–5

Susan Randolph left high tech corporate America shortly after 9/11, and she hasn't looked back. Or slowed down. She has become a Master Gardener, Master Naturalist and Certified Nursery Professional since establishing this serene, but quite upscale nursery in the little town of Bartonville. Specializing in native and well-adapted trees and shrubs, she offers 67 varieties of antique and shrub roses, a huge variety of perennials, grasses, succulents and vines, and some really unusual annuals and tropicals. "Along with providing the finest quality of competitively priced plant material available, we emphasize education and attentive customer service," she says. "We pride ourselves on carrying the largest selection of organic products in the Denton County area, including bagged mulches, fertilizers and composts." What really make this place special are the constantly changing shade and sun demonstration gardens built into two gently sloping acres. The greenhouse is filled with seasonal greenery and such essential items as Felco pruning shears, gloves, gardening supplies and whimsical garden art. There's an elegant selection of pottery, fountains and ironwork here, as well.

Specialty Nurseries

Argyle Acres Iris Gardens
910 Pioneer Cir E
Argyle, Texas 76226
940.464.3680
www.argyleacres.com
Hours: Open every afternoon for two weeks in April. Check website.

Over 430 modern and historic varieties of iris are available here! Joe and Donna Spears' mail order company grew out of their passion for tall bearded iris. These delightful folks are members of the Historic Iris Society, and they've spent years testing iris for hardiness and adaptability to the Texas climate.

Directions: From I-35 W take Exit 76 east about 1.6 miles to Stonecrest, turn right (south) and continue 0.5 miles. Turn right (west) on Forest Trail for another 0.5 miles. Turn left (south) on Pioneer Cir. Park along the street. Mobility impaired visitors may park at the house.

The Pond Depot
301 Round Grove Rd (FM 3040)
Lewisville, Texas 75067
214.488.7400 (store), 817.491.0929 (construction division)
www.sublimewatergarden.com
Hours: Mon–Fri 10–6, Sat 9–5, Sun 12–5

Dan Martinez sells pond and aquarium equipment and supplies, tropical and pond fish and water plants (plus a few carnivorous plants) in this 3,500-square-foot indoor showroom. You'll find lots of decorative containers and fountains, lighting and six running-water features here, too. This industrious man operates fish farms near Gainesville and in Costa Rica, but his biggest business is in turnkey pond design, installation and maintenance. In addition to ponds, the construction division builds arbors, gazebos, decks, trellises, bridges and playhouses.

Garden Furnishings

Yard Art Patio & Fireplace
490 Oak Bend Dr
Lewisville, Texas 75067
972.459.6919
   See complete listing on page 36.

Arlington/Mansfield (southeast Tarrant County)

Garden Centers

Calloway's Nursery, Inc.
1424 North Center St
Arlington, Texas 76011
817.861.1195

4940 South Cooper St
Arlington, Texas 76017
817.465.2838
www.calloways.com
Hours: Daily 9–6; generally open until 8 in spring and during Christmas holiday season
   See complete listing on page 27.

Mike's Garden Centers
4800 South Cooper St
Arlington, Texas 76017
817.466.8400
Hours: Mon–Sat 8–8, Sun 8–6 (closing times vary with the seasons; call to confirm)
   Michael Cook Sr. studied horticulture at Texas Tech and worked for growers in the nursery industry for several years before opening the first of his four garden centers in 1972. There are few Texas nursery professionals with whom he isn't on a first name basis, and no Texas plant is unknown to him! His son Mike, Jr. joined him in the business, and they've expanded into landscape design and installation. Their nurseries have an extensive inventory of plants, supplies and accessories. Each is about four acres in size, complete with greenhouses that allow them to keep a big inventory of tropicals, water plants, cacti and succulents and to grow some of their Texas natives and bedding plants on-site. They also have a growing facility near Weatherford. The Cooks are adamant about having qualified people on staff to answer questions. "With all we know, it has to grow!" said Mike Sr. with a satisfied smile.

The Plant Shed
737 US Hwy 287
Mansfield, Texas 76063
817.473.6657
www.plant-shed.com
Hours: Mon–Thurs 9–6, Fri 9–7, Sat 8–7, Sun 10–6 (spring); closes at 6 on weekdays in summer and fall and at 5 everyday in winter except between Thanksgiving and Christmas, when stores stay open until 8 for tree sales.

The Plant Shed's tagline is "Where Affordable Landscaping Begins." Owned by the Holzbach family since 1981, this company has five retail locations across Tarrant County and maintains a huge wholesale business. With 30 greenhouses in Benbrook and 40 in White Settlement, the company grows much of what it sells. Each autumn, it produces over a million pansies! "Our goal is providing quality plant material at competitive prices." The tidy, well organized nurseries not only provide common nursery stock (trees, shrubs, colorful bedding, ground covers, tropicals, etc.), but also plants native to Northeast Texas. You'll find good selections of hard goods, dry goods and organics. The company offers delivery and installation, and a professional friendly staff, as well. The website is one of the best we have found. There are web coupons and advertised specials, plus colorful photographs of plants and many informative features on gardening.

Redenta's Garden
5111 West Arkansas Ln
Arlington, Texas 76016
817.451.2149
www.redentas.com
Hours: Mon–Sat 9–6, Sun 10–5

This "100% organic garden shop" specializes in perennials (over 200 varieties in season), herbs (over 200 varieties), own-root roses (over 300 varieties) and selected native and adapted trees and shrubs. The organic-only philosophy also rules at Redenta's in Dallas (2001 Skillman). These relatively small garden shops also carry an outstanding selection of garden gifts and accents. "We are constantly searching for garden art, statuary and gift items that we would be excited to have in our own gardens," says owner, Ruth Kinler. "Gardening should be a personal experience, improving the quality of life!" The staff is dedicated to spreading the gospel since all are avid organic gardeners themselves. There's also extensive free literature to help gardeners at every level of experience.

A special service offered by the company is organic lawn maintenance, a five times-per-year program that utilizes only non-toxic fertilizers and insect controls. The company has a design/build landscape division specializing in residential landscape design and organic installation. There is detailed information about the company's services on the website.

Garden Furnishings

The Chair King
1100 West Arbrook Blvd
Arlington, Texas 76015
817.719.1700
www.chairking.com
Hours: Tues, Wed, Fri 10–6, Mon, Thurs, Sat 10–8, Sun 12–6 (all stores)
See complete listing on page 118.

Breckenridge (Stephens County)

Garden Centers

H & H Garden Center
3005 West Walker
Breckenridge, Texas 76424
254.559.7389
Hours: Mon–Fri 9–5:30, Sat 9–5

Connie Kilburn is the plant person here, and her husband Benny does the installation. "In a small town, you have to be all things to all people," says Connie. "We're a full-service nursery with trees, shrubs, herbs and seasonal color. We do lots of combination baskets and custom planters, and our specialty is unusual perennials, including a good supply of natives." She carries organic, as well as the usual garden supplies, and says that she and her husband answer questions from "daylight to dark." She is known for scouring the countryside for the best nursery plants. "I'm always hunting for new things, and people come from as far away as Abilene and Fort Worth to see what we have," she adds. "We're having a good time."

Specialty Nurseries

Turner Seed Company
211 County Rd 151
Breckenridge, Texas 76424-8165
800.722.8616 or 254.559.5860
www.turnerseed.com
Hours: Mon–Fri 7–5, Sat 7–12

Turner Seed Company traces its beginnings to 1961 when Bob Turner started Turner Soil Conservation Service. Today this family-owned business is a significant supplier of grass seed and grass mixes, turf seed and wildflower seeds.
Directions: Turner's is 3.5 miles south of Breckenridge on the east side of Hwy 183.

Brownwood (Brown County)

Specialty Nurseries

Lake Brownwood Plants & Pottery
7341 Hwy 279
Brownwood, Texas 76801
325.784.7521
Hours: Mon–Sat 9–5

This one-woman operation primarily serves the many West Texas folks who spend summers at the lake. For the past nine years Carol Agan has carried such sun-tolerant perennials as lantana and verbena, as well as yuccas, grasses, oleanders, crepe myrtles and whatever else the deer won't eat. "We have to work with Mother Nature around here."

Trees Forever Nursery
3803 Hwy 377 S
Brownwood, Texas 76801
325.646.8234

Hours: Mon–Sat 8–5

Patricia Michael opened this nursery in 1995, and hasn't stopped learning since! She says, "We began with one little greenhouse and, with lots of hard work, have grown into a full-service landscaping business." She has become a Texas Certified Nursery Professional and continues taking classes at Tarleton State to stay abreast of new plants and new trends. "Every plan we do is different, so we have to be able to cater to the individual and either answer every question or find the answer!" Three greenhouse/shadehouse structures protect the shrubs, roses, tropical plants, perennials and annuals from the harsh climate here, and more than a dozen running fountains make this a very pleasant place to shop.

Burleson/Grandview (Johnson County)

Specialty Nurseries

Artistic Plants Bonsai
608 Holly Dr
Burleson, Texas 76028
817.295.0802
Hours: By appointment only

Estella Flather is a founder and active member of the Fort Worth Bonsai Society and a past vice president of the Lone Star Bonsai Federation. She specializes in miniature Japanese-style trees and carries pots, tools and soils. Advice and instruction are happily offered.
Directions: Take Renfro St exit off I-35 W and turn east. Go 2.5 miles and turn right on County Rd 602. The fourth turn to the left is Holly Dr.

Aqua-Tec Aquatic Farms
5916 Johnson County Rd 402
Grandview, Texas 76050
817.996.1741
www.aqua-tec.net
Hours: By appointment only

"We have been in business for 32 years and are water garden specialists at Aqua-Tec," owner Wiley Horton told us. However, a lot has happened since our last visit. While Wiley and Wanda still own Aqua-Tec, the second generation of Hortons — Dave, Kyle and Disa — have opened Hortons Water Display, Inc., which is an on-site pond building and service company. A certified Texas-grown aquatic plant source, Aqua-Tec offers a large collection of marginal and bog plants, koi and goldfish and hard to find pond keeping products and equipment. Throughout the year, there are several display ponds, designed by Hortons Water Display, which are a great source of inspiration. The web site is sure to make you want your own water feature!

Colleyville / Euless / Grapevine / Hurst / Keller / North Richland Hills / Southlake (northeast Tarrant County)

Garden Centers

Blooming Colors Nursery & Landscaping
2221 Ira E. Woods
Grapevine, Texas 76051
817.416.6669
www.bloomingcolorsnursery.com
Hours: Mon–Sat 9–6, Sun 12–5

In its eighth year in this handsome brick building, Blooming Colors sits on four acres of wooded hillside bounded on one side by a natural spring-fed stream. You can walk down through the shade garden and view native pecans, elms, cedars and plant displays. This nursery specializes in large trees and will plant them for you, as well as change the seasonal color in your garden. As its name would imply, there's plenty of color with over 4,000 square feet of greenhouse space dedicated to growing high-quality plants for their retail and landscape operations. Beneath a 40 feet high clerestory ceiling, the 7,000-square-foot building houses a vast selection of indoor plants, gift items and garden accessories.

Calloway's Nursery Inc.
760 Grapevine Hwy
Hurst, Texas 76054
817.581.6361

100 South Parkwood Dr
Southlake, Texas 76092
817.416.0736
www.calloways.com
Hours: Daily 9–6; generally open until 8 in spring and during Christmas holidays
See complete listing on page 27.

Gilley's Nursery and Landscaping
1823 Keller Pkwy
Keller, Texas 76248
817.431.9490
Hours: Mon–Sat 8–5, Sun 12–5

Gilley's (formerly Sutton's) is a complete garden center that sits on 5.5 acres brimming with plants, pots and fountains. The depth of inventory in shrubs, trees and seasonal color really impressed us since the building gives no hint of the vast space behind it. Owner Stephen Gilley, who is only 23 years old as we write this book, says he has gotten this wonderful opportunity by the "grace of God." He explains, "I started mowing lawns when I was 12. While a student at Keller High School, I began working at Sutton's. When I started my own landscaping company, the Suttons began recommending my work. When they wanted to retire, they asked if I wanted to buy the nursery, and I said, 'You bet'." He'll continue the landscaping services, as well as sod sales, the latter something of a specialty here. Asked his vision for ten years down the road, he says, "I want everyone to leave here satisfied that they have gotten good service and quality plants at reasonable prices." We're betting on him to succeed!

Mike's Garden Centers
555 East Hwy 114
Southlake, Texas 76092
817.251.2620
Hours: Mon–Sat 8–8, Sun 8–6 (closing times vary with the seasons; call to confirm)
   See complete listing on page 30.

The Plant Shed
1501 West Airport Freeway
Euless, Texas 76040
817.685.0932

8810 Davis Blvd.
Keller/Southlake, Texas 76180
817.906.1591
www.plant-shed.com
Hours: Mon–Thurs 9–6, Fri 9–7, Sat 8–7, Sun 10–6 (spring). Closes at 6 on weekdays in summer and fall and at 5 everyday in winter except between Thanksgiving and Christmas, when stores stay open until 8 for tree sales.
   See complete listing on page 30.

Specialty Nurseries

Green Mama's Organic Garden Center
5324 Davis Blvd (Hwy 1938)
N Richland Hills, Texas 76180
817.514.7336
www.greenmamas.com
Hours: Mon–Sat 9–6, Sun 11–5
   Our first hint that we were going to really like this exquisite little nursery was the wonderful native demonstration garden at the entry. (The garden is a cooperative of Green Mama's and the Texas Native Plant Society.) Strolling through the plant displays, owned and lovingly tended by the Ross family, you will feel as if you've been invited into a friend's private, intimate garden. There are shaded seating areas, arbors, water features, delightful signage made by Doug Ross and, of course, plants, plants, plants! Green Mama's carries mostly natives, along with Earth Kind roses and some from the Antique Rose Emporium, herbs and water gardening plants. You will also find koi, everything for the bird lover, and the Rabbit Hill organic product line. The sign at the counter reads, "Knowledge is your best gardening tool." We agree. The sociable, relaxed atmosphere here made for a most pleasant visit!
Directions: The garden center is about 0.75 miles north of Loop 820.

Hurst Park Daylily Garden
405 Crosstimber Dr
Hurst, Texas 76053
817.268.5189
Hours: By appointment

Hurst Park Daylily Garden is an AHS Display Garden that features labeled daylilies and some iris and other perennials. "Growing and hybridizing daylilies has been a pleasure of mine for over 45 years," says Mabel Matthews. She carries over 700 named cultivars and approximately 10,000 seedlings from which the most distinctive ones are selected to introduce into the National AHS. There is a wide variety from which to choose (large flowered, small flowered and eyed in tall, medium and short, as well as doubles, spiders and spider variants). You will find *The Beginner's Handbook* and instruction sheets. Special sales are held in March and October, when the weather is best for planting. "I like to have customers take time to discuss their problems and my planting and growing procedures. I encourage everyone who is interested in daylilies to visit and relax in a quiet atmosphere where daylilies are Queen!" *Directions: From Hwy Loop 820 at Precinct Line Rd (near Northeast Mall), go east and exit at Precinct Rd. Turn right (south) and go approximately 0.5 miles. Turn left on Rosebud and proceed several blocks to Crosstimber Dr.*

Garden Furnishings

The Chair King
2705 Grapevine Mills Cir
Grapevine, Texas 76051
682.651.9100
www.chairking.com
Hours: Tues, Wed, Fri 10–6, Mon, Thurs, Sat 10–8, Sun 12–6 (all stores)
See complete listing on page 118.

Yard Art Patio & Fireplace
6407 Colleyville Blvd (Hwy 26)
Colleyville, Texas 76034
817.421.2414
www.myyardart.com
Hours: Mon–Sat 10–7, Sun 12–6 (All stores)

Since opening the original Yard Art Patio & Fireplace in Colleyville in 1994, this company has added three more stores, all of which strive to offer the ultimate shopping experience...you can't beat fresh baked cookies! Yard Art Patio & Fireplace features over 20 of the country's most respected casual furniture manufacturers: Tropitone, Lloyd/Flanders, Hanamint, Mallin, O.W. Lee, Windham, Tommy Bahama and Gloster, to name a few. You'll find tubular and cast aluminum, wrought iron, all-weather wicker and teak in a multitude of styles and colors. There are umbrellas by Treasure Gardens and FIM, as well as Ancient Mosaic table tops in all sizes and shapes, Olympic outdoor lamps and cushions galore, both in-stock and special order. The knowledgeable staff will assist you in creating the perfect outdoor living space to complement your lifestyle.

Comanche / De Leon (Comanche County)

Specialty Nurseries

Comanche Nursery
201 N.W. Hwy 36
Comanche, Texas 76442
325.356.7106
Hours: Mon–Sat 9–5:30; Sun 1–4 (March–June)

This company calls itself "a best kept secret," but, in fact, its wholesale arm serves customers within a 150-mile radius. Kristina Johnson manages the one-acre nursery in town, with its winter greenhouse on-site and several demonstration water features. She designs landscapes for area residents, as well. Kristine and her husband manage 18 greenhouses on their nearby farm where they grow annuals, perennials, shrubs, roses and trees (mostly Texas natives and deer-resistant species that can tolerate the heat and drying winds typical of this area that's known as "the devil's backbone.") They explain, "We can be extremely competitive because we grow our products from seedling to finished plants. Our staff provides professional care throughout the growing process, so the plant will not suffer shock when it goes into the ground. We get constant positive feedback from our customers about that."

Womack Nursery Co.
2551 Hwy 6
DeLeon, Texas 76444
254.893.6497
www.womacknursery.com
Hours: Mon–Fri 8–5, Sat 8–12 Jan–Mar; closed remainder of year

Since 1937, Womack's has been a respected name in the Texas nursery business. There's no online catalog here because the family is too busy growing and shipping thousands and thousands of grapevines, berry plants and fruit and nut trees to customers across the country. You'll find several varieties of peach, pear, plum, apricot, nectarine, persimmon and fig trees, plus various berries available. They also grow pecan and some shade trees. This is a great source for top-quality tree pruning tools and everything you need for budding and grafting. Call for a catalog or send an e-mail (pecan@womacknursery.com) Shipping season for the bare-root plants is from mid-December to mid-March.

Decatur (Wise County)

Garden Centers

Decatur Garden Center
1551 Preskitt Rd
Decatur, Texas 76234
940.627.3453
Hours: Mon–Fri 8:30–5:30, Sat 8:30–5; Sun 10–4 March 15–May

"Home owned and home grown" is the maxim of this tidy nursery owned by Paige and James Haynes. Paige began working for a local nursery when she was in high school, and when the owner decided to retire, she told Paige, "Open your own nursery — you have a knack for it, you love it." So in 2002, she and her husband disassembled and moved the greenhouses and built this new garden center on their own 10-acre property to house garden accessories, seeds, supplies and tools. The five greenhouses are now brimming with the annuals, perennials and roses they propagate, and the colorful outdoor area is filled with #1-grade trees and shrubs they buy from other Texas growers. They use a special organic potting soil (bark, peat and rice hulls) as medium for the plants they grow, and they make the same mix available to their customers. "Good soil preparation is so important in the variable soils of this area where gardeners may encounter black gumbo, red clay, good loam or solid rock."

Specialty Nurseries

Main Street Home and Garden
603 West Main St
Decatur, Texas 76234
940.627.0235
www.mainstreethomeandgardens.com
Hours: Wed–Sat 10–5, Sun 12–4

In 2006, Cary and Beth Hardin opened a most charming display garden and nursery on the grounds of an 80-year-old Tudor-style home and buggy barn. Located just west of Decatur's handsome courthouse, their venture has become a destination for master gardeners, organic gardeners and wannabe gardeners alike. Unusual native plants, old roses and a great selection of herbs are the specialties of the house. It's all about quality merchandise to "complete" a garden and good information to promote "responsible gardening". The website keeps folks informed about upcoming classes. Beth's family founded Green Mama's in the Fort Worth area, so the Hardins' fan base is extensive.

Denton (Denton County)

Garden Centers

Calloway's Nursery Inc.
1601 Dallas Dr
Denton, Texas 76205
940.591.8865
www.calloways.com
Hours: Daily 9–6; generally open until 8 in spring and during Christmas holidays
See complete listing on page 27.

Four Seasons Nursery
3333 East University
Denton, Texas 76208
940.566.2172
www.fourseasons91.com
Hours: Mon–Sat 9–5, Sun 10–5

This lovely garden center specializes in natives and plants that are well-adapted to North Texas. *D* magazine named it one of the area's best nurseries in 2006. All plant material is container-grown, and the vast majority of the plants are grown in Texas. "The most diverse soil types in the state of Texas occur within 60 miles of our nursery, so it's important to choose the right plants. We are competitive, but our main emphasis is on quality," says owner Michael Nack. Four Season's one-acre-site is brimming with trees (shade and fruit), shrubs, ground covers and large selections of perennials, seasonal color and herbs. You'll also find tropical houseplants, hanging baskets and container gardens planted and ready to go. At least 65% of the pest control supplies and soil amendments are organic. There are trellises, wind chimes and birdhouses, as well. Sales are advertised in local newspapers. Staff members welcome groups, speak to garden clubs, and are always accessible for friendly, professional advice.
Directions: Four Seasons is east of I-35 and Hwy 288 on Hwy 380 towards McKinney.

Meador Nursery
2612 Fort Worth Dr
Denton, Texas 76205
940.382.2638
www.meadornursery.com
Hours: Mon–Fri 8–5:30, Sat 8–5

Founded in the early 1940s by R.L. Meador, this is the oldest full service garden center in the city. It has stood the test of time at the same location and is operated by the third generation, Ted and Tim Meador. "As a family-owned business we are proud of the fact that we have continued to offer the same excellent customer service as in the good old days," says Tim. His brother Ted, who holds a degree in horticulture from TAMU is often asked to speak to garden clubs. You'll find everything you need here, from a flat of pansies and decorative items to a custom landscape design. "We see to it that you get the individual attention and expert advice that you need," says Tim, noting that there are many first-time homeowners in the neighborhood, as well as people new to the area. They carry a significant stock of large trees, lots of native shrubs and perennials and several excellent brands of organic products.

Suncrest Flowers
2757 Greenleaf Cir
Denton, Texas 76208
940.566.5761
www.suncrestflowers.com
Hours: Daily 9–5 (spring and fall), Mon–Sat 9–3:30 (summer and winter)

With over an acre under cover, Suncrest grows four crops of seasonal bedding plants every year for wholesale and retail customers. Since 1985, this impressive facility has been owned by Rob Day, who received his degree in horticulture from Cornell. The company is adding perennials to its extensive list of flowering plants, and the retail garden center is expanding to include shrubs and trees, as well as organic gardening products. General Manager Lee Kasprzyk is a Master Certified Nursery Professional with 25 years of experience. She's an enthusiastic gardener and a great source of information. The prices and wide selection here are unbeatable.

Directions: Take University Dr (Hwy 380) east 1.0 mile beyond Hwy 288. Turn left at Geesling and right on Fishtrap Rd. Go 0.25 miles and turn left into the nursery.

Specialty Nurseries

Painted Flower Farm
3801 Lariat Rd
Denton, Texas 76207
940.382.3789
www.paintedflowerfarm.com
Hours: Mon–Fri 9–1 or by appointment

Donald and Marilee Kenny specialize in native and other herbaceous perennials adapted to "the rigors of growing in North Texas — primarily resistance to the hot dry summers." We were impressed by the wide variety in the greenhouse beside their home. There was an especially great selection of sedums. A microbiologist by training, Donald calls their enterprise "a hobby out of control," but the couple has succeeded with many plants that are hard to find and difficult to propagate. They've trademarked the name "TexasTuff" to describe the plants that meet their high standards. He notes, "Some may require protection in the winter but have been chosen because they have such good performance in the heat. Check the zone listing for each plant and give winter protection when required. We are dedicated to producing a quality plant at the best possible price." All of the plants are sold in 1 gallon containers.

Directions: Travel west on University Dr, about 0.5 miles west of I-35. (Take Exit 469 off I-35). Turn right on Marshall Rd. The nursery is on the left about a block from the turn. (It appears to be on Marshall.)

Garden Furnishings

Lone Star Forge
6691 Hawkeye Rd
Krum, Texas 76249
940.482.6982
www.lonestarforge.com
Hours: By appointment

The artist/owner Paul Matthaus got his initial training when he lived with a master blacksmith in Germany from ages fifteen to eighteen. He came to America when he was 31, and moved to Texas in 1977. Paul is an artist who pays loving attention to the details. His artworks and tables shown on the website can be customized to the buyer's specifications or new works commissioned. He and his wife, Becky, make an effective team with whom you feel comfortable doing business.

Fort Worth Metropolitan Area (Tarrant County)

Garden Centers

Archie's Gardenland
6700 Camp Bowie Blvd
Fort Worth, Texas 76116
817.737.6614
www.archiesgardenland.com
Hours: Mon–Sat 8:30–6, Sun 10–4 (spring); Mon–Sat 8:30–5:30 (other seasons)

Situated on two city blocks bought by the company in 1952, Archie's Gardenland is still a wonderful nursery brimming with good looking merchandise. We were very impressed with the large assortment of trees, shrubs and seasonal color. The greenhouse held an array of orchids, bromeliads, bonsai, topiaries, cacti and lots of the more unusual tropical plants. In addition, shoppers will find materials for garden structures, soil and soil amendments, drip irrigation equipment, pest management supplies, books, tools and gift items. We learned that this appealing garden center was actually founded in 1934 by N.E. Archie Sr. as a business focusing on landscaping. An expert in the planting and maintenance of large trees, Mr. Archie became well known for his landscaping jobs from Wichita Falls to Dallas. Today the company is owned and run by Rick Archie (a grandson) and staffed by horticulturists, arborists and landscape architects. Archie's still installs hundreds of landscapes every year, and true to the founder's love of large trees, still has crews that plant and maintain trees of all sizes. The company's basic philosophy is to provide top quality plant material with the best service possible to its customers. The nursery stresses organic gardening and grows many of its bedding plants, shrubs and trees in greenhouses located adjacent to the nursery and on its tree farm located in Azle.

Calloway's Nursery Inc.
2651 South Hulen St
Fort Worth, Texas 76109
817.923.9979
www.calloways.com
Hours: Daily 9–6; generally open until 8 in spring and during Christmas holidays.
See complete listing on page 27.

Mike's Garden Centers
5703 Crowley Rd
Fort Worth, Texas 76134
817.293.8800
Hours: Mon–Sat 8–8, Sun 8–6 (closing times vary with the seasons; call to confirm)

This is the original Mike's, the company headquarters and the site of its landscape design and installation department. See complete listing on page 30.

The Plant Shed
7445 South Hulen
Fort Worth, Texas 76133
817.346.8700

5050 Hwy 377
Benbrook, Texas 76116
817.244.2109
www.plant-shed.com
Hours: Mon–Thurs 9–6, Fri 9–7, Sat 8–7, Sun 10–6 (spring). Closes at 6 on weekdays in summer and fall and at 5 everyday in winter except between Thanksgiving and Christmas, when stores stay open until 8 for tree sales.

See complete listing on page 30.

Weston Gardens In Bloom, Inc.
8101 Anglin Dr
Fort Worth, Texas 76140
817.572.0549
www.westongardens.com
Hours: Mon–Fri 6–10, Sat 9–6, Sun 12–5 (spring thru fall); Mon–Sat 10–5, Sun (November 1–mid–February)

We still recall our excitement when we arrived at Weston Gardens nearly fifteen years ago. At that time, there were few such gentle, earthy nurseries and certainly no others that invited customers to visit extensive display gardens surrounding the owners' home. We are happy to report that the Weston's homeplace still looks like a public botanical garden; its lily ponds, water falls, fountains, English-style perennial and mixed border gardens remain picture-perfect. And their garden center and gift shop across the street has resisted becoming "slick." Even as the city is growing out toward their property, this place is an island of serenity. At least 20 magazines have extolled their success story over the years, and D magazine listed it in the Best of Everything in 2004. Specialties here include Texas natives and acclimated shrubs and ornamental trees, a truly impressive selection of perennials and one of the largest antique rose collections in the South. "We try new things, but we don't sell them until they are proven," says Randy Weston. The company has over 20 years of experience designing natu-ralistic, English-style mixed borders. Weston's offers water-wise gardening expertise, free workshops and handouts, plus a monthly e-mail newsletter. This place is not to be missed! The demonstration gardens are open during spring-fall hours when the garden center is open, but some areas may be difficult for people with wheelchairs or strollers.
Directions: From I-20 east of Fort Worth, take Anglin Dr (Exit 441) south for 2.3 miles.

Specialty Nurseries

Elizabeth Anna's Old World Garden
2825 8th Ave
Ft. Worth Texas 76110
817.922.0930
www.elizabethanna.net
Hours: Mon–Sat 9–5, Sun 12–5

Elizabeth Anna Sumudio's passionate commitment to sustainable, organic gardening is evident not only in her nursery, but also in her books, lectures and teaching through TCU Extended Ed. She and her husband James have started With My Own Two Hands, an organic urban gardening program, and they hold an organic Farmer's Market at the nursery on Saturdays. From planting one container in front of a Starbucks, Elizabeth Anna has branched out into garden design and landscape installation, as well as indoor planters and healing gardens. As a cancer survivor, she has just completed her book, *Gardens That Heal, Creating Your Sacred Space.* Elizabeth Anna's Old World Garden carries mostly perennials and old garden roses with some annuals, trees and shrubs. The web site not only informative, but also inspirational.

Metro Maples
4890 South Dick Price Rd
Fort Worth, Texas 76140
817.797.3419
www.metromaples.com
Hours: Sat 8–2, Mon–Fri by appointment

Now in its 15th year, Metro Maples grows Japanese and Shantung (Chinese) maples, plus a few Ginkgo. Owner Keith Johansson has an inventory of over 15,000 trees — 75 varieties in all colors and sizes (from 1 gallon to 25 gallon containers) for sunny or shady locations. He's currently most excited about Fire Dragon®, a Shantung maple he discovered. It offers brilliant fall color and tolerates full Texas sun and alkaline soils. The grounds of Metro Maples have become a small arboretum that conducts research and supports conservation. A member of the Azalea Society and the Maple Society, Keith describes himself as "grafter, salesman, yardman, hose dragger, web updater and bookkeeper." If there is a better place to explore the many forms and hues of Japanese maples that can thrive in Texas, we haven't heard of it!

Tropical Greenery
7421 Grapevine Hwy
Fort Worth, Texas 76180
817.485.2100
www.tropicalgreenery.com
Hours: Mon–Sat 8:30–6, Sun 9:30–5:30

Founded in 1973, Greer, Gary and Gavin Phillips' family-owned nursery specializes in tropicals with 75% of the business involving installations in malls and large office spaces. Not to worry, there is a vast selection of tropicals from which a homeowner can choose, and you will be hard pressed to find happier, healthier plants. We were quite taken with a huge ming aralia and were delighted to find the prices so reasonable. There is also a large array of bedding plants, starter vegetables, organically grown herbs in 4-inch pots, "winter hardy" palms and luscious hanging baskets here. The sizeable selection of pots includes Gainey Ceramic Pottery, polypropylene accent planters and Riverside planters. There are lots of fountains

(LISTING CONTINUED ON THE NEXT PAGE)

(especially in the spring), a full line of organic products and good advice readily available. Don't miss the end of summer sale. Tropical Greenery is an attractive, friendly place to shop for special plants.

Garden Furnishings

Fort Worth Botanical Garden
3220 Botanic Garden Dr
Fort Worth, Texas 76111
817.871.7668

The Fort Worth Botanical Garden gift shop carries wind chimes, birdhouses and garden ornaments, as well as books and tapes (predominately on waterscapes and Japanese gardening). For complete listing, see page 24.

Into the Garden
4600 Dexter Ave (Hulen at Camp Bowie)
Fort Worth, Texas 76107
817.336.4686
www.intothegardentx.com
Hours: Mon–Sat 10–6, Sun 12–5

We were enchanted by this charming old ice house with its high ceilings, sophisticated displays and flowing fountains. The store carries such furniture lines as Woodard, Brown Jordan, Kingsley-Bate teak, Gloster and beautiful mosaic tables from KNF. There are planters and statuary by Compania, trellises, fountains, wind chimes by Music of the Spheres and Woodstock, birdhouses and birdbaths, as well as a lot of interesting garden accessories. Lush indoor tropicals are artfully displayed, and both this store and its sister branch in Dallas have patios with a nice selection of organically grown perennials, herbs, flowering shrubs, topiaries and seasonal color. There are garden books, potting soil and very substantial garden tools to make the job easier. And, both locations offer a series of seminars on organic gardening, perennials, bulbs and other topics. They also sponsor book signings, lectures and open houses, so be sure you're on the mailing list. The company's Garden Design Center can meet all of your gardening needs. Their idea is to "bring the garden indoors and take the concept of interior design out into the garden." Be sure to check the website for ideas, information and directions.

Texas Patios
5232 South Hulen
Fort Worth, Texas 76132
817.292.6999
Hours: Daily 9–6 (spring and summer); Mon–Sat 9–5:30 (fall and winter)

"A family-owned and -operated business for going-on 30 years, Texas Patios believes in service and helping the customers with all their outdoor patio needs," reports owner Mark Campbell." The furniture lines represented are O.W. Lee, Winston, Patio Renaissance and Mallin. You will find tables, chairs, lounges, gliders and outdoor weather wicker. In addition to a large display of concrete statuary, fountains, and birdbaths, the company carries hammocks, umbrellas, replacement cushions and many other patio accessories.

Gainesville (Cooke County)

Specialty Nurseries

Calla Lily Garden Center
1207 South Grand
Gainesville, Texas 76240
940.665.1484
Hours: Mon–Sat 9–5:30; Sun 1–5 (spring); closed Jan & Feb and July & Aug

Diane Rigler wants people to enjoy the hometown feel of her charming nursery and garden accessory shop. With 26 years of experience in the business (at this location for 13 years) she has developed close ties with Texas and Louisiana growers who supply her with quality trees, shrubs, perennials and all the rest. "Then we take good care of them after they get here." She maintains two greenhouses onsite and uses the off months to rearrange the shop so that it will always be "fresh." Loyal customers know they can find good looking iron work, arbors and pottery here and expect to be surprised with pretty new things to see each season.

Graford / Mineral Wells (Palo Pinto County)

Specialty Nurseries

Boudreau Herb Farms
5545 Hwy 281 N
Mineral Wells, Texas 76067
940.325.8674
Hours: Wed–Sat 10–5

Jo Anne Boudreau told us that herbs were looked upon with distain 40 years ago when her husband took a job in Texas. "People would cross the street to avoid me. Now they mob me," she says with a twinkle in her eye. "Not only have people discovered culinary herbs, but also good research is proving medicinal herbs to be more remarkable than we imagined." The program she does on Thursday mornings from 8–9 on QX radio is wildly popular, and because it's available by pod cast on the web, she gets calls from all over the country. Customers flock to her store and greenhouse to buy herb plants and the teas she packages from her own organically grown plants. In addition to herbs we all know, she has such hard-to-find plants as Chaya (aka Mexican medicine tree) and He-Shou-Wu, the most popular tonic in Japan where it's called herbal Viagra. "I've been into herbs all of my life. My grandmother was the town healer in Muscatine, Iowa," she explains. In addition to selling herbs and organic garden supplies, she spends a lot of time educating people at her shop, where the logo reads: "Making your life, and the world, better with herbs."
Directions: It's located 6.0 miles north of town on Hwy 281.

Naturescapes Nursery
615 North FM 2353
Graford, Texas 76449
940.779.3795 or 940.445.1265 (cell)
Hours: Sat 10–4; by appointment during the week

James Turner's nursery is geared to the needs of people who live on or near Possum Kingdom Lake. Sustainability and deer resistance are the only two traits that really matter to gardeners out here! The majority of James' extensive inventory is native to the area — lantana, sages, verbenas, grasses, a variety of yuccas and agave. He also carries rosemary, which is the only thing deer won't touch no matter how hungry they are. There are two greenhouses on the premises in which he grows some pretty houseplants, as well. "What I like is meeting interesting people and talking with them about plants," he says.

Directions: The nursery is west of Graford on Hwy 254 toward Possum Kingdom Lake. Turn left (south) on FM 2353.

Garden Furnishings

Texas Hill Country Furniture
19280 Hwy 281 S
Lipan, Texas 76462
254.646.3376
www.txhcountry.com
Hours: Tues–Sat 9–5:30, Sun 1–5

Sherry Dennis does all of the design work for this retail store, which is between Mineral Wells and Stephenville. It's filled with rustic accessories and furniture. Her husband Larry constructs gliders, rockers, swings and barstools out of native cedar, oak, mesquite and pecan. While not all of his attractive, rustic furniture is recommended for use out in the garden, most of it is perfect for country porches and covered patios. His signature piece is a beautiful wooden rocking chair with a five-point star meticulously carved into the headrest. Much of his work is custom. You may find a piece you like on the website, and he will make it in unfinished cedar for garden applications, if that is where you want to use it.

Directions: The store is located about 5.0 miles south of the Hwy 120 intersection.

Granbury (Hood County)

Garden Centers

Guerin Nurseries
1418 Fall Creek Hwy
Granbury, Texas 76049
817.326.2507

Hours: Mon–Sat 9–6, Sun 10–5

Phyllis and Glenn Guerin have owned this nursery for over 25 years. It's on eleven acres, and when we visited there were a number of greenhouses under construction. The owners are expanding their capacity to grow more of their own perennials and annuals. There are two wells and water collection tanks on site, and sustainable plants and natives are a significant part of the inventory. There are three designers on staff who work with customers on a one-on-one basis to help them select plants for their landscapes. (They suggest that people seeking help arrive with digital pictures of their properties.) Good signage guides shoppers to the trees, shrubs and other plant materials on this large site. Says Mark Tunstall, a longtime employee, "The staff here is very passionate about helping people improve their gardens."

Directions: Take Hwy 377 east of Granbury. Turn right (south) on Fall Creek Hwy It's about a mile on the right.

Specialty Nurseries

Plantastik Nursery
713 Spring St
Granbury, Texas 76043
817.736.0833
www.plantastikdaylilies.com
Hours: Tues–Sat 9–6, Sun 12–5

Tana Tomlinson's daylilies are sold across the country through her website, but you can visit her lovely nursery, where these plants (and lots of others) can be enjoyed onsite. Here, Tana specializes in Texas hardy perennials. Some of her favorites — columbines, cannas, coneflowers, cardinal flowers, salvias and a particularly pretty penstemon — are pictured on her website. Tana purchased the half-acre Plantastik Nursery property as a residence several years ago, but decided to convert it into a business with display beds in front, craft/gift shop inside and greenhouse in the rear. She keeps busy maintaining the flowering trees and shrubs, tropicals, vines, grasses, and aquatic plants she sells here and grows on 17 acres near Lipan. She swears she's loving every minute!

Lampasas (Lampasas County)

Specialty Nurseries

Lucas Landscaping, Inc.
404 East Ave J (FM 580)
Lampasas, Texas 76550
512.768.9920 or 512.734.3305
(LISTING CONTINUED ON THE NEXT PAGE)

(CONTINUED)

Hours: Mon–Sat 8–5; Sun 12–6 in spring thru Mother's Day

Lyndel Lucas grows everything he sells. Everything! It's a business he started with his mother in 1985, and it is unlike any other nursery of its size in that all of the plants here are propagated onsite in mist houses and lovingly tended until ready for sale. He calls it "a different business model" and explains that by eliminating the middlemen, he can keep costs to a minimum and pass savings along to his customers. We knew we were going to like this place when we observed a customer carrying out the largest, most healthy looking fern basket we had ever seen. The place is crammed with wonderful trees, shrubs, perennials and tropicals, some of which are pretty hard to find.

Poolville / Springtown (north Parker County)

Specialty Nurseries

Willhite Seed Company
199 Sparks
Poolville, Texas 76487
817.599.8656 or 800.828.1840
www.willhiteseed.com
Hours: Mon–Fri 8–12 & 1–5; Sat 8–12 in spring (call ahead).

Our grandmothers probably ordered from this Texas "institution" that began selling seeds in 1901! Today the company carries all types of vegetable seeds, old-fashioned annuals and perennials and such garden products as Jiffy pots, gloves, green twine, spreaders, soil testing kits and animal traps. There are standard and open pollinated vegetable varieties as well as hybrids described in its state-of-the-art online catalog. You can search for exactly what you need or peruse it page by page. (Everything is in alphabetical order, with Precision Garden Seeder falling between 'Pot Luck' cucumbers and 'President' zucchini.)
Directions: About 15.0 miles west of Springtown, take Hwy 920 S (towards Weatherford) 3.0 miles to Poolville. The company is located next to the Post Office.

Garden Furnishings

David's Patios
3001 East Hwy 199
Springtown, Texas 76082
817.677.2759
Hours: Mon–Fri 8–5, Sat 9–5; Sun 12–5 (best to call and check)

As owner Cecelia Grimmett told us, "After 45 years in business, David's Patios is the largest onsite manufacturer of concrete garden products in Texas. We're a 'landmark' in this area!" True enough ... you can't miss this one! Cecelia's son Mark O'Reilly is president of the company, which does a huge wholesale business. There are at least 80 different fountains displayed, along with statuary, bird baths, table sets and benches, stepping stones, flowerbed edging, planters and Japanese lanterns. The company also stocks wind chimes, sundials, terra cotta and ceramic pots, bird houses, bird feeders and wind socks. You will find no lack of selection here!

Directions: Take the Hwy 199 W exit off of Loop 820. David's Patios is about 18.0 miles, midway between Azle and Springtown.

Rising Star (Eastland County)

Garden Centers

Hardwick Nursery
1990 East Hwy 36
Rising Star, Texas 76471
254.643.1708
Hours: Mon–Sat 8–6, Sun 9–6

The comments you hear from people who frequent Hardwick Nursery are "to die for" and "unbelievable!" At this complete garden center, 80% of the plants are grown onsite, and customers insist that they are bigger and healthier than anywhere else. The specialties of the nursery, owned by Jana and Mike Hardwick, are geraniums, mums, ferns and bougainvillea. And lots of them! You will also find trees, shrubs, cacti and tropical houseplants as well as organic supplies, soil amendments and garden accessories. We can guarantee that you won't leave Hardwick's empty-handed.

Stephenville (Erath County)

Garden Centers

GreenMaker Nursery
3030 NW Loop
Stephenville, Texas 76401
254.965.7273
Hours: Mon–Fri 8:30–5:30, Sat 8:30–5, Sun 12–5

Karla Young, who has been the manager of this delightful full-service garden center since 2002, told us its story. "My husband is one of a group of local partners who invested in it. Originally I just came to fill in, but I loved it and I'm still here. My goal from the beginning has been to create an atmosphere where busy people could come to relax," she explains. "I've been so fortunate to have the right people arrive at the right time to help me." She mentions Gail Rankin who orders the plants — "such a knowledgeable gardener. She has taken lots of

(LISTING CONTINUED ON THE NEXT PAGE)

(CONTINUED)

classes to keep us informed about sustainability issues." She names Cathie McDonald, a horti-culturist from Scotland, who takes care of the thousands of plants. For the company's especially tasteful gift shop, she gives all credit to interior decorator Donald Sparks. "Green-Makers," she says, "carries a lot of herbs because everyone is becoming health conscious. We use organic products as much as possible to take care of all of our plants and never apply any chemicals to the herbs and vegetables."

Specialty Nurseries

Littlejohn Produce & Nursery
513 Lingleville Rd
Stephenville, Texas
254.968.0077
www.littlejohnproduce.com
Hours: Mon–Sat 9–7, Sun 1–5 (closes at 6 weekdays in winter)

This lively open air produce market and nursery is operated by Mark, Sherri and Lyndsi Littlejohn. The Littlejohn family lives and grows their crops in fields and greenhouses in nearby Comanche County. Crops are picked and brought in fresh daily in season. In 2002 they built a greenhouse beside their highly successful produce stand and began offering a vibrant array of bedding plants and tropicals. Now they've added some landscape plants, mulches, fertilizers and soils. They bribed us with a box of fresh strawberries, but of course we were only there to see the nursery...(the yummiest strawberries we've tasted in the past 40 years.) "We stand behind everything we sell," says Mark, who brings over 30 years of farming experience to this new ornamental gardening venture.

Weatherford (Parker County)

Garden Centers

Stuart Nursery
2317 Fort Worth Hwy
Weatherford, Texas 76087
817.596.0003
www.stuartnurseryinc.com
Hours: Mon–Sat 8–5

In business since 1950, this nursery carries or can order and install just about everything you could want for your garden from plants and ponds to stone walkways and irrigation systems. There are three garden designers on staff, owners Tommy Cain, Paul Simpson and Pete Sigler (a licensed irrigator), as well as Nichole Heck, a Texas Master Certified Nursery Professional. "We don't just carry it, we know about it," said Nichole. Although the company offers all the familiar plants for North Central Texas, you will find a real depth of inventory in Stuart's natives and perennials. According to Paul and Tommy, "We are always looking for new and different plant material and merchandise." They had added a line of locally made cedar furniture when we visited. "We support this community, and we try to offer personal and cheerful service to all of our customers!" Their informative web site will tell you all about this wonderful place.

Weatherford Gardens
2106 Fort Worth Hwy
Weatherford, Texas 76086
817.594.6055
Hours: Mon–Sat 9–6, Sun 10–6

Across the highway two blocks away, we found another great garden center. (Few small towns in Texas offer such a wealth of horticultural services.) Manager David Coats' card reads "Plant Guru." There's no doubt that this Tarleton State University graduate knows his subject. The emphasis here is on good soil preparation and organic gardening methods. He emphasizes Texas-grown native and hardy adapted plants. You'll find lots of perennials and ornamentals of all kinds here, including cacti. There are vegetables and herbs in the greenhouses. Tropicals and water gardening plants are available, as well as a very good selection of handsome containers.

Specialty Nurseries

Weatherford Farmers Market
217 Fort Worth Hwy
Weatherford, Texas 76086
817.599.4080
Hours: Daily 8–6

We met Heather Hutton one morning last spring when this place was literally packed with tropicals, flats of bedding plants, hanging baskets of all descriptions, and colorful mixed containers. We were surprised to see vegetable starts, herbs, trellises and fountains, too. Her father and uncle own the place, but they weren't there, and she was working hard to take care of all the customers filling their vehicles with seasonal color!

2
Trinity Blacklands

Trinity Blacklands

Dallas and its surrounding suburbs (Irving, Farmers Branch, Carrollton, Plano, Richardson, Garland, Mesquite, Lancaster and Duncanville) are located on the western edge of the Trinity Blacklands. McKinney, Dennison, Sherman, Waxahachie, Greenville, Paris and Corsicana also fall within this distinct region of Texas. The Trinity Blacklands region was cotton country in the late 19th and early 20th centuries, but now the land that hasn't been paved and subdivided has been mostly converted to grazing.

Blackland soil is deep, dark and clayey. Many farmers considered it the best in Texas. Originally, the region was a sea of big and little bluestem, Indiangrass and switchgrass. The smooth rolling hills of this part of the state were once described as enormous green waves that crested every couple of miles. The thick, 4 feet high grasses were punctuated with such tall colorful wildflowers as gayfeathers, coreopsis, butterfly weed, cardinal flowers and firewheel.

Only one-tenth of one percent remains of this formerly luxuriant blackland prairie. The grasses and flowers are found only in pockets left undisturbed by cultivation, but the region's signature trees — hackberries, oaks, pecans, soapberries and cedar elms — still thrive in the riverbottoms. **Pioneer Plaza** in downtown Dallas where a herd of bronze cattle are crossing a stream beautifully captures the way the Trinity River landscape might have looked in the early nineteenth century. Remnants of real tallgrass prairie can be seen in the hiking trails at the **Heard Natural Science Museum** in McKinney, which also takes you into areas of rich bottomland.

Gardeners in the Trinity Blacklands can draw from a wide variety of imported and native plant materials, provided that they are willing to loosen the soil with compost and keep it sufficiently moist through the summer months. Beneath the rich black clay soil, which is subject to deep cracks in dry weather, is a limestone base, which means that its pH registers in the alkaline range.

Rainfall averages 45 inches per year in Paris. Just a hundred miles southwest of Paris, Dallas County's average annual rainfall drops to less than 36 inches. Another 30 miles to the west, Fort Worth's average annual rainfall is 31.3 inches. The northeastern portion of this region falls within USDA Zone 7; Dallas and the southern counties lie in the upper reaches of Zone 8. Winter ice storms and short periods of 10-degree temperatures sweep down into the region with greater regularity than in the blacklands of Central Texas.

For design inspiration, the region's not-to-be-missed public gardens include the **Dallas Arboretum and Botanical Society** on White Rock Lake, and in downtown, the **Nasher Sculpture Center** and **The Water Gardens at Fountain Place**.

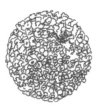

Public Gardens and Nature Preserves to Visit

Dallas Metropolitan Area (Dallas County)

Cedar Ridge Preserve
7171 Mountain Creek Pkwy
Dallas, Texas 75249
972.709.7784
www.audubondallas.org
Hours: Tues–Sun 6:30 am–8:30 pm (April–Oct.), 6:30–6 (Nov.–March)
Admission: free

Dr. Geoffrey Stanford, who founded this 633-acre preserve as The Dallas Nature Center, truly embraced the rugged Texas landscape. I once heard him make a speech in which he wryly observed (with his wonderful British accent) that Texas developers name their subdivisions in memory of the trees they cut down (Oak Hills, Mesquite Ridge, etc.)! After he died in 2000, the property he loved was saved from development as part of the Dallas Parks and Recreation Department and Dallas County Open Space Preserve. Under the management of Audubon Dallas, its ten miles of scenic hiking trails and shady picnic facilities offer a rare opportunity to view unspoiled blackland prairie and escarpment vegetation. There's a lively butterfly garden near the administration building that is maintained by the Native Plant Society.

"Although there is no official admission fee to the Preserve, but donations (around $3/person) are strongly encouraged on an honor system. We are almost completely volunteer-run, and depend on donations to keep the Preserve open to the public and well maintained," said Julie Mobley, a CRP Volunteer. In 2009, Audubon Texas will be opening a new preserve, Dogwood Canyon, nearby that will feature 250 acres of "lost dogwoods" and a critical habitat that sustains the Metroplex's greatest variety of rare and endangered species. Dogwood Canyon can be accessed from FM 1382.
Directions: Take I-20 between Dallas and Fort Worth. Exit Mountain Creek Pkwy and go south 2.7 miles.

Dallas Arboretum and Botanical Society
8525 Garland Rd
Dallas, Texas 75218
214.515.6500
www.dallasarboretum.org
Hours: Daily 9–5
Admission: $6 (adults); $5 (seniors); $3 (children 6–12); free (children under 6)

The designers of this magnificent 66-acre garden on the southeastern shore of White Rock Lake incorporated two elegant 1930s-era residential estates and built upon their existing trees and shrubs to create the state's most sophisticated display garden. Managed by an exceptional Board of Directors, the grounds are meticulously maintained, with seasonal color beds changed four times from March through November. The main entrance leads to the misty, relaxing Palmer Fern Dell, then opens up to the 6.6-acre Jonsson Color Garden with its azaleas (billed as "the country's largest collection") and seasonal plantings designed to awaken all the senses. Pathways surround the historic Mediterranean-style Everette DeGolyer House. A Woman's Garden occupies almost two acres in the back of the home, subtly divided into seven garden rooms, including a magical reflecting pool on an overlook above the lake.

(LISTING CONTINUED ON THE NEXT PAGE)

(CONTINUED)

Directly behind the house, the estate's 1940-era landscape includes a newly refurbished sunken garden. Across from the east wing of the house, the Crepe Myrtle Allée terminates at Toad Corners where four giant bronze toads spray 20 feet streams of water, much to the delight of children of all ages.

The adjacent estate, built in 1938 for Alex and Roberta Camp by John Staub of Houston, now serves as headquarters for the Arboretum and Botanical Society. On the north side of this building, you'll find the Lay Ornamental Garden, which was designed as a Texas Cottage Garden, with more than 75 varieties of woody plants and 200 species of perennials. Its native limestone cascading walls feature free-flowing water windows for an inimitable view of the garden. Here, you'll find the Hardy Palm and Tropical Collection and a Wollemi Pine, a tree once thought to be extinct for millions of years. A quarter-mile-long central pathway that connects all of the arboretum's gardens is aptly named Paseo de Flores. "Dallas Blooms", the organization's five-week spring festival attracts thousands of people to experience 400,000 bulbs, the bedding plants, and the garden's 2,000 varieties of azaleas in full bloom.

Directions: From downtown: travel east on I-30 to the East Grand exit, and go north on East Grand, which becomes Garland Rd. From I-635 E, take the Garland Rd exit and travel south approximately 5.0 miles.

Nasher Sculpture Center
2001 Flora St
Dallas, Texas 75201
214.242.5100
www.nashersculpturecenter.org
Hours: Tues, Wed, Fri, Sat, Sun 11–5, Thurs 11–9; closed Thanksgiving Day, Christmas Day and New Year's Day.
Admissions: $10 (adults); $7 (seniors); $5 (students); free (children 12 & under). All admissions include a free audio tour and entrance to special exhibitions. Joint Admission with the Dallas Museum of Art: $16 (adults); $12 (seniors); $8 (students)

Raymond Nasher's vision was to create an indoor/outdoor museum for the 300 works of 19th and 20th-century sculpture he and his wife had begun collecting in the 1950s. Every museum director on the planet coveted the collection, but he decided it should remain in Dallas. The site he selected in 1997 was an unremarkable two-acre parking lot between the Dallas Museum of Art and the Meyerson Symphony Hall. To turn it into a "peaceful retreat for reflection of art and nature," he chose a stellar architectural team: Pritzker Prize winning architect Renzo Piano of Genoa and Paris and Berkley-based landscape architect Peter Walker. Sketches began flying across the world, and when the Center opened six years later, the critical acclaim was unanimous.

Spend time in this deceptively simple, world-class garden. Walk on the grass. Let the art play with your mind. What you will experience with each visit will be different from what you think you saw before. As Mr. Nasher was fond of pointing out, "A piece of sculpture has 360 different sides." Formal symmetry within an asymmetrical lay out, a difficult balance to achieve, is masterfully used in the one and a half-acre, rectangular garden. The building's five galleries frame uninterrupted views into the landscape. Step down from a wide terrace across the rear of the galleries onto an expansive plane of grass that becomes parallel walkways of varying widths. Live oaks, cedar elms, groves of Afghan pines, weeping willow and crepe myrtles are subtly aligned with the six parallel interior walls of the museum. Its inspiration recalls an archeological site where one might find "the ruins of stone walls and an ancient orchard."

Granite plinths are used as organizing elements, providing areas for the placement of art and for people to perch. The linear walkways terminate in water features and raised planters that form the garden's rear wall. A handsome boardwalk bisects the water, serving as the garden's only cross-axis. Two factors prevent visual clutter. First is the strong, sensible design concept. The second is that no more than 25–30 sculptures in the Nashers' collection will be on display at any one time. Logistics prevent the casual moving of Richard Serra's 44 feet long curving weathered steel walls or Mark di Suvero's monumental steel construction. Barbara Hepworth's elegant monolith, "Squares with Two Circles," is likely to remain a focal point of the primary walkway. As its landscape architect said, "One becomes more aware of nature when the setting is simple."

Directions: The Nasher Sculpture Garden is located in the Dallas Arts District, between Olive and Harwood, 1 block south of Woodall Rodgers, adjacent to the DMA.

Pioneer Plaza
Young St at Griffin St
Dallas, Texas 75201

Hours: Day and night, (year-round)

Admission: free

Award-winning sculptor Bob Summers of Glen Rose cast the larger-than-life bronze steers and cowboys "to capture the full impact of a trail drive." The site of this 4.2-acre plaza in front of City Hall and the Convention Center was actually along the Shawnee Cattle Trail, the earliest and easternmost of the principal routes by which Texas Longhorns were taken to railheads in Kansas. With its native trees and grasses, a waterfall and a flowing stream, the landscape architects who worked with the sculptor beautifully captured the feel of grassland prairie as it existed throughout this region of Texas in the 19th century.

Directions: Pioneer Plaza is located in downtown, just north of the Dallas Convention Center, next to City Hall.

Texas Discovery Gardens at Fair Park
3601 MLK Blvd
Dallas, Texas 75210
214.428.7476
www.texasdiscoverygardens.org

Hours: Mon–Sat 10–5

Admission: $3 (adults); $2 (over 60); $1.50 (children 3–11); free (children under 3)

The first certified organic public garden in Texas, this education-based organization attracts 300,000 visitors annually to its 7.5 acres in Fair Park. Texas Discovery Gardens was the recipient of the Benny J. Simpson Texas Native Plant Collection, donated by the intrepid collector, educator and writer who spent 40 years championing the beauty and diversity of Texas flora. Children and parents can share the experience of nature's intricate web of life at family events throughout the year. Workshops and guided tours provide expert advice on using native and adapted plants to create backyard habitats for butterflies, birds and other native wildlife. The garden is 100% organic, and all plants are maintained using sustainable methods that conserve water and help to protect the environment. In the summer of 2009, the gardens will open a tropical conservatory filled year-round with butterflies and insects.

Directions: From downtown, take I-30 E to the 2nd Ave exit. Curve to the right, take a left at the second light onto MLK. To park, enter Fair Park at gate # 6 (the intersection of Martin Luther King Jr. Blvd and Robert B. Cullum Blvd). Just inside the gate, turn right on Second Ave, which curves left and becomes Pennsylvania Ave. Enter the parking lot on your left.

Dallas

Public Gardens and Nature Preserves to Visit

The Water Gardens at Fountain Place
Ross Ave at Field St
Dallas, Texas 75201
Hours: Day and night, year-round
Admission: free

Landscape architect Dan Kiley was famous for combining modernist functionalism with classical design principles. Here, he appears to have drawn inspiration from Villa d'Este, Tivoli, Italy's terraced extravaganza of shady trees and show-stopping fountains. Beneath the 60-story prism of green glass that is the Fountain Place office building, water cascades down terraced concrete walls and circular pots that sustain an orderly forest of bald cypress trees. Nearby, from holes cut into a rectangular marble surface, synchronized fountains shoot into the air to create hypnotic dancing water effects. If you sit and observe it long enough, you will begin to see the choreography repeat itself. In summer, kids run and play in the water, shrieking when they receive a surprise spraying. Adults who get too close sometimes get doused, as well. Mr. Kiley's many notable projects, often done with the great architects of his time, included the Gateway Arch in St. Louis, Lincoln Center in Manhattan; I. M. Pei's addition to the National Gallery of Art in Washington and the campus of the Air Force Academy in Colorado. This four-acre site in downtown Dallas remains one of his best efforts and has received recognition as one of the great urban spaces in America.

McKinney (Collin County)

Heard Natural Science Museum & Wildlife Sanctuary
1 Nature Place
McKinney, Texas 75069
972.562.5566
www.heardmuseum.org
Hours: Mon–Sat 9–5, Sun 1–5; self-guided trails open until 4
Admission: $8 (adults); $5 (children 3–12 and seniors)

The Heard's native plant garden has a new look. In addition to natives, gardeners will find well-adapted perennials, antique roses and heirloom bulbs. These Texas-tested plants have been chosen because they blend with the existing entry garden, share similar cultivation requirements and enhance the garden's color displays. Reflecting this new direction, the annual spring plant sales now include heirloom plants and herbs in addition to Texas natives. Visit the website for current details. You'll also find a nature store that includes garden accessories, books and other garden related items.

This 289-acre sanctuary offers a place where gardeners and other visitors can enjoy five different habitats: bottomland forest, upland forest, blackland prairie, wetlands and white rock escarpment. More than 4 miles of nature trails meander throughout the sanctuary, harboring streams, ponds and meadows. (One is paved for wheelchair access.) Trails are open only during museum hours and visitors must check in by 4 P.M. Guided walks are available on weekends. First come, first serve; weather permitting. Call ext. 237 for times and to reserve a trail guide. Fees may apply. Museum memberships are also available and reward participants with an informative e-newsletter and various discounts.

Directions: Exit 38A off US 75. Proceed east to SH 5, then go south. The museum is 1.0 mile east of SH 5 on FM 1378.

Trinity Blacklands Resources

Allen / Fairview / Frisco / Plano / Prosper / McKinney (Collin County)

Garden Centers

Bruce Miller Nursery
445 West Prosper Trail
Prosper, Texas 75078
972.346.2760
Hours: Mon–Sat 8–6, Sun 10–5

After more than 30 years in Richardson, Bruce Miller Nursery opened this location in March 2002. Howard Little is the manager of the Prosper location, which offers over 11 acres of plant materials and nursery supplies. There's an even bigger selection of perennials here than the original store caries. See complete listing on page 64.

Calloway's Nursery, Inc.
1000 Preston Rd
Plano, Texas 75093
972.964.3084

1621 Custer Rd
Plano, Texas 75075
972.596.5211

2460 State Hwy 121
Plano, Texas 75025
972.649.6228

4050 West Eldorado Pkwy
McKinney, Texas 75070
972.540.0707
www.calloways.com
Hours: Daily 9–6; generally open until 8 in spring and during Christmas holidays
See complete listing on page 27.

Classic Gardens
401 West FM 544
Murphy, Texas 75094
972.424.9929
www.classicgardensnursery.com
Hours: Mon–Sat 8–6, Sun 12–5

Manager Don Talefski maintains that he wasn't born with a green thumb, but he was strongly influenced by his mother's great love of flower gardening and by his late brother, Albert, who opened this family nursery over 25 years ago. Having learned horticulture hands-on, he enjoys selecting the flowers, plants, shrubs, and trees that will accent and enhance his customers' gardens. Now a Certified Nursery Professional, he also likes talking with customers and helping them with what they perceive to be gardening challenges. Classic Gardens designs and installs complete landscapes, so the inventory here includes a large number of specimen trees and shrubs. We were excited to find such handsome accent plants as smoke trees and weeping yaupons, which the company will plant and guarantee. There were also lots of planters, seasonal color, and a good selection of organic garden supplies here.

Puckett's Nursery
811 East Main St
Allen, Texas 75002
972.727.1145
www.puckettsnursery.com
Hours: Daily 9–7; 9–5 (winter)

"We give individual attention to individual needs," says owner Mark Puckett, who opened this full service, independent nursery in 1991. His company offers a wide range of quality trees, shrubs, and seasonal color and numerous landscaping services, including design, bed prep, masonry work and sprinkler installation. It is Puckett's extensive variety of plant materials that most impresses the customers. For the past several years, this tidy nursery has been emphasizing natives and organics. Now there is a whole room filled with organic products, and lots of good tools and accessories are available, as well. The company employs a landscape architect and five Texas Certified Nursery Professionals.

Directions: From Dallas, take I-75 N to McDermott or Main St and go east 4.0 miles. It's on the left next to Braums.

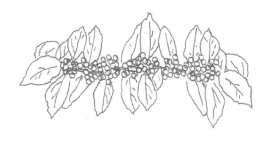

Shades of Green Inc.
8801 Coit Rd
Frisco, Texas 75035
972.335.9095
www.shadesofgreeninc.com
Hours: Mon–Sat 8–5:30, Sun 10–5

Owners Rob Weir and Jeff McCauley, friends since 4th grade, began their venture with a neighborhood lawn mowing service, which has since grown into one of the most prestigious nurseries in the Dallas Metropolitan area. With seven acres of plants ranging from large specimen trees and native plants to perennial color, this "destination nursery" employs a host of experienced designers, contractors and horticulturists. Shades of Green has been on the forefront of the organic movement, promoting sustainability for over 30 years. Rob and Jeff also maintain a nearby farm where they grow wonderful native perennials for the nursery. We were especially excited about their 20 varieties of salvia, including *Salvia greggi* 'Teresa,' for which they pay royalties to the Lady Bird Johnson Wildflower Center. The company's reputation as landscape contractors has been built (word of mouth) on landscaping everything from "charming butterfly gardens to beautifying entire neighborhoods."

In addition to gorgeous, healthy plants, you'll find great garden accents and an array of handsome pottery and fountains here. "We are active gardeners ourselves!" Ask any question, and you will receive copious information. Or pick up a free copy of their newsletter, *The Greenleaf*. The nursery offers seminars throughout the year, and from mid-March through May you can enjoy their popular Thursday evening "garden happy hours" with complimentary beverages and talks on such topics as composting or perfect perennials for shade. Shades of Green has an awesome website that allows you to tour the nursery, view current promotions, watch for scheduled events and link to other useful sites.

Directions: The nursery is 2.0 miles north of Hwy 121 on the left side of the road.

Specialty Nurseries

Cristina's Flowers
6250 Mapleshade Ln
Dallas, Texas 75252
972.599.2033
www.cristinasflowersinc.com
Hours: Daily 8–7 (summer), 8–6 (winter)

The address says Dallas, but this bustling seasonal color nursery is in Collin County (barely), a block off Preston Rd, just south of the Bush Freeway. The quality and prices are so good here that landscape professionals shop alongside the general public. In addition to annuals in flats and hanging baskets, you'll find a good selection of perennials, ground covers and some flowering shrubs. There is a fixed price per flat of 18 4-inch pots. The website pictures all the varieties and colors of the most popular plants available each season. So if you want, for example, 12 flats of 'Crown Golden' pansies or 15 flats of dwarf mondo grass to fill in between steppingstones, this is the place you can find them! Almost everything they sell is grown at Thomas and Cristina Wilson's farm in nearby Pottsboro.

Crump's Garden, Inc.
3163 FM 543
McKinney, Texas 75071
972.542.3346 or 877.801.0700 (metro)
Hours: Mon–Sat 8–5

Kathi Crump Smith represents the fourth generation in a family-owned florist and nursery business that opened its doors in 1939. Serving both the retail and wholesale trade, Crump's has 75 greenhouses full of spring and fall bedding plants, hanging baskets of every description and seasonal plants such as Easter lilies and poinsettias. While the greenhouses are only open to the public during the Christmas season, everything available wholesale to florists and landscape professionals is offered to the public at the retail store, including fresh flowers and fabulous planted gift baskets. The company offers lots of pots with mixed arrangement plantings, but they also invite clients to bring in their own containers to be planted. There are half-price sales at the end of the fall and spring planting seasons, so ask to be added to the mailing list.
Directions: Take Hwy 75 north of McKinney to Exit 43. Go west on Weston Rd about 0.5 miles. Crump's is on the left side of the road.

Fairview Ponds and Gardens, Inc.
690 South State Hwy 5
Fairview, Texas 75069
214.327.7663
www.fairviewpondsandgardens.com
Hours: Tues–Sat 10–5, Sun 12–5

Owner Michael O'Keefe has embraced "agritainment," a new word that incorporates garden display and entertainment center. Since purchasing the 2.5-acre site in 2001, he has transformed a natural drainage ravine into fabulous outdoor rooms with nine full-scale water gardens and 20 running water features. There are hammocks for relaxing, a cliffhanging G-scale railroad, a Japanese meditation garden and teahouse, a landscape lighting display and two putting greens. "Deadwood Village" mimics an abandoned mining town and showcases fire pits and retaining walls. (Individuals or businesses can rent this space for parties.) There's even a demonstration kitchen garden maintained by Cub Scouts who harvest and distribute the bounty. You'll find hardy shrubs and small trees, including several varieties of Japanese maple, and an array of native perennials for sale in the nursery section. Fish and aquatic supplies are also available here, as well as organic garden supplies. Resident chickens and rabbits provide compost for the demonstration gardens. "We're 110% organic here," says Michael. Note: due to the terrain, access for wheelchairs and strollers is very limited.

Fannin Tree Farms
15700 State Hwy 121
Frisco, Texas 75035
972.747.9233
Hours: Mon–Sat 8–5, Sun 1–5

This firm provides large (3" caliper and up) native and hardy adapted trees for customers all over North Texas. Live oaks, bur oaks, red oaks, cedar elm, Eastern red cedar, bald cypress and Chinese pistache, yaupon holly and eldarica pine are among the species that are available all year. Crepe myrtles are only in stock seasonally so that you can select the variety you want while it is in bloom. Fannin Tree Farms delivers, plants and guarantees everything it sells. The company will also transplant trees, which is a rare service indeed.
Directions: Fannin's is located just west of Custer Rd on 121.

Garden Furnishings

Casual Living Patio & Fireside
8700 Preston Rd #103
Plano, Texas 75024
972.668.6040

7223 Central Expressway (US Hwy 75)
Plano, Texas 75025
972.527.5000
www.casuallivingltd.com
Hours: Mon–Fri 10–7, Sat 10–6, Sun 12–6 (all stores)

Casual Living bills itself as a middle-to-upper-end garden furnishings shop and now has grown to four locations in the Dallas area. Its slogan is, "Going the extra mile," and that means giving customers extra, unexpected attention and effort. The company carries outdoor chairs, tables, swings, gliders and hammocks in cast aluminum, steel and outdoor wicker, and handsome Ancient Mosaics table tops. The furniture lines include Lloyd Flanders, Mallin, Hanamint, Windsor, Woodard, O.W. Lee, and Tropitone, to name a few. You will also find fountains, planters, pergolas, fire pits, gas grills, umbrellas, outdoor rugs, wind chimes and a host of decorative accessories. Look for good sales advertised in the newspaper and coupons and specials on the website.

Heard Natural Science Museum
1 Nature Place
McKinney, Texas 75069
972.562.5566

The gift shop at the Heard Natural Science Museum & Wildlife Sanctuary carries books, gardening gloves and tools as well as birdhouses and feeders. There are two plant sales annually, one in the spring and one in the fall. For the museum's complete listing, see page 58.

Yard Art Patio & Fireplace
3500 Preston Rd
Plano, Texas 75093
972.769.0093

111 North Central Expressway, Suite 114
Allen, Texas 75013
214.547.8144
www.myyardart.com
Hours: Mon–Sat 10–7, Sun 12–6 (all stores)
See Complete listing on page 36.

Bonham (Fannin County)

Specialty Nurseries

Chloe's Plant & Garden Mercantile
709 W. Sam Rayburn Dr (Hwy 56)
Bonham, Texas
903.583.6001
www.chloesnursery.com
Hours: Tues–Sat 9–6 (summer), 9–5 (winter)

Chloe is not the owner here, but rather an adorable lapdog (Coton de Tulear) that presides as if this charming nursery had been her idea. The actual owner is Brenda Daglow, who has restored buildings and transformed three neglected acres at the edge of Bonham's historic district into a series of colorful vignettes with a goldfish pond and an array of old garden favorites. Brenda handpicks the very best plants available from local growers, stocks organic soil amendments, and makes the gorgeous stained glass garden ornaments she sells. You can see her glass flowers, butterflies and dragonflies mounted on trellises and stakes (and a photo of Chloe) on the website. Brenda's custom-made containers are also feasts for the eye. She has an extensive library of garden books, which she's happy to let customers use, and she's more than willing to answer gardening questions. This is not just another place to shop.

Dallas Metropolitan Area (Dallas County)

Garden Centers

Bruce Miller Nursery
1000 E. Belt Line Rd (Main St)
Richardson, Texas
972.238.0204
www.brucemillernursery.com

Hours: Mon–Sat 8–6, Sun 10–5; closes at 5:30 (winter)

What began with a lawn mower in 1969, blossomed into a family of nurseries providing its customers with a wonderful selection of plants, plus professional gardening and landscaping expertise. Bruce Miller Nursery serves both retail customers and landscape professionals; 90% of what the company sells is grown just 40 miles east of Dallas at its huge wholesale nursery. The 10-acre Richardson site has nine greenhouses, which is why you can expect to find 40–50 varieties of herbs, for example, in addition to the large variety of trees, shrubs, perennials and annual color.

The nursery staff is professionally trained to help gardeners with solutions for every landscaping and gardening need. "Our staff is so qualified and knowledgeable," says Kay Miller. "They really love what they're doing and love to answer questions about gardening and plants." Additionally, the nursery regularly brings in distinguished seminar speakers. Steve Bayouth, partner and son-in-law of Bruce and Kay Miller is the general manager here. He notes that many landscape professionals send their own customers to Bruce Miller Nursery to select plants. The company will also plant and guarantee trees for individual customers. You'll find lots of organic gardening options here, as well as big sales at Memorial Day, Fourth of July and Labor Day.

Calloway's Nursery Inc.
14120 Marsh Ln
Addison, Texas 75001
972.484.0784

7410 North Greenville Ave
Dallas, Texas 75231
214.363.0525

723 South Cockrell Hill Rd
Duncanville, Texas 75137
972.283.8021

4220 North Galloway Rd
Mesquite, Texas 75150
972.686.0048

2100 North Plano Rd
Richardson, Texas 75082
972.644.0144
www.calloways.com
Hours: Daily 9–6; generally open until 8 in spring and during Christmas holidays
See complete listing on page 27.

Doan's Nursery Inc.
622 South Belt Line Rd
Irving, Texas 75060
972.790.3500
Hours: Mon–Fri 8–5, Sat–Sun 9–6

Owner John Doan and six employees keep this 2.5-acre nursery humming! You'll find everything for the garden here. Along with all of the landscape plants, there are nine

(LISTING CONTINUED ON THE NEXT PAGE)

(CONTINUED)

greenhouses on site, brimming with tropical houseplants, container plants and hanging baskets. There are materials for walks, patios and walls, soil and soil amendments, irrigation equipment, tools, and garden accessories. The prices are very reasonable. Mr. Doan caters to Irving's large Asian-American population, but gardeners of every cultural background will find this expansive nursery inviting.

Directions: Doan's is between Thousand Oaks Blvd and East Shady Grove.

Landscape Systems of Texas
608 South Pearl
Dallas, Texas 75201
214.748.1435
www.landscapesystems.com
Hours: Mon–Sat 7–6, Sun 8–6

Ed Ruibal founded this company 25 years ago, and has built it into a significant player in the large-scale residential design/build niche. He will be opening another nursery and landscape contracting business in Argyle in the spring of '09. He and his brother Mike (see Ruibal's Plants of Texas) have invested heavily in the Farmers Market District. This nursery carries everything for the garden. Many of the plants are specimen-size, and it's known for the largest selections of Japanese maples and dogwoods in town. Ed has begun gravitating toward drought resistant plants, as well. He notes that with water restrictions in place in 2008 (even though the lakes are presently full), his nursery is stocking an increasing number of native shrubs and perennials.

Mike's Garden Centers
7227 South Westmoreland Rd
Dallas, Texas 75237
972.283.5600
Hours: Mon–Sat 8–8, Sun 8–6 (closing times vary with the seasons; call to confirm)
See complete listing on page 30.

Nicholson-Hardie Nursery & Garden Center
5725 West Lovers Ln (Garden Shop)
5060 West Lovers Ln (Nursery)
Dallas, Texas 75209
214.357.4348 (Garden Shop), 214.357.4674 (Nursery)
www.nicholson-hardie.com
Hours: Mon–Sat 9–6, Sun 12–5 (both locations)

Nicholson-Hardie specializes in top-of-the-line merchandise. In business since 1899 and under present ownership since 1974, this company needed two locations to contain all of the plant materials and home and garden accessories its discriminating clientele requires. Owners Josh and Michael Bracken grew up in this business and learned early that there is no substitute for quality. The Garden Shop is overflowing with gorgeous tropical plants, professionally designed gift baskets and container gardens, seasonal color, herbs, books, diverse containers and accessories and top quality gardening implements. You will also find some bulk as well as packaged seed (wildflower seeds, too) and a large assortment of chemical and natural pest controls.

The Nursery is especially strong in small accent trees (Japanese maples, dogwood, etc.), modern and antique roses and other unusual trees and shrubs, as well as hard-to-find perennials and herbs. Carefully interspersed among the plants, are works of fine art by Texas sculptors and special garden art from around the world. In addition to the owners, there are 16 Certified and Master Certified Nursery Professionals here. "Above all, we specialize in success for our customers," notes Garden Shop Manager John Allen. The company offers seminars on such topics as organic gardening, cooking with herbs, container gardening and attracting birds. To stay informed, use the website and subscribe to their E-Newsletter. "Again, our goal is to sell success," reiterates Nursery Manager Bob Wilson. "Every product we sell comes with the guarantee of 100% satisfaction. Every plant, every tool, every seed and every bulb. Everything."

North Haven Gardens Inc.
7700 Northaven Rd
Dallas, Texas 75230
214.363.5316
www.nhg.com
Hours: Mon–Sat 9–6, Sun 10–5:30 (April–Oct); Mon–Sat 9–5:30, Sun 10–5 (Nov–Mar)

Why has North Haven Gardens been a top destination for gardeners since 1951? It has the largest selection of quality plants and unusual varieties year round. Free educational programs are offered weekly so you can stay up-to-date on the best new plants and gardening techniques. Plus, the staff is extremely knowledgeable and friendly; many are degreed horticulturists, Texas Certified Nursery Professionals or Master Gardeners. You'll find an impressive selection of tools, books, gifts and accessories. North Haven Gardens takes pride in its huge selection of eco-friendly and organic products — everything from a full line of organic garden products to composters and rain barrels. Everything you need for a great garden experience!

The first weekend of March, North Haven Gardens holds its Rose Weekend with more than 300 rose varieties from which to choose. If you grow your own veggies and herbs, the company is well known for a wide selection and for its spring and fall Herb Festivals. In fall, the nursery offers hundreds of varieties of spring blooming bulbs, and it's the only nursery in North Texas that will store and chill your tulip, hyacinth and crocus bulbs until planting time! "Here at North Haven Gardens, we pride ourselves on having beautiful plant material year around, excellent customer service and an emphasis on education. When our customers have successful gardens, we feel we have done our job," says general manager Leslie Finical Halleck. For events, programs, and great gardening info, visit the website.

Directions: North Haven Gardens is located on Northaven Rd (between Royal Ln and Forest Ln), 0.1 mile west of Central Expressway.

Petal Pushers Garden Emporium
813 Straus Rd
Cedar Hill, Texas 75104
972.291.7650
www.petalpushersgarden.net
Hours: Mon–Sat 9–6, Sun 12–5

Located only 15 minutes south of downtown Dallas, this complete, all-organic garden center may be the most relaxing environment in the busy Metroplex. Formerly known as Kings Creek Gardens, it was designed by landscape architect Rosa Finsley. Lovely demonstration beds brimming with unusual plant material surround the weathered building. "Our staff

(LISTING CONTINUED ON THE NEXT PAGE)

(CONTINUED)

has always consisted of real gardeners! We're constantly testing and propagating new plants," says owner Angela Groom. The specialties here include natives, herbs, unusual perennials, English and antique roses and aquatic plants. There's also a nice selection of large trees. In this comfortable atmosphere you can browse through books and peruse the accessories and twig furniture. "We want you to visit us for the experience alone — hopefully finding something to add to your own garden." Throughout the year, the website invites customers to attend various programs and lectures for inspiration. There's an online newsletter and lots of great gardening tips.

Directions: From Dallas, take I-35 S to 67 S and exit at FM 1382. Turn right and cross the bridge. After crossing the bridge, stay in the left lane and turn left on Straus. Look for the sign on the right.

Rohde's Nursery and Nature Center
1651 Wall St
Garland, Texas 75041
972.864.1934
www.beorganic.com
Hours: Mon–Sat 7:30–5:30, Sun 10–5

Rohde's Nursery and Nature Store was one of the first nurseries in Texas to carry only organic fertilizers and employ pest control that uses beneficial insects, microorganisms and bacteria products. The staff's knowledge in the use of organic gardening techniques is unsurpassed. You'll find a great selection of native plants, big trees, lots of perennials and herbs, as well as everything to attract birds. About this earth-friendly store, owner Gregory Rohde says, "We try to carry unusual plant material and products at prices lower than our competitors' for products normally stocked everywhere. We manufacture our own organic fertilizers and other organic products, so we have an edge. You'll also find garden books, gifts and accessories and products for pets here." The company has added organic spraying and an organic fertilization program to its list of services. Watch the website for sales, and plan to attend the frequent seminars in Rohde's little red schoolhouse.

Directions: From LBJ, go North on Garland Rd 2 blocks to Leon Rd. Turn right onto Leon Rd and go 1 block to Wall St. Turn left onto Wall.

Walton's Garden Center
8652 Garland Rd
Dallas, Texas 75218
214.321.2387
www.waltonsgarden.com
Hours: Mon–Sat 8:30–6, Sun 11–5

Located across from the Dallas Arboretum, this is a popular stop for people inspired to revamp their own gardens. In addition to flowering shrubs, Walton's well-organized 1.5-acre site is just brimming with perennials, herbs and bedding plants. We were surprised to find such a wonderful selection of Japanese maples, but much of the site is shady, which suits them fine. The tree canopy helps provide a pleasant browsing experience for people, as well. We thought the pots were especially handsome and found a good selection of fountains and garden accessories as well as tools, books and some furniture. Manager Greg Fairchild told us that there has been a nursery on this property since 1944. The old stucco house where most of the accessories are displayed was a speakeasy during prohibition. The Walton family bought the property over twenty years ago with the goal of keeping this valuable eastside nursery viable. It's fully organic now, with tons of Texas native plants and a well-informed staff. The company also offers landscape design and installation services.

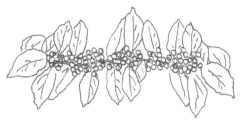

Specialty Nurseries

Cristina's Garden Center
4617 West Lovers Ln
Dallas, Texas 75209
214.357.5626
www.cristinasflowersinc.com
Hours: Daily 8–7 (summer) 8–6 (winter)
This is a much smaller version of the Collin County store, but the same good values apply. See complete listing on page 61.

Dallas Farmers Market District
1010 Pearl St
Dallas Texas 75201
214.939.2808
www.dallasfarmersmarket.org
Hours: Daily 7–6
It can easily take a whole day to explore the garden shops in this huge area bounded by Central Expressway on the east, I-30 on the South, St. Paul on the west, and north to Commerce St. The whole market is blooming with fresh flowers, garden decorations and a mélange of indoor and outdoor plants. Plan to load your car or truck with flats of seasonal color! Only two nurseries are within the actual Farmers Market. Sunset Plants (at the corner of Marilla & Harwood) is packed with houseplants and bedding plants. Caliper Flower Market (on Marilla St in front of Shed 2) specializes in seasonal color. Near the market is Amigo's Pottery (Cadiz at Harwood), where you'll find a huge collection of rustic decor. Also nearby are numerous plant purveyors worth exploring. Texas Palm Trees & Plants, Ruibal's Plants of Texas and Landscape Systems of Texas are so large in scale that we are giving them stand-alone listings in this edition of the book.

Dickson Brothers, Inc.
204 North Galloway
Mesquite, Texas 75149
972.288.7537
www.dicksonbrothers.com
Hours: Mon–Fri 8–5:30, Sat 8–5
As manager Mary Traveland proudly proclaims, "We have been your water gardening headquarters for 35 years, and we only carry the best!" You will find absolutely everything

(LISTING CONTINUED ON THE NEXT PAGE)

(CONTINUED)

you could ever need in this company's 20,000-square-foot showroom and 0.5-acre outdoor site. In the way of hard goods, Dickson Brothers has both flexible pond liners and green fiberglass pre-formed basins imported from England. You'll also find a wide array of pumps, filtration systems, underwater lighting systems and floating fountains from an impressive array of manufacturers. There are freestanding fountains, decorative bridges and benches here as well. And, of course, fish and fish supplies. All of the water plants here are Texas-grown. The hardy, tropical day- and night-blooming water lilies are potted, established and ready to go. Also offered are marginal bog plants, oxygenators, and aquatic fertilizer tabs. You will find informative books, brochures and handouts (we particularly liked the seasonal check lists), as well as a most helpful, informative staff. If you are even thinking about a water garden, see this company's website. Dickson Brothers ships its products all over the country.

Directions: From Hwy 635 E, take the Military Pkwy exit and go east. Take a left on Galloway toward downtown Mesquite.

Jackson's Home and Garden
6950 Lemmon Ave
Dallas, Texas 75209
214.350.9200
Hours: Mon–Sat 9–6, Sun 12–5

This small, sophisticated nursery surrounds two sides of a garden furnishings store that is second to none in the state! The outdoor garden offers every kind of plant material except trees. Not only is there copious seasonal color, with special emphasis on unusual perennials, but also Jackson's is well known for its large selection of herbs and ground covers. See complete listing on page 73.

Plants & Planters
1050 North Greenville Ave
Richardson, Texas
972.699.1281
Hours: Mon–Sat 9–6, Sun 10–5; open an hour later mid–March–Memorial Day

The best-kept secret in the Metroplex may be this little nursery wedged between Central Expressway and the new DART line. Welcome to Paradise! You'll be wowed by the tropical plants. Owners Shelley Rosenfeld and Jerry Duncan hand-select all the pots and plants that go into their shop. You'll find good statuary, fountains, containers and wall decor. They carry a large selection of indoor cactus from a grower in Florida. (Shelley has 35 years of experience with houseplants.) They also carry some hard-to-find shrubs, and everything is native to Texas or Louisiana. And, they offer more than 200 varieties of perennials.

Directions: Exit Hwy 75 at Arapahoe. Travel east to Greenville and turn left.

Redenta's Garden
2001 Skillman
Dallas, Texas 75206
214.823.9421
www.redentas.com
Hours: Mon—Sat 9—6, Sun 10—5

The herbs and perennials really make this small store special. See complete listing on page 31.

Ruibal's Plants of Texas
601 South Pearl Expresway
Dallas, Texas 75201
214.744.9100

7219 East Grand Ave
Dallas, Texas 75214
214.324.4800
www.ruibals.com
Hours: Daily 8–6 (same at both locations)

Ruibal's is always breathtaking with its wall-to-wall seasonal color. In addition to every imaginable annual plant, you'll find perennials and herbs. The wall-to-wall flats of annuals at the Farmers Market remind one of a giant quilt! This company grows most of the bedding plants it sells on a thirty-acre farm nearby. Mike Ruibal and his brother Ed (see Landscape Systems of Texas) grew up in Colorado and moved to Texas in the early '80s. Mike began selling bedding plants with a small truck, a 10' x 20' daily rental space at the Dallas Farmers Market and a desire to satisfy every customer. Now the entire Ruibal family works to expand their reputation for excellence, both in service and in the quality of plants. They've added pottery and statuary, and they offer their own patented topiary system that includes iron basket planters, obelisks and arbors.

Sunshine Miniature Trees
7118 Greenville Ave
Dallas, Texas 75231
214.691.0127
www.sunshinebonsai.com
Hours: Daily 9–6

This premier source for bonsai in North Texas has been the darling of plant enthusiasts since 1966. Although we have shopped here many times, we only recently learned that it got its name from Robert and Mayme Sunshine, not from the sunny spirit of the staff or the yellow hue of the building. Their son Richard left a law practice to work with his parents in the early '70s, and he has continued to built the company's reputation on attentive customer service and a splendid array of plants and pots. "We like to talk about bonsai as much as you do," says Richard. The store carries a lot of rare plants for indoor and outdoor uses — exotic fruit trees as well as maples, cypress, zelkova, azaleas, a wide assortment of cacti and succulents. You'll find lush tropical houseplants and hanging baskets, too. It's a one-stop source for books, tools, wire, planters and all related bonsai supplies. "We use our buying power to give our customers the very best prices possible. If we don't have what you want, we can probably get it for you quickly or help you find it elsewhere. Our goal is 100% customer delight," says Richard. Some of his plants are imported from Asia and Central America or obtained from California, Florida and Texas growers, but many are propagated onsite. There's a wide range of finished bonsais as well as a lot of "rough" plants for customers who want to create their own works of art. "We will pot the plants you purchase in your own container or one here at the nursery, finishing it with ground cover, rocks and moss," he promises. Many customers have plants potted as gifts. Sunshine delivers locally and ships nationwide.

Texas Palm Trees & Plants
NW corner of Harwood & Cadiz in Farmers Market District
Dallas, Texas 75201
214.741.2310

7807 East I-30 (R.L. Thornton Freeway)
Dallas, Texas 75228
214.741.2310
www.texaspalmtreesdallas.com
Hours: Mon–Sat 8–5, Sun 9–5

Texas Palm Trees and Plants, Inc. has brought the Southern Texas tropical trail to Dallas, but here the palms are cold hardy, and the company also carries tropical-looking, winter-hardy trees and shrubs. The large selection of cacti impressed us, and we were especially surprised to find a good selection of orchids and bromeliads. There's a huge selection of terra cotta pots and an array of freestanding and wall fountains, as well. Family-owned and operated, it has been in business for over 17 years.

Water Gardens Galore
2530 Butler
Dallas, Texas 75235
214.956.7382
www.wggalore.com
Hours: Tues–Sat 9:30–5

Barbara and Steve Moeller, a mother and son team, design, install and maintain small garden features. "We exist in a highly-specialized niche," says Steve. "There is more to water gardening than digging a hole and dropping something in it. To be successful, you must have a clear goal in mind and get solid information and quality materials." Since the company moved from the old Lovers Lane location, the showroom is entirely indoors, but there's more room for displays of ponds and fountains, as well as high-quality pumps, filters, plants, fish and food. The Moellers cheerfully provide all the advice a "do-it-yourselfer" may need or want. Their website offers images of lovely ponds, instructions for winter care and an interesting Q & A.

Garden Furnishings

Casual Living Patio & Fireside
17390 Preston Rd # 120
Dallas, Texas 75252
972.735.9493

3400 North I-35E
Carrollton, Texas 75007
972.245.7789
www.casuallivingltd.com
Hours: Mon–Fri 10–7, Sat 10–6, Sun 12–6 (all stores)
Casual Living is headquartered in Carrollton. See complete listing on page 63.

Dallas Arboretum
8525 Garland Rd
Dallas, Texas 75218
214.515.6500
Hours: Daily 9–5
In addition to an extensive collection of garden related books, the gift shop at the Dallas Arboretum and Botanical Society has many other items of interest to the gardener...seeds, tools, aprons, gloves and garden ornaments. The annual plant sale is held in April. For the Arboretum's complete listing, see page 55.

Jackson's Home and Garden
6950 Lemmon Ave
Dallas, Texas 75209
214.350.9200
www.jacksonshomeandgarden.com
Hours: Mon–Sat 9–6, Sun 12–5
Whether you are planning to furnish an elegant terrace or outdoor kitchen, looking for handsome ceramic pottery or decorating for Christmas, there's probably exactly what you want right here. Housed in a lovely red brick Williamsburg-style building, which has been recently expanded to 37,000 square-feet, Jackson's will simply knock your socks off! The awesome selection of containers (largest in the Southwest) includes cast stone, Italian terra cotta and Asian glazed pottery in every shape and size. It's personally chosen and of exceptional quality! Cast stone pots and fountains can be beautifully faux-finished to your specifications. You'll also find handsome bronze fountains and statuary, plus gifts and accessories and a roomful of top-quality barbeque grills.

Upstairs you'll discover a huge selection of teak, cast aluminum, wicker and wrought iron garden furniture from 10–12 manufacturers and gorgeous marble tabletops from Italy. Jackson's has added a custom-design department offering specialty gift baskets, which can be made as you desire and shipped to any destination. At Christmastime, Jackson's really "decks the halls." Sales are held Memorial Day, July 4th, Labor Day and the "really big one" after Christmas. As reported in the Park Cities News, "Personalized service and satisfaction to the customer is guaranteed, and Mr. Jackson is in the store daily to answer any questions." It is his attention to detail that has made this store what it is. Trust us, you will find something you "just have to have."

Into the Garden
4527 McKinney Ave
Dallas, Texas
214.351.5125
www.intothegardentx.com
Hours: Mon–Sat 10–6, Sun 12–5
(LISTING CONTINUED ON THE NEXT PAGE)

(CONTINUED)

This Dallas store, which opened 1999, was modeled after Into the Garden in Fort Worth, which had began attracting a discriminating clientele six years earlier. The stores are somewhat different in atmosphere, but both offer the same alluring selection of plants, outdoor furniture, garden art and accessories. See complete listing on page 44.

Landscape Lighting Supply Co.
780 South Floyd Rd
Richardson, Texas 75080
972.480.9700 or 800.238.0346
www.landscapelight.com
Hours: Mon–Fri 8–5, Sat 10–4

As far as we know, this is the state's only store devoted exclusively to outdoor lighting. The showroom is set up to turn off all other lights and let you see the illumination pattern of whatever fixture you are considering for your property. Products from all of the major manufacturers (including Focus, FX, Kim, Greenlee, Lumiere, Hevilite, Hadco, Unique and Kichler) in solid copper, painted brass and cast aluminum are available here. You can also order from the company's excellent website where you'll find all of the components involved in an outdoor lighting system. The website has a photo gallery of lighting techniques and helpful installation tips. The company has experts to assist you with the design and wiring plan for your lighting system. "We know landscape lighting!" says owner Ed Barger. "If you aren't the 'do-it-yourself' type, we would be more than happy to recommend reputable lighting contractors in your area."

Sunnyland Furniture
7979 Spring Valley Rd
Dallas, Texas 75254
972.239.3716
www.sunnylandfurniture.com
Hours: Tues, Wed, Fri & Sat 9–6, Mon & Thurs 9–9 (closes at 7 from Oct thru Feb), Sun 12–5

When owner David Schweig told us that he carries the largest selection of outdoor/casual furnishings and accessories available in the Southwest, we had no reason to quibble! Since 1970 Sunnyland has grown into a 35,000-square-foot showroom and clearance center and 30,000-square-foot on-site distribution center. There are over 300 outdoor patio sets and umbrellas on display at any given time, plus patio accessories and a huge selection of replacement cushions in every imaginable size and color. The website takes you into the product lines of 30 different manufacturers whose products range from quite moderate to very upscale. "We have quality furnishings at competitive prices backed by our complete parts, service and umbrella repair department," says David. There is even the promise of "free glides for life." A family-owned and operated store, Sunnyland seeks to give each customer "the personal attention you deserve." Once a month during the spring and summer, David appears on Good Morning Texas (WFAA Channel 8) to discuss ways to maximize the comfort of your outdoor spaces. "We specialize in extreme comfort."

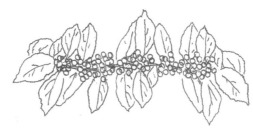

Denison / Sherman (Grayson County)

Garden Centers

Twin Oaks Landscape and Nursery
2107 Hwy 691
Denison, Texas 75020
903.463.2205

2120 Hwy 1417
Sherman, Texas 75092
903.870.7800
Hours: Mon–Sat 8:30–5:30, Sun 1–5:30 (March–Sept)

Luella and Bob Graham sold their little grocery store in Waterman, Illinois and moved to Dennison where their two sons, Bruce and Brian had begun a landscape business. Daughter Linda Graham-Taube and her family joined them soon after. The nursery they started "from scratch" in 1980 has since blossomed into a seven-acre site that includes 20 greenhouses and serves both retail and wholesale customers in a wide area of North Texas. Luella modestly explained the secret to Twin Oaks' success, "We try to handle the highest quality plant materials we can find. We have well informed sales personnel (the company is staffed with numerous Certified Nursery Professionals and master gardeners). We feel that our operation is an asset to our community and a pleasant experience for all who shop here." She might have added what we observed: the success is due to one very energetic family! Their plant selection is huge. Twin Oaks takes pride in providing specimen trees and shrubs, grows over 600 varieties of perennials and annuals, carries its own brand of lawn fertilizer and a full line of organics. Over the years the nursery has expanded into water gardening supplies, tools, books and handsome garden accessories as well as landscape design, irrigation and installation. It's hard to imagine a livelier place to find absolutely everything for the garden. The Sherman store is more of a boutique, with seasonal color its specialty.

Specialty Nurseries

Gardenland Nursery
810 Frisco Rd
Sherman, Texas 75090
903.868.1938
Hours: Mon–Sat 8:30–5:30; closes at 3:30 in summer and is closed on Monday in winter.

LISTING CONTINUED ON THE NEXT PAGE)

(CONTINUED)

Gary and Judy Milton, who grew up in the area, bought this somewhat rundown little nursery in 2007. When we visited they were hard at work remodeling the building, cleaning up the creek that runs through the property and creating paths. They plan to create a collector's nursery with hard to find native shrubs and perennials, hummingbird and butterfly attractors, vegetable and herbs and organic supplies. They've set up a potting bench where customers can bring in their own pots to fill with colorful plants, and folks are coming by to browse, buy and learn. We wish these passionate gardeners well with their new venture!
Directions: Turn south on Broughton off Texoma Pkwy and take an immediate left onto Frisco.

Forney/Terrell (Kaufman County)

Garden Centers

Homesley Nursery & Landscape
707 West Broad St (FM 688)
Forney, Texas 75126
972.564.1426
Hours: Mon–Sat 9–6, Sun 11–4

There is a very good selection of healthy plant material from which to choose at the tidy nursery. Third-generation nurseryman John B Homesley assumed its operation in the early '80s. He now has four acres that include 11 greenhouses in which he grows a lot of spring and fall annuals and perennials as well as vegetables and herbs. Homesley's also carries a good selection of trees and shrubs; the live oaks and red oaks here are grown onsite. Nature's Guide organic products are among the garden supplies the company offers. The staff is very friendly and knowledgeable.
Directions: Take Hwy 80 to FM 688 (old Hwy 80).

J & T Nursery
5126 West Hwy 80
Terrell, Texas 75160
972.524.0806
Hours: Mon–Sat 8:30–5, Sun 1–3

An engineer by training, John Doan emigrated from Viet Nam and found his true passion in the landscape business. His "no frills" garden center is simply two-acres of carefully tended plants and all the supplies you'll need to keep them healthy. He has a large section of organics that includes Back to Earth soil amendments, compost tea, green sand and lava sand. He also does landscape design and installation.

Greenville (Hunt County)

Garden Center

Steve's Nursery
4386 Hwy 34 S
Greenville, Texas 75402
903.883.2911

Hours: Daily 8–6:30; closed Christmas

Since 1977, Steve's Nursery has provided customers with top quality plants, as well as seeds, organic fertilizers, soil amendments and mulches. Here you'll find friendly people ready to offer sound garden advice. Four staff members here are Texas Master Certified Nursery Professionals. We found owner Steve Goode to be especially charming and knowledgeable. "We grow many of the shrubs and roses we sell, which helps keep prices down and quality up," he explained. "We regularly receive our bedding plants, vegetables and herb plants, perennials and container-grown trees from select growers nearby." Their printed plant lists are very, very impressive.

December through February the company sells bare-root fruit and pecan trees, which are handled "the old-fashioned way" in large bins of sawdust to keep the roots from drying out. "You choose your trees, and we will prune them and bag them for your trip home," he says. To provide the best-quality roses, he pots up Jackson & Perkins roses in January for sale in late March, when the plants are established and beginning to bloom. At a nearby farm, the company grows a wide array of old garden roses, hard-to-find flowering shrubs and perennials, an array of berries and small fruits, plus several varieties of crepe myrtle that have proven to be hardy and mildew resistant. Steve actively promotes organic garden products, and although he carries some chemicals, he "refuses to sell anything that is highly toxic." *Directions: The nursery is located 5.0 miles south of I-30 across from the Cash Water Tower.*

Paris/Detroit (Lamar County)

Garden Centers

Bratcher's Nursery & Landscaping
1744 FM 1502
Detroit, Texas 75436
903.982.5918

Hours: Mon–Sat 9–5:30

Family-owned and operated for 30 years, Bratcher's is a complete garden center that offers friendly professional customer service and landscape design. The nursery's forte is its large selection of container-grown shade and fruit trees. Other plant materials include shrubs, herbs, seasonal color, seeds, vegetable starts and water plants. Arbors, trellises, statuary, fountains and ponds complement the plant list. Gift items include custom-made gift baskets, books and antiques. Says owner Wynell Bratcher, "Both my husband and I are Texas Certified Nursery Professionals, and our service and low prices make our company worth the drive." *Directions: Turn north off Hwy 82 between Blossom and Detroit.*

Mulberry Creek Nursery
4645 Lamar Ave
Paris, Texas 75460
903.784.0146
Hours; Mon–Sat 8–6; closes at 1 on Sat in hot weather

In 1991 Jo Blackburn began working at this 1.2-acre general nursery her husband founded. When he died three years later, it became her "labor of love." The five greenhouses and three shade structures hold a large assortment of plants from trees to grasses and water plants. She propagates some of what she sells and buys all of the rest from reliable Texas growers. She observes that landscape installation is her favorite part of the business, and she also enjoys making container gardens and hanging baskets for her loyal clientele. "The best ad is a happy customer," she notes.

Waxahachie/Midlothian (Ellis County)

Garden Centers

The Greenery
3708 North Hwy 77
Waxahachie, Texas 75165
972.617.5459
810 East Main St
Midlothian, Texas 76065
972.723.0702
www.thegreenerytx.com
Hours: Mon–Sat 8–6; Sun 1–5 (March–May)

There are over four acres of colorful plants and delightful pottery and iron work to be discovered at the Waxahachie store. Founded in 1987 by lifelong Ellis County residents Deborah and Scott Green, the company has expanded to include their grown children, Cassie and Bruce. The staff, which they describe as "awesome", includes three certified nursery professionals, three people with degrees in plant science and a licensed irrigator. These folks know the local soils and local plants! Scott now spends most of his time managing their wholesale tree farm, and the family has opened a second, smaller retail store on a beautiful site in Midlothian.

Both locations specialize in native Texas plants and trees of all sizes, including a huge selection of crepe myrtles. You'll also find a complete line of organic products including Nature's Guide, Rabbit Hill Farms, Lady Bug and Garden-Ville to name a few. Their website features a comprehensive chart of products and how to apply them. Landscaped with seasonal color, fountains and arbors, the entire Waxahachie property feels like a garden. A wonderful old house and formal garden on the grounds can be rented for business dinners, weddings and private parties. The most popular events here are public plant auctions in February, July and October. Check the website for details.

Will's Point (NW Van Zandt County)

Garden Centers

Chitty's Garden Center
817 Hwy 80 E
Wills Point, Texas 75169
903.873.2553
Hours: Mon–Sat 8–5

As Randy Chitty told us, "This garden center has been in our family since 1953, and we carry a little bit of everything." You will find 20–30 species of trees, a good selection of hardy shrubs and the most popular perennials. There are accessories and everything for maintaining the garden here, including some organics. Chitty's offers a large array of houseplants in the spring as well as lots of seasonal color.

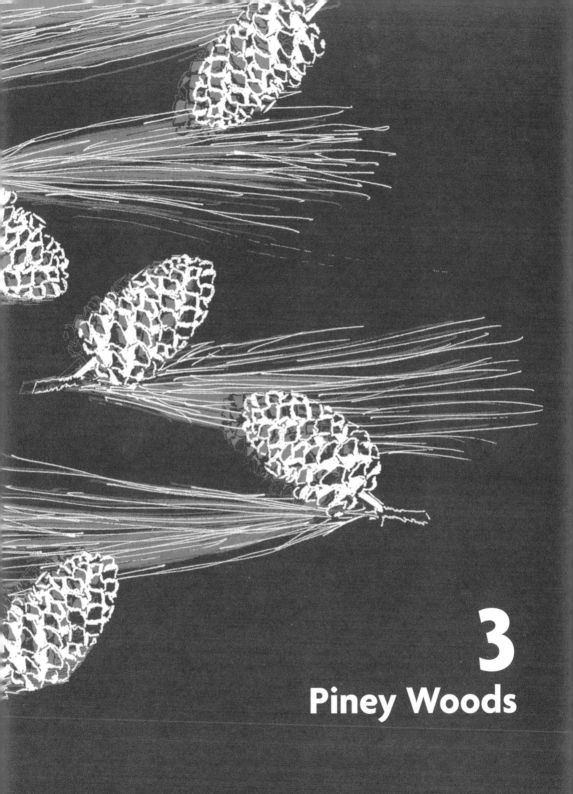

3
Piney Woods

Piney Woods

Although named for its three species of pine (longleaf, shortleaf and loblolly), the woods were originally replete with other venerable trees as well — beech, elms, hickories, magnolias, maples, oaks and sweet gums. Unlike most urban areas in Texas, which are visible from miles around, the cities of Tyler, Longview, Marshall, Nacogdoches and Lufkin are tucked into dense forests. The region extends from Texarkana south through the Big Thicket National Preserve, which is one of four National Forests in East Texas.

The landscape appears uniformly luxuriant. However, with few exceptions, the second-growth forests that we see today do not contain the rich ecological mix that existed before the first sawmills were built here in the early nineteenth century. By the 1940s, almost all of the native forests had been timbered. In many areas, including the National Forests, pine plantations have replaced the mature forests that nurtured a mix of pines and hardwoods and an abundance of wildlife.

Selective breeding has produced fast-growing pines, and while the planted seedlings quickly grow tall, all of them mature at the same rate. Such a monoculture supports fewer plant and animal species and is more vulnerable to insects and diseases. Where the forests are left natural, a thick understory of dogwood, yaupon holly, paw-paw, plum, cherry laurel and wax myrtle can make these gently rolling woodlands almost impenetrable.

The Piney Woods is far more diverse than it appears. Five major plant communities reflect differences in soils, moisture levels and elevation. The northern portions vary from dry uplands to moderately moist upland forests, with swampy areas alongside the creeks and riverbanks. **Governor Hogg State Historical Park** at Quitman provides an excellent example of a dry upland landscape. A transition zone between pine and post oak woodlands, this park is of interest to East Texas gardeners and history buffs alike. Here, you'll find a 0.5-mile nature/interpretive trail where the vegetation has remained undisturbed since 1900. At nearby **Daingerfield State Park**, springtime brings breathtaking color to the rolling hills when the dogwoods, redbuds and wisteria burst into bloom. In autumn, sweetgum, oak and maple trees produce dazzling shades of red and gold.

One of the most ethereal landscapes of Northeast Texas can be discovered in **Caddo Lake State Park**. While most Texas lakes are manmade, a vast natural logjam created this one. Ultimately the jam was removed, and the Army Corps of Engineers drained the lake in 1873. It was dammed in the early 1900s, but it still looks much as it might have in mid-nineteenth-century with dense vegetation that includes lotus and lily pads and hundreds of swampy cypress islands. The park consists of over seven thousand acres along Little Cypress Bayou, which feeds into Caddo Lake. There's an interpretive center, 1.5 miles of hiking trails, and a 0.75-mile nature trail. According to the Parks and Recreation Department, "Naturalists will enjoy the stately cypress trees, the lotus and lily pads, the waterfowl, alligators, turtles, frogs, raccoons, minks, nutrias, beavers and snakes." ("Enjoying" snakes may be what separates naturalists from other folks.)

The central portion of the Piney Woods is often called "Deep East Texas." Palestine stands on its western edge, straddling the line between Trinity Blacklands and Piney Woods. In late March, Texans stream to **Davey Dogwood Park** in Palestine to see the dogwoods in bloom, as well as flowering plum and wisteria, redbud and tulip trees. Five miles of narrow paved roads wind through the hills, leading to scenic overlooks, trailheads and sparkling brooks. In the center of East Texas is Nacogdoches, the oldest city in Texas, which was named for the Caddo family of Indians who once lived in the area. Spain established a mission here in 1716 on the old El Camino Real, and later Nacogdoches became a gateway from the newly formed United States to the Texas frontier.

All of the trees and understory plants of the Piney Woods are labeled at the wonderful **Mast Arboretum** at Stephen F. Austin State University in Nacogdoches. It features an impressive azalea garden, and other themed gardens display a wide array of cultivated plants. Closer to the Louisiana border, **Wild Azalea Canyons Trail** in Newton County allows visitors to walk deep into the forest where native azaleas (*Rhododendron canescens*) bloom on rocky cliffs under a canopy of long-leaf pines. Begun as a project of the Magnolia Garden Club, this breathtaking wild area is now maintained by the Newton Chamber of Commerce on Temple Inland Forest Products Corporation's private land.

The southern forests are more moist than the sandy hills of Northeast Texas. **Mission Tejas State Park** at Weches occupies 363 acres at the northern tip of the Davy Crockett National Forest. Built in 1934 by the CCC as a representation of the first Spanish mission, this 363-acre park is all rustic beauty beneath a canopy of tall pines. There are 3.5 miles of trails, plus a large nature pond, which offers an opportunity to explore aquatic life. A wealth of garden-worthy plants grow wild in **Martin Dies, Jr. State Park**, which lies in the heart of the Big Thicket between Woodland and Jasper. This 705-acre park showcases genuine old growth forest. Its numerous sloughs are lined with mature cypress, willow, beech, magnolia and sweet bay. In autumn the golden hues of beeches are brilliant against the reds of blackgums, maples and oaks, mixed among the evergreen pines. A garden area displays native East Texas plants and medicinal, culinary and fragrant herbs.

Although greatly reduced from its original three and a half million acres, the remaining 86,000 acres of the **Big Thicket National Preserve** are the least altered area of the Piney Woods. It was saved from destruction partially because settlers avoided the area (wagons routinely became mired down in its bayous). These swampy bottomlands still nurture bald cypress and water tupelo, beneath which grow numerous rare and endangered species, including orchids and pitcher plants.

The Alabama and Coushatta Indians preserve about four thousand acres on their reservation east of Livingston at the northern edge of a section of the Big Thicket. The major access point to the forest is from the Visitor Information Center north of Kountze. The Big Thicket is designated an International Biosphere Reserve by the United Nations. Its several distinct plant communities range from cypress bogs to upland forests. The forests are richly layered, with tall, medium and small trees towering over an understory of shrubs and ground covers (including ferns and mosses) that retain moisture around the tree roots. Ecologists estimate that it would take about a thousand years for such a forest to regenerate.

Decomposing leaves and an average 46 inches of rainfall each year combine to make sandy loam soil in the Piney Woods register acid on the pH scale. Such acid-loving plants as azaleas, camellias and blueberries flourish naturally here. In a few areas where the post oak is the dominant native tree species, however, the soils are too sandy to hold moisture for very long. The entire Piney Woods region falls within USDA Zone 8. Winter temperatures will occasionally dip down to into the teens, but compared to most other regions of Texas, gardening is almost effortless. In addition to the Mast Arboretum in Nacodoches, the **East Texas Arboretum & Botanical Society** in Athens and **Tyler Municipal Rose Garden** offer inspiration and instruction for gardening here. Find complete descriptions of these great public gardens in Chapter Two of *Texas Gardening for the 21st Century*.

Public Gardens and Nature Preserves to Visit

Athens (Henderson County)

Public Gardens and Nature Preserves to Visit

East Texas Arboretum & Botanical Society
1601 Patterson Rd
Athens, Texas 75751
903.675.5630
www.eastexasarboretum.org
Hours: 7:30–7:30 (spring and summer), 8–6 (fall and winter)
Admission: suggested $2 donation per person over 12 years of age

An abandoned truck farm covered with debris and carpeted with tenacious Bermuda grass would seem an unlikely site for an arboretum. Its only asset was a small creek where a tangle of cherry laurel, poplar and a variety of hardwoods grew. Unfortunately, dense underbrush made this marshy area virtually impenetrable! In 1991, a small group of dedicated visionaries began to dream of restoring the 100-acre property as a regional botanical garden. Board members refer to its purchase a "leap of faith" since the organization had "no funds, no assets and few members." In less than 20 years, volunteers, generous donors, grants and foundation awards have transformed the place into an "attraction," replete with colorful gardens, historical structures (moved from other sites), hiking trails and classrooms. The rear garden of the 152-year-old Wofford House is designed to replicate a 19th-century kitchen and medicinal garden.

Nacogdoches (Nacogdoches County)

Mast Arboretum at Stephen F. Austin State University
2900 Raquet St
Nacogdoches, Texas 75962
936.468.1832
www.arboretum.sfasu.edu
Hours: Daily dawn to dusk
Admission: free

Begun in 1985 as a small planting area beside the Agriculture Building, this facility has quickly risen to national stature under the direction of Dr. David Creech. The Mast Arboretum's twenty-four acre site is on the main campus of SFASU. Through trades with many of the nation's top arboretums and the gifts of numerous Texas growers, the Mast Arboretum has evolved into an outstanding collection with over 8,600 plants representing over 300 taxa. Its trees, shrubs, vines, ground covers, grasses and herbaceous perennials are arranged into a series of theme gardens. The Ruby M. Mize Azalea Garden is an eight-acre site bisected by LaNana creek, a stream that wanders through the canopy of the University's loblolly pines. In addition to 6,500 hybrid evergreen and native deciduous azaleas, it showcases new plants being introduced by growers from across the South. The sandy loam soil of this floodplain makes it a prime location for such plants as Japanese maples, camellias and other species that thrive in acid soil. A visitor can easily spend a day exploring the arboretum, which features a Texas heritage garden, a "dry" garden that features new plants from western states and Mexico, and the "woodland glen" with its collection of native ferns, hostas and other shade-loving plants. There is a butterfly garden, an "endangered plants" garden, plus a rock garden just south of the daylily collection and an herb garden, maintained by the Herb Society of Deep East Texas. The arboretum's mission is to promote the conservation, selection and use of native plants and encourage diversity in the landscape philosophy of Texas.

Tyler (Smith County)

Tyler Municipal Rose Garden
420 South Rose Park Dr
Tyler, Texas 75702
903.597.3130 (museum) or 903.531.1212 (garden)
www.texasrosefestival.com

Hours: Daily dawn to dusk. Gardens are closed periodically to treat pest and disease problems. Museum & gift shop: Tues–Fri 9–4, Sat 10–4, Sun 1:30–4
Admission: Gardens free. Museum: $3.50 (adults), $2 (children 3–11)

Spring and fall are peak seasons at the nation's largest municipal rose garden, but its daylilies delight in summer and the Vance Burks Memorial Camellia Garden extends its appeal through the winter. What words can describe nearly 35,000 rose bushes exhibiting approximately 600 varieties of roses? Over 100,000 people from around the world visit each year to see roses of every imaginable color in six acres of terraced beds. The bulk of the collection consists of hybrid teas, floribundas and grandifloras. Of special interest to rosarians is the All American Rose Selection test garden (one of only 24 in the country) where new varieties are evaluated before they can be selected and patented. Our favorite section is the one-acre Heritage Rose and Sensory Garden, which features hardy varieties that date back to the 19th century. The Idea Garden, developed by the Smith County Master Gardeners, demonstrates plants that combine well with roses. Most of the garden's 14-acre site is wheelchair/stroller accessible; it also features a picnic area, fountains and a gazebo. Inside, a gift shop offers potpourris, garden books and other rose-related items. The Rose Museum features historical mementos of the Texas Rose Festival and a film that tells about Tyler's rose industry. *Directions: From Loop 323, take Hwy 31 (which runs east-west through town) to Rose Park Dr.*

Piney Woods Resources

Canton/Chandler (Van Zandt County)

Specialty Nurseries

Blue Moon Gardens
13062 FM 279
Chandler, Texas 75758
903.852.3897
www.bluemoongardens.com
Hours: Mon–Sat 9–5:30, Sun 10–5

Featured in *Southern Living* magazine, Blue Moon Gardens has expanded since our last visit, but it remains an oasis of beauty and tranquility committed to organic gardening. Here, a 90-year-old farmhouse is surrounded by display gardens filled with fragrant herbs and colorful perennials and flowing shrubs. As Sharon Lee Smith and Mary Wilhite explained, "Blue Moon started in 1984 as a wholesale herb growing operation, but now the 12 propagation and production greenhouses are open during business hours for browsing and shopping." We highly recommend doing just that. You will find elegant wood arbors, a large butterfly garden, antique and Knock Out roses as well as unusual and whimsical garden art. The gift shop is brimming with herbal products and decorative accents for the home and garden along with lots of informative handouts. This area, however, is not wheelchair/stroller accessible. Check the web site for workshops and, if possible, take advantage of the Fall Festival the second week in October, the Spring Open House the last Saturday of April and the Christmas Open House the weekend following Thanksgiving. This is serious gardening with a sense of humor. A real treat!

Directions: Blue Moon is located 15.0 miles west of Tyler, 5.0 miles east of Edom. Take FM 314 south of I-20 to FM 279 and turn left.

Cactus Ranch
511 CR 1104
Canton, Texas 75103
903.567.5042
www.cactus-ranch.com
Hours: Mon–Fri 9–5, Sat 10–4

As the name suggests, drought-tolerant, winter-hardy cacti, agaves and yuccas can be found in abundance within the ten greenhouses here. Owner Renee Cecil is also proud of the hardy palms, cycads, angel's trumpet, spider lilies, crinums, bananas and "odd tropicals" that she, and the friends who help her, lovingly tend. Since it opened in 1996, landscape designers and interior designers have flocked to this place to buy specimen container plants for their clients. It is only partially wheelchair/stroller accessible, but this is something nobody will want to miss!

Directions: From I-20, take the Hwy 19 exit. Go north over the freeway for 2.5 miles. Look for a sign on the right hand side. Turn onto CR 1104 and proceed less than a mile to the greenhouse.

Pope's Azalea Farm
1960 CR 4125
Canton, Texas 75103
903.829.5921
Hours: Mon–Fri 8–5, by appointment on weekends

As the new owners, Jerry and Beverly Trollinger, explained, "the Popes have retired, but they live across the street and still offer us their expertise when needed." And, this verdant nursery is still committed to growing the finest azaleas — propagated from their own cuttings in a medium of peat moss and fine bark. "We grow over 65 varieties in 50 greenhouses for the landscape trade, as well as for our retail customers." The one thing that has changed is that they are growing the stock to specimen-size plants before releasing them for sale. So if you want large azaleas (including not only the popular indica azaleas, but also kurume, macrantha, pericat, Glendale hybrids and several varieties of native deciduous azaleas), this is the place. You'll also find camellias, ground covers, hostas and daylilies. They also manufacture and distribute 12-foot, 16-foot and 20-foot coldframe greenhouses. Call for quotes. "Better yet, come by and see us in the spring — we're beautiful!"

Directions: Take Exit 530 off I-20 east of Canton. Stay on the south side feeder road, passing 1255, and turn right on VZ (Van Zandt County Rd) 4125. It's on the left, about 0.5 miles.

Center/Tenaha (Shelby County)

Specialty Nurseries

King's Nursery
956 North Bowers Dr (E Hwy 840)
Tenaha, Texas 75974
936.248.3811
Hours: Mon–Sat 8–5

Serious gardeners within a 100-mile radius come to this tiny town for the wares and wisdom of Aubrey King, Master Certified Nursery Professional. A third generation plantsman, Mr. King grows native and adapted species that may be impossible to find elsewhere in Texas. In addition to myriad old roses, he has Portadora elephant ears, and many other bulbs such as hardy amaryllis, crinums and oxblood lilies. We found bald, pond and Montezuma cypresses, dawn redwood and native white fringe trees among the tangle of greenery that surrounds this mecca for savvy shoppers.

The Lily Farm
Rt. 4, Box 1465
Center, Texas 75935
409.598.7556
www.lilyfarm.com
Hours: Open house to public last week of May through June 15th

Jack Carpenter's top-notch hybrid daylilies can be purchased from the field during the two to three week open house which usually runs from the last week of May through the middle of June. Check out his wonderful website!

Directions: This farm is located 19.0 miles northeast of Nacogdoches on State Hwy 7. There is a sign on the highway only during the open house. The site is not wheelchair/stroller accessible.

Henderson (Rusk County)

Specialty Nurseries

Jordan's Plant Farm
7523 State Hwy 42 S
Henderson, Texas 75652
903.854.2316 or 800.635.1147
www.jordansplantfarm.com
Hours: Daily 8–5

This is definitely not your typical nursery. Not only was "The General Store" once part of a movie set, but also there are half a million-square-feet of greenhouses on site! We were impressed by the old-fashioned building that replicates an old-time hotel complete with saloon, a general store, a post office and Grandma's kitchen. Now comes the even better part, the plants. As Betty Gibson says, "The Jordan family started it as a hobby in 1976 with one greenhouse and the hobby ran amuck." Jordan's is a wholesale nursery as well, but retail customers receive one-on-one attention and information. You will find a wide selection of bedding plants, hanging baskets, perennials, bulbs, vegetables, shrubs and trees. The prices are competitive, but the staff is quick to tell you that they won't sacrifice quality. Christmas is a special time at Jordan's. The company grows over 40,000 poinsettias and furnishes every room with spectacularly designed Christmas trees. The place has become a major tourist attraction.

Directions: From Henderson, take Hwy 79 S and turn right on Hwy 42. Go 2.0 miles. Jordan's is on the right.

Jacksonville (Cherokee County)

Specialty Nurseries

Courtyard Gardens at Joe Smith Plant Farm
15305 Hwy 79 E
Jacksonville, Texas 75766
903.589.8024
Hours: Mon–Sat 9–6, Sun 1–5 Mar–June

Betty and Joe Smith opened their wholesale nursery in the '80s and eventually turned it into an operation with 80 greenhouses and three fields that supply bedding plants to retail nurseries all over Texas. At the request of the local citizenry, they've opened this retail division on the property, offering bedding plants, vegetable starts, hanging baskets, shrubs and, in spring, even tropical greenery. In addition, you'll also find fun, funky decorative items for your garden here. People love to just come and sit in this tree-shaded environment in hot weather. For a complete line of cool- and warm-season annuals, this is the place. And, if you need 30 flats of something special, they'll probably be able to supply them. This is truly a family affair.
Directions: From downtown Jacksonville, take Hwy 79 E about 3.0 miles. It's past the golf course on the top of the hill, on the north side of the highway.

Guinn Plant Farm
Hwy 69 S
Jacksonville, Texas 75766
903.586.0651
Hours: Mon–Sat 8–5:30, Sun 1–5 (March–May); Mon–Sat 9–5, Sun 1–5 (mid-Sept–mid-Dec); Mon–Sat 8:30–5, Sun 1–5 (Jan–Feb)

This family-owned nursery has been in business for 24 years and carries a full line of trees and shrubs as well as vines, annuals such as begonias and periwinkles, some perennials (grown from seed and cuttings) and lots of hanging baskets. You will also find potting soil and soil amendments. With 15 greenhouses, Guinn's is most well known for the vegetable starts (tomatoes, peppers, greens, squash, eggplant and more) and a full line of bulk garden seed. Owner Wanda Guinn closes during the summer while she is helping her son run the Guinn produce stand just south of downtown on Hwy 69. Here, they supply the local citizenry with fresh-picked vegetables. As she says, "People not only enjoy shopping with us, they also enjoy eating our veggies!" On a cold, rainy, windy day in the Piney Woods, Wanda's warm personality was most welcome.
Directions: From downtown Jacksonville, take Hwy 69 S about 6.0 miles. Turn left immediately after the concrete barricade, and make a U-turn back to the nursery, which is on the east side of the highway.

Garden Centers

Ellis Pottery
3110 North Eastman Rd
Longview, Texas 75605
903.663.9111
www.ellispottery.com
(LISTING CONTINUED ON THE NEXT PAGE)

(CONTINUED)

Hours: Mon–Sat 9–8, Sun 1–6

This fifth generation business, started by Richard Ellis, carries everything from pottery to quilts, but it is, indeed, a complete garden center with a 10,000-square-foot greenhouse. In this well-maintained environment, you will find lush greenery and healthy bedding plants and ornamentals. Natives, herbs, and perennials are prominently featured, and we were impressed with the large selection of fountains. Ellis Pottery occupies three acres of landscaped grounds and employs two Texas Certified Nursery Professionals. The leisurely nature trails wind into lovely garden settings, and, as Dennis Rowden says, "Fountains bubble, birds sing and our staff is friendly and helpful. We encourage everyone to experience our store." We second that suggestion.

Emerald Gardens
5006 Judson Rd
Longview, Texas 75605
903.663.4757

Hours: Mon–Sat 8–5:30, Sun 1–5

Opened in 1990 by Master Certified Nursery Professional Bonnie Holloway, Emerald Gardens closed briefly but is on the way up again. As Bonnie says, "It's my work in progress." This very pleasant full service nursery offers consulting, landscaping, herbs, lots of color, tropicals and butterfly plants. In addition to birdhouses and garden ornaments, you will find two charming water features and plenty of water plants from which to choose. The irrigation pond is not only a conservation measure, but also it provides the plants with chlorine-free water. Dedicated to organic gardening, Bonnie is happy to share her expertise with customers. We found Emerald Gardens a most delightful place to visit.

Smotherman's Scenery, Inc.
1122 West Marshall
Longview, Texas 75606
903.753.4290
www.smothersscenery.com

Hours: Daily 8–5 (fall and winter), Mon–Sat 8–6 (spring and summer)

Smotherman's Scenery has been providing quality service to professional landscapers as well as do-it-yourself gardeners in East Texas for over thirty years. Owner Mike Smotherman prides himself on the "quality of the plants and the personnel." This complete garden center carries everything from trees and shrubs to bedding plants and roses. There is a wide selection of turf grasses from which to choose. In addition, you will find bulk materials, flagstone, rock, sand, fertilizer, Keystone pavers and retaining walls and organic products. The garden center also provides concrete statuary, books, tools, pottery and gifts. Sales are held periodically. When we asked manager William George what Smotherman's specialty is, he good-naturedly replied, "The usual and the unusual. If we don't have the plants or the answers for you, we'll find them." And the finishing touch — free delivery!

Lufkin (Angelina County)

Garden Centers

Lufkin Farm Nursery
1217 East Lufkin Ave
Lufkin, Texas 75901
936.634.7414
Hours: Mon–Sat 7–5:50, Sat 7–1

This 40 year old nursery, now owned by Stephen Corley, has grown since our last visit, but it still offers the same "happy plants" and helpful service. We found a complete and assorted selection of trees, shrubs, bulbs, vegetable seeds and starts as well as bedding plants. Also offered are pest management products, soils, organic products such as mushroom compost and organic humus, tools, books, gifts and garden accessories. Staff member Craig Corley is a licensed irrigator, and additional services include lawn maintenance, landscaping and sprinkler systems. As manager George Woods said, "We used to specialize in vegetables, but now it is just about everything. There is even an archery section!" Sales are held from time to times, and seminars are also offered. We found this nursery tidy and well organized, and the plants spoke for themselves.

Malakoff (Henderson County)

Garden Centers

Malakoff Nursery and Garden Center
724 West Royall Blvd
Malakoff, Texas 75148
903.489.1521
Hours: Mon–Sat 8–4 (closes at 2 on Wed); Sun 11–2 (spring)

After 32 years in business, Gary and Randy Reaves know exactly how to provide their customers with quality plants and service. You will find trees, shrubs, annuals, and perennials as well as pest control, soil amendments, mulches, soils and some organic products. The gift department offers wind chimes, birdhouses and other accessories for the garden. Cedar Works furniture is available, and a 30-foot x 60-foot area features a nice selection of pots. As Gary commented, "I've done a lot of landscaping over the years."

Directions: The Nursery is 9.0 miles west of Athens on Hwy 31 (West Royall Blvd)

Marshall (Harrison County)

Garden Centers

Pottery Tent
5015 Hwy 59 N
Marshall, Texas 75670
903.927.1041
Hours: Mon–Sat 9–6, Sun noon–6

This garden center is a bit smaller than Ellis Pottery in Longview (see page 89), but you'll find a wealth of plant material and pottery here.

Garden Furnishings

Marshall Pottery
4901 Elysian Fields Rd
Marshall, Texas 75670
903.938.9201
Hours: Mon–Sat 9–6, Sun 10–6

W.F. Rocker settled in East Texas because of the abundance of the two natural resources he needed for his business — white clay and water. There he founded Marshall Pottery Works in 1895, and, after a series of owners, the company fell into the hands of Sam Ellis in 1905 — "tools, clay, manufacturing ware, one wagon and two mules." Today, Marshall Pottery is still the place to find red clay pots. They come in all sizes from 1.5-inch to 18.5-inch standards, plus several shapes, round and square, plain and decorative. Their hand-turned pottery can serve a multitude of purposes.

Nacogdoches (Nacogdoches County)

Garden Centers

Cook's Nursery
3535 State Hwy 21 W
Nacogdoches, Texas 75964
936.564.6359
Hours: Mon–Sat 9–5:30, Sun 1–5

What we discovered here was "an oasis!" Tucked into the woods about three-quarters of a mile past Loop 224 on Hwy 21 W, Cook's is the largest retail nursery in the Nacogdoches/Lufkin area. This family-owned nursery has been in business for 50 years and since 1978 been under the guidance of Richard Cook. The company carries a large quantity of quality plants, including unusual perennials, annuals, azaleas, shrubs, ferns, trees and Knock Out roses, with much of the stock grown on site. You will find books, tools, Carl Pool products for roses and azaleas and other organic supplies. There are periodic sales. Although not all of the garden center is wheelchair/stroller accessible, friendly, professional advice is always available and the atmosphere is most pleasant. This experienced staff wants "to help you get things growing." As Mr. Cook says, "If we don't have the answer, we will find it!"

Texarkana (Bowie County)

Garden Centers

Ellis Pottery
3920 Summerhill Rd
Texarkana, Texas 75503
903.792.2246
www.ellispottery com
Hours: Mon–Sat 9–8, Sun 1–6

This garden center is a bit smaller than Ellis Pottery in Longview (see p. 89), but you'll find a wealth of plant material and pottery here.

Tyler/Lindale (Smith County)

Garden Centers

Breedlove Nursery & Landscape
11576 State Hwy 64 W
Tyler, Texas 75704
903.597.7421
Hours: Mon–Sat 8–5:30, Sat 9–5

Breedlove's "roots" go back to 1927 when founder Jesse Breedlove pioneered Tyler's famous rose industry. Today Ray Breedlove, a landscape architect, and Paul and Laurie Breedlove, both horticulturists, manage the nursery and landscape business. The grounds cover four acres and include three display gardens: a formal garden complete with fishpond, a cottage garden, and a Victorian Knot garden. The nursery carries a full line of trees, shrubs, ground covers, seasonal color, herbs and perennials. It has a wonderful selection of camellias, sasanquas and Japanese maples. The whole effect is fabulous! According to Laurie, "During the Spring Azalea Trail, Breedlove's is a rainbow of color!" The garden center carries fertilizers, chemicals, organics and a refreshing selection of garden gifts. Breedlove's is also known for its "Special Mix," a fertilizer especially for East Texas soil. The company carries a very extensive line of statuary, pottery, fountains and planters. As Laurie says, "We love what we do, and it shows!"

Harris Nursery
10940 County Rd 490
Tyler, Texas 75706
903.593.8646
Hours: Daily 8–7. Shorter hours in winter. Call ahead.

This family-owned business has been serving customers in the Piney Woods for 39 years, and, as manager Cindy Allen says "has a very loyal following." Harris Nursery, owned by Gene and Zelda Harris, carries stock grown at their wholesale location. You can rest assured that the plants you buy here will grow well in the area! The nursery is a complete garden center and sells trees, shrubs, bedding plants, ground covers and more. You will find soils, pest control products and tools as well as garden accessories such as wind chimes, birdbaths, fountains and statuary. Look for sales advertised in the local papers, and be sure to check out the summer Anniversary Sale.

Directions: The Nursery is located at the corner of 490 and Hwy 69 N.

Hughes Plant Farm
19980 Hwy 69 S
Tyler, Texas 75703
903.894.7737
Hours: Mon–Sat 8–6, Sun 11–5 (spring); Mon–Sat 8–5, Sun 11–5 (fall); closed in August

Hughes Plant Farm may be short on frills, but it definitely has what counts — great depth of inventory and really good prices. Having been in business for 22 years, Hughes boasts 40 greenhouses in which the owners grow a vast array of bedding plants. You will also find trees from 5- to15-gallon, shrubs and Encore azaleas as well as bulbs, bulb food and grass seed. The organic supplies carried include Nature's Guide and Garden-Ville, and there are lots of ceramic pots from which to choose. For the "hands-on gardener," Hughes is certainly worth exploring.

Directions: Hughes is located south of Tyler, 2.76 miles from Bullard.

Specialty Nurseries

Bob Wells Nursery
17160 CR 4100
Lindale, Texas 75771
903.882.3550
www.bobwellsnursery.com
Hours: Mon–Sat 8–5 except off-season; calling ahead is advised

This highly regarded, fourth-generation company specializes in fruits and berries. It is an excellent source for the best varieties of blackberries, blueberries, boysenberries, raspberries and strawberries as well as grapes, asparagus and rhubarb. The nursery carries a large selection of shade and nut trees, crepe myrtles, roses and other flowering shrubs. They offer bare root trees and plants from November 1st to May 1st and container grown in most varieties all year. According to owner Bob Wells, "We sell one tree or any amount — hundreds or thousands." Bob, who works with horticulturalists at Texas A&M and the University of Arkansas, is happy to visit with and advise the retail customer, and the website provides an order form for convenient on-line ordering. The company does have occasional sales, usually shade and fruit trees.

Directions: Bob Wells Nursery is located 2.0 miles east of Lindale on Hwy 16.

Chamblee's Rose Nursery
10926 Hwy 69 N
Tyler, Texas 75706
903.882.5153
www.chambleeroses.com

Hours: Mon–Fri 8–5 and weekends except summer

As Mark Chamblee will tell you, "We have the largest retail inventory of roses in East Texas. We ship Earth Kind landscape roses and own-root garden roses nationwide." This 55-year-old, family-owned business boasts two Texas Master Certified Nursery Professionals, owner Mark Chamblee and Ron Hill, as well a Texas Licensed Irrigator, general manager, John Willbanks. Chamblee's carries over 50 varieties of miniature roses, over 120 varieties of old garden roses and over 75 varieties of hybrid tea, grandiflora, floribunda, and climbing roses. They do a brisk mail order business, offer a free catalog, and mark down merchandise throughout the year. Mark hosts seminars for various interested groups, and there is always plenty of free literature pertaining to roses and their care at the nursery. Books and magazines are available as well. Mark and wife, Sharon, also own and operate a Bed and Breakfast, the Lott House, in Mineola, which features their own private rose garden. A real treat to behold!

Directions: The nursery is located 3.0 miles north of Loop 323.

Hand Nurseries
15522 Hwy 64 W
Tyler, Texas 75704
903.593.6589
Hours: Mon–Sat 8–6, Sun 10–6 (March–July 4); Mon–Sat 8–5, Sun 12–5 (Sept–Dec 1)

We happened upon this inviting nursery and felt compelled to check it out. We learned from Karen Hand, who owns the nursery with her husband Scott, that Scott's family has been growing roses in the area for three generations. This nursery defines decorative gardening with its iron trellises, topiary, perennials, vegetables, herbs and lots of seasonal color. As Karen explained, "We have such good quality because we know which growers have the best of any particular plant." The four greenhouses are very attractive and well kept, and we found visiting Hand Nurseries a serendipitous experience.

Directions: The nursery is 1.5 miles west of the airport.

Senter's Nursery
608 Railroad Ave
Whitehouse, Texas 75791
903.839.2626
Hours: Mon–Fri 7:30–5

"Although Senter's Nursery is primarily wholesale," says owner Gerald Senter, "we welcome retail customers! We've been in business since 1977 and try to do the best for our customers." The company must be doing something right! This nursery, located just a few miles south of Tyler, carries 82 kinds of container native trees, shrubs and vines. The company collects its own seeds, ensuring that the trees will grow in the area.

Directions: Take Hwy 110 south to 346. Go east 0.25 miles to the railroad track. The nursery is 1.0 mile on the right.

Garden Furnishings

Patio Center at East Texas Brick
3901 SSW Loop 323
Tyler, Texas 75711
903.561.1670, 800.256.1750
www.etbrick.com
Hours: Mon–Fri 8–5, Sat 9–4

The Patio Center at East Texas Brick is absolutely brimming with everything you could possibly need to furnish your garden. As Steve Davenport graciously gave us the tour, we could hardly take it all in. The outdoor furniture lines include Woodard, Winston, Lloyd Flanders, Rockwood teak, New River swings and gliders, and gorgeous iron and mosaic tables by KNF. There's everything an outdoor chef could want — a complete line of Weber (this is a five-star dealer), Fire Magic and Twin Eagles grills to Orion smokers, Big Green Egg and Cajun Grill, plus all the tools you'll need. The spacious showrooms also feature the components for a complete outdoor kitchen. In the garden accessories department, the Patio Center offers everything from hand-tuned wind chimes, Hatteras hammocks and outdoor rugs, cushion replacements and umbrellas to fountains, mailboxes and weather vanes. Also available are Palapa structures, children's play equipments, spas and factory-built home enclosures. The service department offers free delivery and assembly on most products and reasonable for-fee services all over Northeast Texas. The "brick" part of the company carries cut stone and pool coping.

Tyler Rose Museum Gift Shop
420 Rose Park Dr
Tyler, Texas 75702
903.597.3130
Hours: Mon–Fri 9–4:30, Sat 10:30–4:30, Sun 1:30–4:30

As they say at the Tyler Rose Museum, "We are Tyler's gift shop specializing in items that reflect the city's status as 'Rose Capital of the Nation'" You will find a large selection of gifts and garden ornaments from birdhouses and feeders, topiary, sun catchers and wreaths made from Tyler roses to Christmas ornaments to rose reference books. A great place to find a present for a friend or purchase a remembrance of your visit. For the garden's listing, see page 85.

4

Coastal Prairies & Marshes

Coastal Prairies & Marshes

The upper Gulf coast is the most heavily populated and industrialized area of the state, yet its principal cities, Houston, Galveston and Beaumont, are remarkably green. This topographically flat region is well known for steamy summers and mild winters, both of which make for a hospitable growing environment. The region as we define it in this book also includes the growing cities that ring Houston: Seabrook and Webster to the southeast; Sugar Land, Katy, Rosenberg and Richmond to the southwest, and to the north, The Woodlands, Spring and Conroe. The region extends east to the Louisiana border to include Orange and Port Arthur.

"Fragile" is the word The Nature Conservancy uses to describe this "interlocking mosaic of fresh and saltwater wetlands and estuaries, coastal prairies, and coastal woodlands." The organization has several projects aimed at preserving the region's dwindling natural resources while creating a balance with such compatible human activities as rice farming and cattle grazing, which produce its primary agricultural income.

The Gulf has inundated Texas many times in geological history. Although the water is slowly rising at present, it is too soon to invest in oceanfront property in College Station! The last invasion was 40 million years ago. Houston is sinking, however, not because the Gulf is rising, but because so much ground water has been pumped out from beneath it. Slow drainage is a common problem for gardeners throughout the region.

Soils here are mostly clayey and acid, but there are pockets of sandy soil within the region. The clay soils are particularly rich, heavy and nutritious. Live oaks and elms predominate in the slow-draining "gumbo" alongside sluggish bayous, while pines and post oaks are indicators of sand. Beneath the towering live oaks of the coastal woodlands you'll often find a thick understory of tropical-looking palmettos with their beautiful fan-shaped leaves. The live oaks are frequently festooned with long strands of Spanish moss, which is not a parasite, but rather an epiphyte that feeds on dust and rain.

While trees are plentiful, the region's principal vegetation is grass — big and little bluestem, Texas wintergrass and gulf cordgrass on the drylands; saltgrass, sedges and bullrush in the marshes. Where farming and heavy grazing have disrupted the natural composition of species in this fertile region, oak underbrush, mesquite, Macartney rose, ragweed and other weedy plants readily invade.

Barrier islands protect almost the entire Texas Gulf Coast. These huge sandbars created by the accumulation of shells and sand provide shelter for the inland marshes, mudflats and saltflats that nourish everything that lives in the sea. Marsh environments are disappearing at an alarming rate, however. They've been filled in for real estate, decimated by upstream dams that withhold vital fresh water and silt, and used as dumping grounds for chemicals. One of the least-spoiled environments can be experienced at **Sea Rim State Park** between Port Arthur and Sabine on State Hwy 87. With over 15,000 acres of marshland and 5.2 miles of shoreline, this park is named for that portion of the seashore where marsh grasses extend into the surf. The Harrington Beach Unit features a Visitors' Center with exhibits, observation deck and nature trail (on a boardwalk through the marsh) with a self-guided booklet.

Just ten miles north of Beaumont, **Village Creek State Park** is a rainforest environment filled with cypress and water tupelo swamps, river birch, mayhaw and yaupon trees. These 1,004 acres remain virtually unspoiled. Several environmentally oriented botanical repositories can also be found in the Houston area. **Armand Bayou Nature Center** in Pasadena, the **Mercer Arboretum** in Spring and the **Houston Arboretum and Nature Center** provide miles of nature trails.

Southeast of Houston, you'll find 5,000 acres of upland coastal prairies and lush bottomland forests in **Brazos Bend State Park**. Sycamore, cottonwood and black willow line the creek banks. Picnic areas are sited among huge, moss-draped live oaks, and nature trails run along oxbow lakes and through the woodlands

Rainfall in the Coastal Prairies region varies from an average annual 59.2-inches in Orange County to 43.2-inches in Matagorda County. Rain falls heaviest in July, August and September. Poor drainage aside, from the gardener's standpoint this region has much to offer. Lush ground covers and such exotic flowering shrubs as bottlebrush and pineapple guava, which are marginal in gardens as far north as Austin, can be grown with impunity here in Zone 9. Acid-loving plants positively thrive.

Places you'll want to visit for design ideas include **Beaumont Botanical Gardens**, **Shangri La Botanical Gardens and Nature Center** in Orange, **Moody Gardens** in Galveston, and Houston's **Bayou Bend**, **Cullen Sculpture Garden** at MFAH, and Hermann Park (which hosts the **Houston Garden Center**, **Houston Japanese Garden** and the **Cockrell Butterfly Garden** at The Museum of Natural Science). Although it is only open a few days each year, don't miss **Peckerwood Garden** near Hempstead, which has been accepted by the Garden Conservancy to ensure the preservation and continued development of this exquisite private garden. The **Robert A. Vines Environmental Science Center** and the **Texas AgriLife Extension Center Display Garden** feature more modest (realistic for the average homeowner) ideas for backyard gardening.

Public Gardens and Nature Preserves to Visit

Beaumont (Jefferson County)

Beaumont Botanical Gardens
Tyrrell Park
6088 Babe Zaharias Dr
Beaumont, Texas 77705
409.842.3135
www.beaumontbotanicalgardens.com
Hours: Daily dawn to dusk (gardens); Warren Loose Conservatory: Wed, Thurs and Fri 10–2, Sat 10–5, Sun 1–5

(LISTING CONTINUED ON THE NEXT PAGE)

(CONTINUED)

Admission: Gardens free. Conservatory: $3 (adults), $2 (seniors over 60), $1 (children 6–12), free (children under 6)

This 23.5-acre garden includes displays of both sun and shade-loving plants, a native plant and wildflower garden, herb garden and an informal antique rose garden. You'll also see a small Japanese Garden, several color-coordinated garden areas (green and white, all violet, etc.) and ponds all connected by a paved "Friendship Walk" which allows easy access for strollers and wheelchairs. The Warren Loose Conservatory houses tropical plants from around the world. You may also want to visit Cattail Marsh, which is located about a mile south of the Botanical Gardens in Tyrrell Park. Billed as Beaumont's best-kept secret, this wetlands wildlife refuge features hiking trails where you'll find iris, cattails, arrowhead and other marsh-loving plants. It is home to some 350 species of birds.

Directions: Turn south off I-10 at Walden Rd exit (west of the city) Follow Walden Rd about a mile to the park entrance.

Orange (Orange County)

Shangri La Botanical Gardens and Nature Center
2111 West Park Ave
Orange, Texas 77630
409.670.9113
www.shangrilagardens.org
Hours: Tues–Fri 9–5, Sat 9–7, Sun 12–5 (Daylight Savings Time); Mon–Sat 10–5, Sun 12–5 (Central Standard Time)
Admission: $6 (adults), $5 (seniors &students 13–17), $4 (children 4–12), free (children under 4)

The term "Shangri La" has represented a place of beauty, peace and enlightenment since the publication of the book Lost Horizon in 1933. The Nelda C. and H.J. Lutcher Stark Foundation has recreated a modern Shangri La with handsome new buildings, gardens and a large nature preserve. The unique ecosystem here provided an ideal opportunity to carry on the vision of Mr. Stark, who originally developed it more than 60 years ago. The formal Botanical Gardens contain more than 300 plant species in five formal "rooms" as well as four sculpture "rooms." You'll also discover a Children's Garden, Exhibition Greenhouses, Café and Garden Store. Adjacent to the botanical gardens is a bird blind that allows visitors to observe nesting birds in Shangri La's heronry. A Nature Discovery Center, laboratory, and three outdoor class-rooms are located deep in the cypress swamp. This is the first project in Texas and the 50th project in the world to earn the U.S. Green Building Council's Platinum certification for LEED®-NC, which verifies the design and construction reached the highest green building and performance measures. As one of the most earth-friendly projects in the world, it offers a glimpse of how people can live in harmony with nature, as well as the opportunity to explore, discover and learn.

Galveston (Galveston County)

The Moody Gardens
1 Hope Blvd
Galveston, Texas 77554
409.744.4673; 800.582.4673
www.moodygardens.com
Hours: Daily 10–8

Admission: Rainforest Pyramid: $9.95 (adults), $8.95 (seniors), $7.95 (children)

The late Sir Goeffrey Jellicoe's original intent for The Moody Gardens was to reflect the full scope of his book, *The Landscape of Man*. Only a small portion of the great landscape architect's vision has been realized, but the garden's tropical rainforest is truly spectacular. The ten-story glass pyramid displays over 2,000 plant and animal species from the Americas, Asia and Africa. The structure encloses an acre at its base, and flamingos wade in a pool at the entrance. The garden's paths skirt various waterfalls, cross over streams and wander through thickets of ferns, bromeliads, orchids, bamboo, gingers and palms. Colorful birds and butterflies flit through the tree canopy overhead. Bat caves and a Mayan colonnade are but a few of the surprises contained within this verdant greenhouse. Outside the rainforest, the grounds are lush, but given over to numerous commercial enterprises.

Directions: From I-45 S, exit 61st St. Right on 61st and again on Seawall Blvd. Right on 81st to Jones Rd. Left on Hope Blvd.

Houston Metropolitan Area

Armand Bayou Nature Center
8500 Bay Area Blvd
Pasadena, Texas 77507
281.474.2551 or toll free 866.417.3818
www.abnc.org
Hours: Tues–Sat 9–5, Sun 12–5
Admission: $3 (adults); $1 (seniors and children); free (children under 3)

One doesn't expect to find 2,500 unspoiled acres at the edge of one the country's biggest cities, and certainly it is a surprise to discover three different wild habitats — tallgrass prairie, estuary bayou and bottomland hardwood forest — next door to the bustling Johnson Space Center. At the entrance to this pristine preserve, a lovely wood bridge crosses a pond that absolutely teems with life. From there, you'll find a Visitor's Center where you can get a trail map and perhaps visit the gift shop before exploring this vast and tranquil place. Its Coastal prairie environment is especially valuable because only one-percent of such wilderness remains. Behind the center is a restored farm where volunteers demonstrate pioneer-era skills during summer weekends. Most of the trails are rough, crushed limestone and not easily negotiated with strollers or wheelchairs. Call for more details about specific access to exhibits.

Directions: From Downtown Houston travel south on I-45. Exit at Bay Area Blvd and travel east to the intersection at Red Bluff Rd and the Center's entrance.

Bayou Bend Collection and Gardens
1 Westcott St
Houston, Texas 77007
713.639.7750
www.mfah.org/bayoubend/

(LISTING CONTINUED ON THE NEXT PAGE)

(CONTINUED)

Hours: Tues–Sat 10–5, Sun 1–5; mansion tours by reservation only

Admission: $3 (age 10 and older)

Out of wild woodlands on the bank of Buffalo Bayou, Ima Hogg created the finest private garden that existed in Texas in the early years of the 20th century. Among the factors that set Bayou Bend apart even today is its exceptionally strong overall design. Starting with what she termed "nothing but a dense thicket," she established a series of graceful gardens that were intended to be outdoor rooms for living and entertaining. But Miss Hogg also appreciated nature, so her desire was to leave the surrounding woodlands natural.

Eight distinctive gardens are woven into the fabric of the designed landscape here. The dense woods open up to reveal the late Miss Ima Hogg's pink stucco house glistening in a sea of bright green grass. Framing the house at the woodland edges are planting beds drawn in sweeping curves and massed with rich evergreen shrubbery. As you walk through the garden, vistas open and close. Formal fountains, charming statuary and colorful, sometimes playful plantings keep your eye moving from place to place.

A broad terraced lawn behind the house leads to a rectangular pool and arching fountain designed to frame a white marble statue of Diana, goddess of the hunt. Here, the sculpture plays dramatically against a backdrop of dark, columnar clipped hedges. Directly west of the Diana Garden is a parterre where Clio, the muse of history, presides on a central pedestal, encircled by brick walks and beds filled with clipped azaleas and boxwoods. Smaller outdoor rooms are tucked into the surrounding woods and designed to be experienced in sequence. Members of the River Oaks Garden Club lovingly (and organically) maintain Bayou Bend. All tours are self-guided; wheelchair/stroller access is limited.

Directions: Take Memorial Dr west from downtown. Turn south on Westcott and park in the free public lot. A suspended footbridge takes you to the Jones Visitor Center.

Cullen Sculpture Garden at MFAH
Bissonet at Montrose Blvd.
Houston, Texas 77005
713.639.7300

Hours: Daily 9 am–10 pm

Admission: free

Created by the famous Japanese-American sculptor and architect Isamu Noguchi, this one-acre site displays masterworks by such nineteenth and twentieth-century sculptors as Matisse, Aristide Maillol, Auguste Rodin, Alberto Giacometti, Frank Stella, Ellsworth Kelly, Louise Bourgeois and Anthony Caro. Working with Houston landscape architect Johnny Steele, Noguchi selected the plants with care, favoring native species when possible. The works animate the space amid a serene envelope of native trees and shrubs. The garden is shaded by more than 80 trees, including Drummond red maples, loblolly pines, Drake elms, bald cypress, magnolias, crepe myrtles and water oaks. Other plantings include giant timber bamboo, pittosporum, and evergreen wisteria. Live oaks and cedar elms line the garden's outer walls.

Houston Arboretum and Nature Center
4501 Woodway Dr
Houston, Texas 77024
713.681.8433
www.houstonarboretum.org

Hours: Building: Daily 8:30–6, the grounds from dawn to dusk

Admission: free

This facility in Memorial Park offers city folk a wonderful way to experience the wonders of nature. The 155-acre wildlife sanctuary offers a wide array of classes for adults, family programs and popular year-round adventures for children. (Membership has its advantages in discounted programs.) Saturday lectures and guided walks that begin at 2 and 3 o'clock are free to the public. Five miles of wooded trails wind under the forest canopy, around ponds, through a swamp and a demonstration prairie. These diverse habitats are a great place to reflect on the complex habitats of the Coastal prairies and marshes. Its Nature Store is a good place to find gifts for fellow gardeners. The Alice Brown Interpretive Trail is wheelchair/stroller accessible.

Directions: The park is located just south of the intersection of I-10 and Loop 610 west of downtown.

Houston Garden Center
1500 Hermann Dr, Hermann Park
Houston, Texas 77004
713.284.1986 / 713.284.1989
Hours: Mon–Fri 8–8, Sat & Sun 10–8; closed Thanksgiving, Christmas and New Year's Day
Admission: free

Houston's Hermann Park offers gardeners and nature-lovers much to enjoy within its 440 acres. The Houston Garden Center and Museum of Natural Science stand at the north end of the park, across the street from the monumental equestrian statue of Sam Houston. The Garden Center's All-America Rose Garden displays about 2,500 bushes of 93 varieties, which are at peak in late March/early April and again in late October/early November. The wildflower garden is also at its most colorful in spring and fall. In summer, the Fragrance Garden's 80 herbal species come into their own. (Nationally known herbalist Madalene Hill selected the plants, which are divided into aromatic themes.) Other favorites to be found along the Center's walkways include a Bog Garden that features lilies and iris, a Bulb Garden and a Perennial Garden. An International Sculpture Garden is also tucked into a corner of this showcase for garden plants. The Museum of Natural Science next door is noted for its Cockrell Butterfly Garden, which is filled with a collection of tropical plants that will thrill indoor gardeners. The new Japanese Garden is another must while you're in Hermann Park. (See next listing.)

Directions: From downtown, take Fannin S and turn left into the park. The Garden Center is just past the Museum of Natural Science; it has a parking lot.

Houston Japanese Garden
Hermann Park
Houston, Texas
713.284.8300
Hours: Daily 10–6 (April–Sept); 10–5 (Oct–March)
Admission: free

One tends to think of a Japanese garden as venerable, but this young garden already possesses magical qualities. Constructed under the canopy of mature oak and pine trees and dedicated in 1992, it features winding paths that crisscross interconnected ponds. Crepe myrtles are used in lieu of traditional cherry trees to create breathtaking vistas, especially when viewed through the opened screens of the teahouse. A garden for all seasons, its Japanese iris, dogwoods and azaleas provide spring color, and the Japanese maples color the

(LISTING CONTINUED ON THE NEXT PAGE)

(CONTINUED)

garden in autumn. Japanese landscape architect Ken Nakajima took a Zen approach to the problems inherent in the site: flat topography, existing tree roots that prevented major changes in grade, and a lack of native weather rock. "I had to induce and create a different concept to design the garden," he noted at its inception. He succeeded admirably. This garden will become even more tranquil with age.

Directions: Located about a block south of the Sam Houston statue and adjacent to the south end of the reflection pool.

Mercer Arboretum and Botanic Gardens
22306 Aldine Westfield Rd
Humble, Texas 77338-1071
281.443.8731
www.hcp4.net/mercer
Hours: Mon–Sat 8–7 (summer); 8–5 (winter); Sun 10–7; closed Thanksgiving, Christmas Eve, Christmas Day and New Year's Day
Admission: free

The Mercer has something for everyone with its displays of cultivated and native plants. Close to the Botanic Information Center, its gardens have been filled with pleasing perennial beds. There's an iris bog, a vine garden, herb garden, bamboo collection, fern gardens, and a tropical garden that's designed to recall a rainforest. Beyond the 0.75-acre lily pond, you'll discover loop trails through unspoiled natural areas. More than simply an outstanding public garden, the Mercer's mission includes education and research. As a participating member of the Center for Plant Conservation, Mercer features one of the nation's first Endangered Species Gardens. It hosts a variety of programs for children, adults and families. Knowledge-able volunteers are heavily involved in its programs and maintenance. A vast expanse of forest on the west side of Aldine Westfield Rd is the arboretum with its outdoor classroom, Big Thicket Loop, ponds, bogs and picnic pavilion.

Directions: From I-45, take FM 1960 E to Aldine Westfield Rd. Turn left (north) to the Mercer entrance.

Peckerwood Garden
20571 F.M. 359
Hempstead, Texas 77445
979.826.3232
www.peckerwoodgarden.com
Hours: Open ten days during the year 1–4. See website for dates and directions.
Admission: $10 per person

John G. Fairey, who came to Texas to teach in the Department of Architecture at Texas A&M University, began this remarkable project in 1971. Because it was reminiscent of his childhood home in South Carolina, a clear, spring-fed brook that runs through the property enticed him to purchase the first part of the 17 acres that are now Peckerwood Garden. Around its edges, Fairey began planting what was to become America's most important collec-tion of rare plants native to a wide region of the southern United States and Mexico. But to call this a "collection" is to miss the fact that it is, first and foremost, an exquisite personal landscape. Its success can be attributed to his passion for the project, years of practical gardening experience, and a genuine concern for preserving little-known plants.

The garden brings together magnificent examples of numerous species of *Acer, Ilex, Liquidambar, Magnolia, Styrax, Taxus, Quercus,* etc., many of which he discovered in remote mountain ranges of Mexico. But again, to focus on the elements of this ethereal place is to miss the "whole." What makes a stroll through this garden unforgettable is the juxtaposition of the plants' forms, textures and hues and the intermingling of distinctive outdoor sculpture and folk art, all brought into harmony by the eye of an artist. In 1998 a nonprofit foundation, the Peckerwood Garden Conservation Foundation, was formed with guidance from the Garden Conservancy to insure its preservation and continued development.

Robert A. Vines Environmental Science Center
8856 Westview
Houston, Texas 77055
713.365.4175
www.springbranchisd.com/instruc/science/vsc/
Hours: Mon–Fri 8:30–5; Botanical Garden: Daily dawn to dusk
Admission: free

This resource facility for the Spring Branch School District brings together a five-acre arboretum, museum of Texas wildlife, geology hall and oceanography study center. The botanical garden in front of the building features plant materials drawn from Northern Mexico and all parts of Texas. Mike Anderson and his father-in-law, the late Lynn Lowrey (an important name in Texas native flora), designed this residential-scale display. In addition to serving the district, the Center's programs are open to the public. It hosts seminars, wildflower and bird identification classes in spring and fall and educational field trips to such places as the Galapagos Islands, Hawaii and Central America.
Directions: Located a mile north of the Katy Fwy (I-10) between Campbell and Bingle Rd.

Texas AgriLife Extension Center Display Garden
#2 Abercrombie Dr
Houston, Texas 77084
281.855.5600
Hours: Mon–Fri 7:30–4
Admission: free

This American Horticultural Society test and display site offers a wealth of practical ideas. There's a vineyard, fruit trees, a floral display area that's changed-out seasonally and vegetables growing in waist-high raised beds for the benefit of folks in wheelchairs. Novice gardeners will appreciate that plants are labeled and advice is freely given. There's a wonderful Children's Garden, as well. This has never been known as a "destination" garden, but it should be. It's really something special.
Directions: From downtown, take I-10 W to Hwy 6. Travel 3.0 miles north on Hwy 6. Turn right on Patterson, left at Bear Creek Rd. The building actually faces Bear Creek.

Coastal Prairies & Marshes Resources

Beaumont / Nederland (Jefferson County)

Garden Centers

Al Cook Nursery
10225 Hwy 105
Beaumont, Texas 77713
409.898.2294
Hours: Mon–Sat 9–5:30, Sun 10–5:30

There is an understated charm about this large, orderly establishment. The site is quite lovely with two creeks and several waterfalls. We were particularly impressed with the many specimen-size trees for sale and a greenhouse brimming with handsome cacti. "We have five greenhouses and a very big selection of quality plants with a knowledgeable staff to answer any questions and offer advice," says Doug Jerome, who purchased this nursery seven years ago. With the exception of water plants, just about everything suitable for the area can be found here. In addition, there are soils and soil amendments, pest management supplies, garden tools, gifts and garden accessories, including a very large selection of pots. Landscaping services are offered, and every Wednesday is "Ladies' Day" with a 10% discount!

Directions: Travel west on Hwy 105 from town. It's on the left, and the unobtrusive sign is easy to miss.

Cook's Nursery & Landscaping
1424 Nederland Ave
Nederland, Texas 77627
409.724.2665
Hours: Mon–Sat 8:30–5:30, Sun 12–4

A sign in the parking lot led us to believe we were going to like this place: "All unattended children will be given a puppy and an espresso!" Inside, we were delighted by the profusion of color. We met the high-spirited owner, Leslie Cook, who escorted us about and introduced us to numerous rare plants such as the magnificent purple-blooming Mona lavender, which is not a lavender, but rather a hybrid *Plectranthus*. Cook's grows about 10% of its plants from cuttings. "This nursery has been in the family forever...at least, three or four generations." There are, of course, the requisite shrubs and trees, and the gift shop has a bit of everything. Added attractions include interior plant lease and maintenance and plant rentals.

Sunshine Plant House
3425 Concord
Beaumont, Texas 77703
409.835.7007
Hours: Mon–Fri 9–5, Sat 9–3

This two-acre Beaumont institution has been in business since 1958 and under the ownership of Richard Tinkle for almost 30 years. When we visited, it was brimming with seasonal color, and the many shade houses were filled with hanging baskets. Sunshine sells to a number of landscape contractors and boasts a real depth of inventory, particularly in trees and shrubs. The company also carries "Texas tough" natives from a major Texas grower in Magnolia. As Richard told us, "I am off the beaten path, and I don't advertise, but our loyal customer base has grown by word of mouth." Judging by the brisk business we witnessed, that certainly seems to be the case.

Garden Furnishings

Ellis Pottery
3737 Calder
Beaumont, Texas 77706
409.839.8473
Hours: Mon–Sat 9–8, Sun 1–6

A branch of Ellis Pottery in Longview (see page 89), but you'll find a wonderful selection of pottery and fountains here.

Galveston (Galveston County)

Garden Centers

Tom's Thumb Nursery & Landscaping
2014 45th St
Galveston, Texas 77550
409.763.4713
www.tomsthumbnursery.com
Hours: Mon–Sat 10–6, Sun 10–4

Tom's Thumb is a family-owned business with 33 years of experience assisting island gardeners. According to Peggy Cornelius, "Although we specialize in tropicals and coastal plants, we carry everything from tools to grasses, from trees to vegetable starts and perennials and much more." We were impressed with the company's garden furniture, the seaside nautical gifts and the large assortment of fountains. According to the locals, "the Christmas store is wonderful!" The best selling furniture is a Seaside Casual's amazingly heavy Adirondack-style, which is made of recycled milk bottles and colored all the way through. This furniture comes with a 20-year warranty and can stand all the salt, wind and sea air Galveston can muster! What a treat to stop by for a visit when the masses are at the beach!

Hempstead/Brookshire (Waller County)

Specialty Nurseries

Bluebonnet Herb Farms
2105 13th St
Hempstead, Texas 77445
979.826.4290
Hours: Mon–Sat 9–5

Although we were a little too early to enjoy the Secret Garden Tea Room, Robin Kwiatkowski treated us to a tour of the charming plant display area and antique shop. Owner Linda Wood carries herbs, vegetables starts, perennials and roses and will order anything on request. The antique collection includes some items for the garden, and landscape design and installation are also available. Bluebonnet, which is well on its way to becoming all organic, provides a delightful shopping and dining experience.

Logans Run Tree Farm
32002 FM 1736
Hempstead, Texas 77445
979.826.8514
www.logansruntreefarm.com
Hours: Tues–Thurs 8–4, Fri & Sat 8–3

"Buy Farm-Direct and Save Big" is the tag line at Logans Run Tree Farm. Owned for 12 years by Mark and Elizabeth Cerny, it is a gorgeous site where everything is picture perfect. No herbicides or pesticides are used, and macro irrigation ensures 80% less water usage. There is a lovely pond filled with fish, and nature trails and bird boxes enhance the bucolic atmosphere. Even the deer, which are fed, don't present a problem! You will find a wide range of native shrubs and trees laid out in tidy rows. The Cernys also grow the five most hardy varieties of crepe myrtle and both yellow and double red Knock Out roses. They have recently added fruit and citrus trees. The Cernys sell mostly to the trade, but welcome homeowners and endeavor to educate the public about earth-friendly growing practices.
Directions: From Hempstead, take Hwy 6 N 3.5 miles. Turn right on FM 1736 and continue 2.5 miles. Logans Run is on the left.

Pecan Hill Nursery
34303 Pecan Hill Dr
Brookshire, Texas 77423
281.346.2001
www.pecanhillnursery.com
Hours: Wed–Sun 9–4 (March thru mid–April)

As owners Michael and Marilyn Pawelek say, "Pecan Hill, established in 1972, is a 'Mom and Pop' nursery with very personalized service and 'in-house' advice from a degreed horticulturalist." In the spring you will find six-inch geraniums and impatiens as well as gallon herbs, annuals and perennials...tens or thousands from which to choose. They are all oversized and AAA quality. Hanging baskets abound, and in 2008 the Paweleks introduced vegetable hanging baskets. Pecan Hill supplies over 6,000 six- and ten-inch containers of poinsettia..."Texas Size!" To take advantage of these lush plants, you will need to order in September. Check the website for details. Pecan Hill Nursery grows all of its plants and rotates the varieties to meet customer demands. As Marilyn explained, "We used to stay open until May, but we are sold out by mid-April." So get there early!

Directions: Pecan Hill Nursery is located between Brookshire and Fulshear off FM 359 at the dead-end of Pecan Hill Dr behind the Pecan Hill subdivision.

Will Fleming Nursery
37592 Porter Ln
Hempstead, Texas 77445
979.826.0510
Hours: by appointment

If Mr. Fleming's name sounds familiar, it's because he found an upright variety of yaupon in the wild, and now this widely used plant bears his name. His nursery is replete with perennials you won't find elsewhere. Most of what he grows is from seed, and the plants' provenance is important to him. Working from his homeplace and drawing mostly from the plants of his region, Will Fleming offers Mexican buckeye from Fort Bend and Washington County, bear grass (Nolina) from Schulenburg, flowering dogwoods from Bellville, as well as several species of native gayfeather, cobaea, silene (iron weed) and euphatorium. What he can't grow, he buys from like-minded wholesalers. When asked how to prevent Will Fleming yaupon from splaying as it ages, he replied, "Cut a 7 feet plant back to two feet in late winter. It will have grown to five feet by the next autumn. Or tie it up to rebar to make an excellent narrow hedge." Native plant enthusiasts and other knowledgeable gardeners sit at his feet to learn from a master.

Directions: From Hwy 290 (business), turn south on Hwy 359. Take the first street to the east (left), south of the fairgrounds. Turn in at the first road past the mailbox and veer left into the property toward the nursery.

Garden Furnishings
Frazier's
23200 Hwy 6
Hempstead, Texas 77445
979.921.2906
www.fraziersconcrete.com
Hours: Sun–Tues & Thurs–Sat 9–6, closed Wed

Frazier's is even bigger and better than on our last visit! Today, Billy Frazier's wares are spread over the eight-acre landscape. There are still a lot of concrete pots, fountains, birdbaths and statues, but now there are all manner of ceramic pots (some of which are very large, some elaborate). There are arbors, lavabos, mosaic and wrought iron tables and chairs...This is a place to linger because there is just so much merchandise from run of the mill to very upscale. Inside the extensive gift shop/garden shop there is, indeed, something for everyone.

(LISTING CONTINUED ON THE NEXT PAGE)

(CONTINUED)

You'll find good garden tools, coconut shell liners for hanging baskets, hose holders, rain chains, wind chimes, and birdhouses and feeders in abundance, as well as a vast array of decorative items for every taste and budget. Mr. Frazier was excited about his plans to build a meditation garden with a 24 feet structure topped by a gold spiral. Yet another addition to this already extraordinary shopping experience.

Houston Metropolitan Area (Harris County)

Garden Centers

Anderson Landscape & Nursery
2222 Pech
Houston, Texas 77055
713.984.1342
Hours: By Appointment

Mike and Patsy Anderson got a head start in natives. She is the daughter of the late Lynn Lowrey, whose name is synonymous with Texas native plants. The Andersons not only carry all the grasses, wildflowers, trees and shrubs her father collected and propagated, but also continue his commitment to natives as resources for a sustainable future. With its lovely little pathways and wealth of unusual plants, theirs counts as one of the most charming places we visited during our travels through the state. Spilling out of the flowerbeds in the different seasons you'll see columbines, turk's cap, dwarf ruellia, unusual strains of purple coneflower and oak leaf hydrangeas, to name a few. You'll find all the tried-and-true native shade trees here, plus the more rare understory trees including two-winged silverbell, fringetree, parsley hawthorn, scarlet buckeye, Louisiana crabapple and wax myrtle, so useful for small gardens. The company offers design and maintenance services. The Andersons also stock seasonal color and lots of container plants, as well as paving materials and soil amendments.
Directions: From I-10, take the Bingle Rd exit. Go north on Bingle to the 4th light, which is Hammerly, turn right and go to Pech St and turn left.

Buchanan's Native Plants
611 East 11th
Houston, Texas 77008
713.861.5702
www.buchanansplants.com
Hours: Daily 9–6

Buchanan's Native Plants is a complete garden center specializing in plants native to the Texas area. It also stocks many other hardy, adapted trees, shrubs and ornamentals. Says Donna Buchanan, "We are known for our varied inventory which includes a wide assortment of antique roses, old-fashioned perennials, herbs, wildflowers and seasonal color, as well as pond supplies and water lilies. We have three Certified Texas Nurserymen on staff who are able to help customers with their most difficult problems, usually recommending natural and organic products as remedies." The gift shop offers a selection of garden-related books, tools, seeds and gift items and lots of terra cotta pottery. This Houston Heights nursery is a fun place to visit. According to Donna, "We always have something new, and our customers love our two resident cats, Cleo and Pumpkin." Sign up to receive the e-mail newsletter, which has news, tips and coupons, and don't miss "Heights 1st Saturday" for plant specials, unique events and speakers.

Cornelius Nurseries, Inc.
1200 North Dairy Ashford
Houston, Texas 77079
281.493.0550

2233 South Voss Rd
Houston, Texas 77057
713.782.8640

1755 FM 1960 W
Houston, Texas 77090
281.444.1210
www.corneliusnurseries.com
Hours: Daily 9–7

Cornelius Nurseries has been serving the Houston and Upper Gulf Coast area since 1937, and after merging with Calloway's Nurseries of Fort Worth in 1999, Cornelius kept its name and its wonderful reputation in Houston. It hadn't missed a beat until the disastrous fire at the Voss Rd store in July, 2008, but it's scheduled to rebuild and reopen as soon as possible. Regarding plant quality, Steve Moore, the company's buyer comments, "We pride ourselves in our selection of gardening products that perform for our customers in this area. Our long suit is the color department. Within this area, we feature new and unusual items for intrepid gardeners, new plant or variety introductions and beautiful bedding plants grown to our specifications. You'll find herbs, vegetables, seasonal specialties, occasion-specific gardening baskets, bulbs and many other related products that encourage success." Affiliated with Turkey Creek, one of the largest wholesale-only nurseries in the state, the company maintains great depth in landscape plant materials. Additionally, its tropical plants are spectacular.

Cornelius carries a complete selection of fashionable home accessories. We were particularly impressed with the handsome pottery. The stores stock a large selection of books on subjects ranging from gardening advice to beautifully illustrated coffee table conversation pieces. Cornelius really sparkles at Christmas. The company has worked for many years compiling free information sheets on many Houston-area plants and gardening projects. Other customer services include delivery, grass pluggers and fertilizer spreaders on loan, landscape design and installation, and business or in-home holiday decorating. "Our goal at Cornelius," says Steve, "is to help you shape your corner of the world." Sales are advertised weekly, and there is a full-time information center staffed with Texas Certified Nursery Professionals to assist customers at each of the stores. Sign up at the web site for a newsletter with coupons and special seasonal information.

Kingwood Garden Center
1216 Stonehollow Dr
Kingwood, Texas 77339
281.358.1805
www.kingwoodgardencenter.com
Hours: Mon–Sat 9–6, Sun 10–5

Tucked behind a colorful and diverse perennial bed, Kingwood Garden Center is the place to fill your gardening needs in the Kingwood area. Here for almost 30 years, this independent shop is owned by Bob and Nancy Robertson and manned by a very professional and helpful staff. All manner of annuals, perennials, vines, roses, seeds, succulents, soils and herbs are in tip top shape and ready to go home to plant today. Kingwood carries a large selection of organic products such as Medina and Lady Bug and has its own 19-5-9 premium lawn fertilizer specific to the Kingwood area. This nursery is not fancy and does not have tons of bells and whistles, but what you will find here are good quality plants, solid advice, and the proper amenities to make your garden grow and flourish.
Directions: Kingwood Garden Center is a block off of Kingwood Dr. From 59 go east on Kingwood Dr, take a left on Chestnut Ridge and then the first right on Stonehollow.

RCW Nurseries Inc.
15809 Tomball Pkwy
Houston, Texas 77086
281.440.5161
www.rcwnurseries.com
Hours: Daily 8–5

What a pleasant surprise it was to find this nursery. Since RCW has its own all-organic tree farm, it has created a lovely, shady atmosphere of its own and built a large inventory of shade and flowering ornamental trees for customers. There are also shrubs, perennials, seeds, herbs, tools, books, vegetable starts and water plants to be found in this country-feeling nursery where gardeners are greeted by a fragrant rose garden and large cages of birds. As customers say, "Not only is the selection great, but this is such a peaceful place to visit." RCW will deliver, and it guarantees all trees it plants. Trees and shrubs are frequently marked down in late-summer, fall and winter.
Directions: RCW is on the NW corner of Hwy 249 and Beltway 8.

Shades of Texas
2618 Genoa Red Bluff Rd
Houston, Texas 77034
281.991.8733
www.shadesoftexas.com
Hours: Mon–Sat 8–5

Shades of Texas is a family-owned garden center that attracts customers with its beautiful trees. The specialty here is home-grown hollies: 'Emily Brunner', 'East Palatka', 'Nellie R. Stevens', 'Foster', 'Burfordii', 'savannah' and yaupons. If hollies aren't on your menu, don't pass up this immaculate nursery for other trees (oaks and magnolias especially), plants, soil, mulch or gravel. In 1967 owner Jon Matthews' father bought a gas-powered edger, and as resourceful 9th grader, Jon paid someone to drive him around to landscape jobs. He has been successfully in business ever since. This nursery can offer everything from trees to complete landscapes, ponds, irrigation, lighting design and myriad soils for any project large or small.

The owner is charming, so friendly, and very helpful. He is usually found behind the counter to meet all customers as they come in. Shades of Texas is absolutely worth the trip if you need trees for your landscape.

Directions: Shades of Texas is just a mile outside Beltway 8 on Genoa Red Bluff. Look for the yellow gates.

Teas Nursery Co. Inc.
4400 Bellaire Blvd
Bellaire, Texas 77401
713.664.4400
www.teasnursery.com

Hours: Mon–Fri 9–7, Sat & Sun 9–6; opens at 8 on Saturdays in spring

Although Teas' acreage has downsized in the last few years, we find the same lovely atmosphere, friendly people and high-quality plants and service from years past. Houston's "super store" for plants, this five-acre nursery in Bellaire offers over 400 varieties of roses and a broad selection of other plants, including azaleas, crepe myrtles, herbs, orchids, bedding plants, bromeliads, succulents, African violets and much, much more. Houstonians have long appreciated the huge selection of high-quality perennial and seasonal plants at market prices and the great selection of bulbs, which are kept refrigerated to ensure healthy blooms. A family-owned business established in Raysville, Indiana in 1843, Teas moved to its present location almost 90 years ago. A home built on the site in 1910 is available for tours and catered luncheons by appointment, and the 1916 family home serves as a Teas museum and landscape office.

Teas Landscape Services employs landscape architects, designers, installers, and maintenance experts working on interior, exterior, home and business plantscapes. Teas *Orchid and Exotic Plant Supply Catalog* is mailed to 50,000 customers each year and provides toll-free ordering service. Says Diann Teas, "We enjoy a well-earned reputation as the best nursery in Houston with the highest quality and selection at reasonable prices." The company holds a "Back 40" sale in late spring and has summer clearances. Almost every weekend you'll find visiting experts speaking on specific topics. As one of the country's oldest nurseries, Teas is certainly "the grandfather of nurseries in the Houston area!"

Thompson + Hanson
3600 West Alabama
Houston, Texas 77027
713.622.6973
www.thompsonhanson.com

Hours: Daily 9–6

Thompson + Hanson is more than a nursery these days with a retail nursery, landscape design team, installation department, full-service maintenance department and even a restaurant on-site! Lance Thompson started landscaping during high school, stored his menagerie of plants on his family driveway, and Thompson + Hanson hasn't stopped growing and inspiring Houston gardens and gardeners ever since. The nursery moved to a charming Austin-style retail space in 2000 which includes a gift shop with constantly changing French antiques for home and garden, a beautifully kept nursery space, and the restaurant, called "Tiny Boxwoods," which serves breakfast and lunch and is overflowing on pretty days. The nursery specializes in perennials, tropicals, ferns, ivies and bedding plants, and the quality and selection is all one could want. All of the plants are beautifully maintained. The nursery

(LISTING CONTINUED ON THE NEXT PAGE)

(CONTINUED)

carries an unusual selection of pots, ranging from handmade Italian to Belgian zinc. Sid Leeah specializes in custom pots, so the nursery overflows with potted seasonal color for the taking on any occasion. Manager Steve Crowson says, "We strive to carry things that work here," and specialty trucks from California bring in different and unusual plants, which "sets us apart from other nurseries." Thompson + Hanson is a great place to start with a new garden or put the finishing touches on an existing one.

Directions: Thompson + Hanson is just 2 lights north of 59 at the Edloe exit, 1 block west of Edloe.

Specialty Nurseries

Another Place in Time
1102 Tulane St
Houston, Texas 77008
713.864.9717
www.anotherplaceintime.com
Hours: Mon 9:30–5:30, Tues–Sat 9–6, Sun 10–5

For 19 years Mike Lowery has been cultivating heirloom plants and collecting handcrafted garden accessories for an appreciative gardening audience. Ferns are a specialty here, along with unusual perennials, water plants, bonsai and tropicals, including orchids. Mike himself says, "We do a ton of container gardens and unique hanging baskets." Another Place in Time has been called "a nurturing place," and staff members who work out of this 1920s-vintage house in Houston's Heights are dedicated to personal service. Avid gardeners all, they're full of "old-fashioned" advice. The accessories here are especially nice. The selection of containers ranges from the dramatic to the whimsical. Landscaping services are available on a limited basis. Look for special offers and sales on the website.

Directions: Another Place in Time is really on 11th St and the NE corner of Tulane, west of Heights Blvd.

The Backyard Gardener
5117 North Main St
Houston, Texas 77009
713.880.8004
www.backyardgardenerhouston.com
Hours: Tues–Sat 9–5

This is another Heights area nursery that is a great resource for culinary, medicinal, and scented herbs and exotic fruit trees, specifically, papaya! After a visit with the manager and a tour of the beautifully designed and planted fountains on the property, we went to peruse the plants which are grown locally so they are acclimated to this balmy Zone 9 climate. Visiting on a hot day in June, the plants were in beautiful shape, and the nursery was a tidy oasis with everything from perennials, tropicals, and water plants to pots, fountains, and arbors. April Cohen and Jim Ruzicka have been selling plants for almost ten years, and this bright shop in an old grocery store has much of the old-style Houston Heights charm. They do offer landscaping services, and check out the website with all kinds of useful information!

Directions: The Backyard Gardener is at the corner of Winston and North Main just west of I-45.

Cactus King
7800 I-45 N
Houston, Texas 77037-4219
281.591.8833
www.bluesguy.com/cactusking
Hours: Mon–Sat 10–6, Sun 12–6

Our visit to Cactus King was quite an "eclectic" experience! This is as much an art stop as a plant source! According to owner and artist Lyn Rathburn, "We carry 3,000 varieties of cacti and succulents and 40 varieties of *Cycas*." We found a wonderful cache of books; garden accessories; stone, metal, and wooden statues; Mexican and African art. There's also pottery from Mexico and other countries, rocks, fossils, skulls, artifacts, pre-Columbian art and swords. Cactus King offers advice and plant identification for "weird succulents." The shop is only partially wheelchair/stroller accessible. There is a mini-documentary on the internet filmed with Cactus King as the backdrop and Lyn Rathburn and his art as the subject. (www.onlyinhouston.org/en/cms/) Click Cactus King! This three-minute bit is a fascinating perspective of this rather unusual shop.

Directions: Cactus King is just east of the Canino Rd exit off I-45 N.

Jerry's Jungle Garden
712 Hill Rd
Houston, Texas 77037
832.978.5358
www.jerrysjungle.com
Hours: check the website for the three open days per year

Don't miss a chance to see Jerry Seymore's myriad tropicals collected during 23 years of traveling. Jerry opens up his garden three times a year and enjoys "distributing the wealth of plant material" to those lucky souls who stop by to peek into his special garden world. Jerry's Jungle is also open for special garden club groups, or other arrangements can be made during the "off season" when the garden is not normally open. (one opening in spring, summer, and fall is the norm). We took home little wisps of a flowerless blue passionflower on our first visit that Jerry dug up and handed to us in black plastic 1 gallon pots, and we felt like new adoptive mothers as he handed his precious plants to us to tend. Jerry gave directions, and that passionflower became the focus of our butterfly gardens. The fritillary caterpillars had quite a buffet that first summer. Visiting this garden is a treat and a special look into Jerry's love and passion, which he shared with his late wife and continues to share with other passionate gardeners.

Directions: Hill Rd is between I-45 and the Hardy Toll Rd north of 610. From downtown on I-45, head north and take the West Mt. Houston exit and head east. Take a right on Airline and a left on Hill Rd.

Joshua's Native Plants & Garden Antiques
502 West 18th
Houston, Texas 77007
713.862.7444
www.joshuasnativeplants.com
Hours: Tues–Sat 10–6, Sun 12–6

Says Joshua Kornegay, "Hardy, aggressive natives and old-fashioned perennials are our specialty...work less and enjoy more! Hard-to-find, yet-easy-to-grow ornamentals, along with "old-fashioned advice" gets your garden just the way you've always wanted!" Bring pictures and measurements of your garden, and they will help you design and plan with your color scheme. Get on the mailing list for workshops, (most of them free), sales, parties, gardening tips, etc. Joshua handpicks every item and plant for this shop — everything from the turn-of-the-century planters and birdbaths to funky '50s garden furniture. He imports fine European cast iron and garden benches, gates, statuary and old watering cans. For gardeners on a budget, there's a huge assortment of reproduction Victorian decor. The recirculating urn fountains are particularly impressive. Not all areas are wheelchair/stroller accessible.

Lucia's Garden
2216 Portsmouth
Houston, Texas 77098
713.523.6494
www.luciasgarden.com
luciasgarden@juno.com
Hours: Mon–Sat 10–6, Tues and Thurs until 7

In a little house in a residential area, you will find Lucia's Garden, the only garden shop in Houston that is exclusively dedicated to growing and using herbs. They retail four-inch to 5 gallon live plants, predominately culinary, and teach classes in growing herbs, cooking and crafting with herbs (potpourri, wreaths, tussie-mussies, etc.), medicinal herbs and aromatherapy. We were most impressed with their large selection of dried bulk herbs and their books...the largest selection in Houston of gardening, crafting and personal health use books on herbs and flowers. Lucia's has a fun spring open house and "Faerie Festival" in May and offers a huge abundance of cooking (and eating!) classes using herbs. Don't miss these! Not all areas are wheelchair/stroller accessible.

Palmer Orchids
1308 East Broadway
Pasadena, Texas 77506
713.472.1364
www.palmerorchids.com
Hours: Mon–Sat 9–5

Although Palmer Orchids carries other tropicals, the company definitely specializes in orchids with some 15,000 plants and all orchid supplies. Palmer Orchids grows and sells in sizes ranging from very small seedlings to large specimen plants. You'll find *Asocendrum*, *Brassia*, *Cattleya*, *Dendrobium*, *Epidendrum*, *Phalaenopsis*, *Paphiopedilum*, *Vanda* and intergenerics. A specialty is heat tolerant varieties that grow and bloom in South Texas. Says Terri Palmer, "We have the largest variety of orchids (blooming and green leaf) in the state! You will find plants at Palmer's that are not available elsewhere." Delivery is available in the Houston area, and Palmer Orchids holds an open house and offers programs for garden clubs. Check the website and order online! Palmer's is not wheelchair/stroller accessible.

Directions: Palmer's is located 20 minutes southeast of downtown Houston. Take the Red Bluff exit off Hwy 225 and turn south to Broadway.

River Oaks Plant House
3401 Westheimer
Houston, Texas 77027
713.622.5350
Hours: Mon–Sat 8–8, Sun 9–7

River Oaks Plant House is best known for fantastic topiary figures. As one of the leading topiary makers in the nation, River Oaks Plant House has revived the ancient art of shaping plants into decorative sculptures. Says owner Daniel Saparzadeh, "Our firm is the largest manufacturer of topiaries in the world." Its artists have handcrafted a menagerie of shapes such as deer, birds, elephants and many more animals, as well as whimsical custom designs. To ensure quality control, all of the topiary is locally made in the company's studio greenhouse. The galvanized metal frames are designed, welded together and stuffed with sphagnum moss while being wrapped with monofilament, which brings out the detail. The frames are guaranteed to maintain their shape for at least 10 years under normal conditions. A sprinkler system, usually for larger pieces, is an optional feature and can be installed prior to filling the frame. The final step in creating topiary is planting either fig ivy or Asian jasmine in the moss. According to *Architectural Digest,* "River Oaks Plants represents the state of the art in topiary design."
Directions: River Oaks Plant House is at the corner of Buffalo Speedway and Westheimer. Look for the topiaries lining the esplanade!

Garden Furnishings

Adkins Architectural Antiques
3515 Fannin St
Houston, Texas 77004
713.522.6547 or 800.522.6547
Hours: Mon–Sat 9:30–5:30, Sun 12–5

Adkins is known for period and reproduction garden decor, street lighting (in 40 styles), patio furniture, fountains, urns, benches, bronze, stone and cement statuary, and wrought iron gates and fencing. Specializing in architectural antiques, its inventory is one of the largest in the Southwest and includes mantels, stained glass windows, lighting and plumbing fixtures, doors and door hardware. As Nancy reports, "Adkins is frequently able to obtain large or unusual architectural embellishments or materials from landmark homes or buildings during renovation projects. The staff is experienced in working with home owners, decorators, and architects to adapt these architectural treasures for use in restoration or new home projects." Most of the areas are wheelchair/stroller accessible.

Armand Bayou Nature Center
8500 Bay Area Blvd
Pasadena, Texas 77507
281.474.3074

The Armand Bayou Nature Center gift shop carries wind chimes, birdhouses and feeders, rocks, books and totes. For complete listing, see page 101.

BBQ Pits by Klose
1355 Judiway
Houston, Texas 77018
713.686.8720 or 800.487.7487
www.bbqpits.com
Hours: Mon–Sat 8–6:30

David Klose founded this company in 1986 with the idea of maintaining the trail-drive style of cooking. His custom-made wood, charcoal and gas-fired barbecue grills and smokers range from a $69 drum to a half-million-dollar catering rig. In addition to standard, pits, you'll find that chuck wagons, trains, old perambulators and automobiles have provided inspiration for his "usable art." Mr. Klose is a man who loves what he does. A great story-teller, he makes visiting the factory an experience. You'll find hundreds of sizes in stock, but if you can't get to Houston, he'll ship his products anywhere in the world. "Steel doesn't lie to you," he observes in a serious moment. "One welder makes each unit. Handmade all the way. These guys are really artists!" The website provides everything from product information to recipes and amusing "delivery tales."

The Chair King
6393 Richmond
Houston, Texas 77057
713.781.7340

5402 W. FM 1960
Houston, Texas 77069
281.893.7130
www.chairking.com
Hours: Tues, Wed, Fri 10–6, Mon, Thurs, Sat 10–8, Sun 12–6 (all stores)

"We make it easy...to take it easy!" This has been the motto of this Houston-based company for 58 years, and its stores continue to live up to that promise. Marvin Barish purchased the Chair King in 1973, and today the 17 stores are still family-owned and operated. As Jackie Barish told us, "We all work side-by-side in a company that has grown from two stores into the largest specialty furniture retailer in the Southwest." The Chair King offers an extensive selection of fine casual furniture in wrought iron, aluminum, molded resins, traditional wicker, "perma-wicker" and teak. The list of manufacturers includes such names as Woodard, Mallin, Tropitone, Hanamint, Castelle and Solaris, which is designed and manufactured exclusively for Chair King. You'll also find hammocks, swings, gliders and a variety of accessories including umbrellas, replacement cushions, furniture covers, torches, garden clocks and thermometers and outdoor tableware. The Chair King prides itself on the large selection, warranty protection, professional, courteous personnel and prompt delivery. The company's brochures are especially helpful, not only for selection purposes, but also for maintenance instructions. Chair King is an institution.

The Garden Gate
5122 Morningside Dr
Houston, Texas 77005
713.528.2654
www.gardengateco.com
Hours: Mon–Sat 10–6, Sun 12–5

As we wandered around The Garden Gate, the gurgling fountain with goldfish and blooming water lilies first caught our attention. Only later were we astounded by the vast array of cast stone English reproduction fountains, urns, planters, birdbaths, and statuary, the English lead and limestone works, the Italian marble pieces, and endless other decorative garden items available here. There is a colorful abundance of glazed French terracotta urns from small to very large (31" pot mouth) and beautiful examples of different metal works: arbors, gazebos, gates and garden furniture. The store carries tools, books, herbs, vines and much seasonal color, offers landscaping services, and even a pond maintenance service for customers. Says Donna Lokey, the owner, "One client referred to The Garden Gate as one giant garage sale, always something different!" The gift shop has lovely French table linens, soaps, candles and fun gifts for any gardener.

Directions: From Hwy 59, take the Kirby exit and head south on Kirby past the light at Sunset. Three blocks past Sunset, take a left on Robinhood and go down 2 blocks to Morningside.

Home & Patio
2525 FM 1960 W
Houston, Texas 77068
713.440.7667
www.houstonhomeandpatio.com
Hours: Mon–Sat 10–6

This store, which opened in 1978, is owned by the same Kelley family as the San Antonio Home & Patio, and is managed by family members Beverly Weeks and her daughter, Kelley Wendt. As Kelley explained, "the two locations carry different furniture lines reflecting the character of their respective locations. Here, you will find Lane, Meadowcraft, O.W. Lee, Mallin, Suncoast, Telescope, Hansen, and Seaside Casual, among others." There are recirculating fountains, statuary, fire pits and a host of accessories from umbrellas, replacement cushions, tableware and outdoor rugs to wind chimes, birdhouses and feeders and outdoor lighting. Commented Kelley, "We have been in business for 30 years, and you will find the same personnel offering the same great customer service each time you visit. Besides, we pride ourselves on our very competitive prices." Home & Patio offers delivery service and has an on-site warehouse for easy pick up.

Houston Arboretum and Nature Center
4501 Woodway Dr
Houston, Texas 77024
713.681.0076

The gift shop here stocks lots of items with a nature or wildflower theme. You will find a large selection of books about Texas plants, as well as wind chimes, birdhouses and feeders, and sun hats. One of the more unusual items is the "bird clock" which features a different birdcall each hour and an informative booklet telling you about that particular bird. There are three or four tree or plant sales during the year. For complete listing, see page 102.

Jerald N. Bettes Company
6105-A West 34th St
Houston, Texas 77092
713.682.7901
www.jeraldbettes.com
Hours: Mon–Fri 8–5; Sat 9–3 (call for exact time on Saturday)

As Jerald Bettes explained to us, "Because we couldn't buy any outdoor furniture that would last, our furniture was originally built for personal use, not to sell." Today, his company produces all types of furniture — swings, gliders, park benches, picnic tables, planter boxes, trash receptacles and more. The company calls its product "lifetime outdoor furniture." Heavy materials (a steel framework and thick wood slats) are used to manufacture the high-quality, commercial grade products, and you have a choice of available wood. You will also find a large selection of gas and charcoal grills and fire pits. At Jerald Bettes, there's a price range to fit every budget. UPS can ship swings and small pieces.

Kay O'Toole Antiques & Eccentricities
1921 Westheimer
Houston 77098
713.523.1921
Hours: Tues–Fri 11–5, Sat 11–4

As Kay O'Toole explained, "Although I don't cater exclusively to the garden at Antiques & Eccentricities, I do carry a good selection of European antique garden furniture and accessories as well as architectural embellishments." In both the indoor and outdoor display area, you will find antique chairs, tables, benches, plant stands and planters, fountains and statuary. There are also garden carts, stone bases for sinks, marble basins, terra cotta and stone wall hangings, concrete jardinières, English stone balls and wrought iron garden surrounds. As Kay laughingly admits, "It seems like one buying trip after another, so the shop is always crowded with new treasurers."

Directions: The shop is on Westheimer, not even a block east of S Shepherd.

Patio One Furniture
5807 Richmond
Houston, Texas 77057
713.977.4455

3105 FM 1960 W
Houston, Texas 77068
281.893.9700
www.patio1.com
Hours: Mon 10–7, Tues–Sat 10–6

Patio One specializes in premium quality patio furniture. See Page 121 for complete listing.

Katy (west Harris County)

Specialty Nurseries

Nelson Water Gardens
1502 Katy Fort Bend County Rd
Katy, Texas 77493
281.391.4769
www.nelsonwatergardens.com
Hours: Mon–Sat 9–6, Sun 10–4

Here you will find the best source for water gardens, water plants, water lilies, koi and goldfish, and "disappearing" fountains anywhere. Rolf Nelson has been in business for 11 years and has built an impressive shop and nursery with a very enthusiastic staff and a fantastic koi pond to keep anyone not interested in the plants occupied! "Almost any pot on the property can be turned into a disappearing fountain," says one employee, save for some of the more fragile Mexican-types." The water features, the ponds, the water plants, and the fountains seem to get customers here, but there is also a wide range of annuals, perennials, and a huge selection of herbs from which to choose. "We are possibly the largest supplier of herbs on the west side of town," according to Mr. Nelson. This is a very friendly place with helpful staff and well-maintained plant material. Nelson subcontracts pond work, but he will send you home with a very detailed "how-to" for installing disappearing fountains, streams or waterfalls. The website has info on water plants and troubleshooting as well as sales, specials, upcoming (free!) classes, and fish info.

Directions: Nelson is just north of I-10. Take Exit 742, Katy Fort Bend County Rd, and go about 0.5 miles. Nelson Gardens is on the right.

Garden Furnishings

The Chair King
20061 Katy Freeway
Katy, Texas 77450
281.599.1818
www.chairking.com
Hours: Tues, Wed, Fri 10–6, Mon, Thurs, Sat 10–8, Sun 12–6 (all stores)

See complete listing on page 118.

Patio One Furniture
20425 Katy Freeway
Katy, Texas 77450
281.578.9100
www.patio1.com
Hours: Mon 10–7, Tues–Sat 10–6

Having been in business since 1978, Patio One specializes in premium quality patio furniture. As founder and owner B. J. Mehrinfar proudly states, "We look all over the world for the newest in design and technology, and we offer traditional, contemporary and classical selections. Here you can buy your 'last set first time.' We are a full-service patio store; in addition to our four-million-dollar inventory, we also design, make and refinish to your specification." High-quality furniture lines are available in teak, cast aluminum, wrought iron,

(LISTING CONTINUED ON THE NEXT PAGE)

(CONTINUED)

extruded aluminum and outdoor wicker. This company manufactures cushions and umbrellas, and there is a huge selection of three- or five-year, no-fade guaranteed fabrics from which to choose. The customer can select a frame from any furniture line, decide on cushion size, color and style, and, even better, the cushions will be ready in five to ten days! Matching bar sets from the best manufacturers are also popular items.

Montgomery / Conroe / Magnolia / Shenandoah / Willis / The Woodlands (Montgomery County)

Garden Centers

The Growers Outlet
11173 North US Hwy 75
Willis, Texas 77378
936.856.5001
Hours: Mon–Sat 8–5, Sun 11–3

The Growers Outlet, owned by Terry Wibberg for the last eight years, occupies two acres, which are mostly covered with seven large greenhouses. Color abounds! Here, they grow bedding plants and hanging baskets, carry tropicals, ferns, trees, shrubs and a large array of attractive mixed planters as well as do a brisk business in special orders. Bagged mulches and soils are available, and organic gardening is being encouraged. We were especially impressed with Tosha's free "Keys to Success" cards. These cards provide invaluable information about a variety of plants including tips on light, watering, fertilizing, pruning and pest and disease management.

Directions: The Growers Outlet is on Hwy 75, 1.0 mile south of Willis.

Specialty Nurseries

Flores Produce & Plants
160 Eva St (Hwy 105)
Montgomery, Texas 77316
936.597.5070
Hours: Daily 9–6

Not only can you buy fresh produce daily at Flores, but you can also find hanging baskets and colorful bedding plants for your garden. There are fruit and shade trees, shrubs, Knock Out roses, Encore azaleas, vines and a large selection of tropicals. And even better, you will be quite pleased with the reasonable prices for these healthy plants. Having been in business for 20 years, Adam and Alice Flores have very successfully combined tasty produce and happy plants with lots of wrought iron, chimineas and colorful Talavera pots. Flores is not wheelchair/stroller accessible.

The Pineywoods Nursery and Landscaping
12437 Sleepy Hollow Rd
Shenandoah, Texas 77385
281.681.2889
www.thepineywoodsnursery.com
Hours: Tues–Sat 8:30–4:30

The Pineywoods Nursery specializes in native plants, but it also stocks such other adapted plants as antique roses and clumping bamboo, plus non-invasive Asian plants with direct family ties to our Texas natives. "Our mission is to create a place where native plants and knowledgeable people provide a landscape of beauty that's friendly to the environment and a habitat for animals and people alike," says Jason McKenzie. He and his wife bought property that belonged to the late Lynn Lowrey, and they are living there with their children. They are caring for the trees and shrubs Mr. Lowrey planted and are striving to follow in his footsteps. It had been abandoned for fifteen years before the young couple took over in 2000 and started cleaning up and reforesting the 2.8-acre site. You'll find such uncommon plants as Florida anise, gordonia, two-wing silverbells, scarlet catchfly, Mexican milkweed and pipevine and native wisteria growing against the backdrop of the old trees now. We expect great things from this place in years to come.

Teas Herbs & Orchids, Inc.
32930 Decker Prairie Rd
Magnolia, Texas 77355
281.356.2336
www.teasherbsandorchids.net
Hours: Mon–Fri 7:30–5, Sat 9–3

There have been some changes since our last visit to Teas Herbs & Orchids; the nursery has moved next door, and Jim Oates has become co-owner, along with Janis Teas. This specialty wholesale/retail nursery carries up to 175 species of herbs, orchids, vegetables, perennials, trees, shrubs and bedding plants. Says Janis Teas, "Our hours are limited, but we will make your trip worthwhile. In our 16,000-square-foot greenhouse, you will find unusual plant material at discount prices, and customers can choose from a crop instead of a few flats." The nursery also carries garden supplies, books, tools and some organic products. This is the place to find "the unusual."

Directions: Travel 3.0 to 4.0 miles north of Tomball on State Hwy 249. Turn west on Decker Prairie/Stagecoach Rd. It is less than 1.0 mile on the right.

Garden Furnishings

The Chair King
27200 I-45 N
Conroe, Texas 77385
281.298.1300
www.chairking.com
Hours: Tues, Wed, Fri 10–6, Mon, Thurs, Sat 10–8, Sun 12–6 (all stores)
See complete listing on page 118.

Rosenberg / Richmond / Stafford (Fort Bend County)

Specialty Nurseries

Caldwell Nursery
2436 Band Rd
Rosenberg, Texas 77471
281.342.4016
www.caldwellhort.com
Hours: Mon–Sat 9–5:30

This nursery may be "off the beaten path," but it is well worth the trip. A labor of love, its immaculate display gardens are richly textured, soft and naturalistic. Says Cay Dee Caldwell, "I tend to like things overgrown and full." Caldwell specializes in natives, herbs, roses, antique roses, unusual perennials, tropicals, bamboo, water plants and bog plants. The owners are enthusiastic about named-variety daylilies, and the samples throughout the display gardens, as well as those for sale, are very healthy with color popping out in the spring. Chuck Caldwell is passionate about growing bamboo, and Caldwell carries unusual and hard-to-find species, from 5-gallon to 200-gallon, just perfect for the Houston area like Timor black, angel mist, Buddha's belly, lemon-lime, golden goddess, and painted bamboo, to name a few. In an effort to help customers, the Caldwells provide personal, informal signs with accurate knowledge on each plant and point out when a specific rarity is available in the nursery. According to Cay Dee, "In using texture and contrast plants, we hope to inspire many gardeners to try different natives and perennials. All plants have their own 'uniqueness' ... like people, I guess. We don't claim to know everything, but we hope our enthusiasm 'wears off' on our customers." What a delight!

Directions: Take the Hwy 36 exit south of Sugar Land and go south. Bear right on Band Rd after the fairgrounds and the nursery is down a mile on the right.

Bill Bownds Nursery
10519 FM 1464
Richmond, Texas 77469
281.277.2033
www.bilbowndsnurseries.com
Hours: Mon–Sat 9–5:30

When we visited this three-acre nursery, we were wowed by the stock of specimen-size native trees. You'll find oaks of all kinds (except post oaks), Drummond red maple, sweetgum, bald cypress, cedar elm and river birch, along with such hardy adapted species as crepe myrtle (6–8 varieties), trident maple, drake and lacebark elms and Chinese pistache. There is also a good stock of native small trees/large shrubs, including wax myrtle, yaupon, possumhaw, Mexican plum and Texas mountain laurel. The late Mr. Bownds left this well established nursery in the capable hands of his son-in-law, John Sieple, who told us that all the trees are now grown in containers (up to 100-gallon) and that the company is happy to plant its wares at your home.

Enchanted Nurseries and Landscapes

Enchanted Gardens
6420 FM 359
Richmond, Texas 77406
281.341.1206

Enchanted Forest
10611 FM 2759
Richmond, Texas 77469
281.937.9449
www.myenchanted.com
Hours: Mon–Sat 8:30–5:30, Sun 10–4

Enchanted Gardens and Enchanted Forest make up the "Enchanted" nursery and landscape group in the Sugar Land area. Enchanted Forest is down from the Greatwood community and is set up like a park and has a wide variety of beautifully maintained plants specific to this area of Texas. A huge selection of roses is available. Professional horticulturists are on staff to help with questions and problems and to guide customers who need an extra hand. Enchanted Forest has a fountain stream running through, and the children were busy watching fish and playing while the parents were shopping. Enchanted Gardens has an equally nice selection of locally grown annuals and perennials, perfect for a Texas landscape. Both nurseries have a little something for everyone on a pretty spring day or even a hot summer one! Enchanted has a long list of seminars: fairy gardening, lawn care, organics, children in the garden and butterfly gardening, and they host special events all through the year. Check the website or get on the mailing list for the information-packed newsletter.

Garden Furnishings

The Chair King
11375 Fountain Lake Dr
Stafford, Texas 77477
281.240.8555
www.chairking.com
Hours: Tues, Wed, Fri 10–6, Mon, Thurs, Sat 10–8, Sun 12–6 (all stores)
See complete listing on page 118.

Seabrook / Webster (southeast Harris County)

Garden Centers

Maas Nursery & Landscaping
5511 Todville Rd
Seabrook, Texas 77586
281.474.2488
www.maasnursery.com
Hours: Mon–Sat 9–5:30, Sun 10–5:30

Jim Maas reports, "At Maas Nursery we specialize in giving our customers a pleasant experience to explore and enjoy. Our out-of-the-way location doesn't lend itself to a quick stop on the way home from work. We therefore cater to the gardener who wants to take more than four or five minutes to shop." When you visit Maas' 14 acres, you'll see why he says, "We are not just another garden center." Not only does this nursery grow almost every plant that's adapted to this part of Texas, but it also offers fun things to see and do. Maas has live music many weekends in the spring. Local artists carve stone or wood, or paint and throw pots as you watch. Some of the most interesting displays revolve around ethnic and native art from foreign lands. You'll find out about canoes from the Cuna Indians, Indonesian folk art and antique and modern yard art (furniture and statuary).

"Our exotic animal compound is very popular with both kids and adults," says Jim. It's a natural environment for all sorts of non-carnivorous animals. We could have anything from rabbits to wallabies to longhorns. Since we rescue, buy, love and sell our animals, the population changes from year to year." The main building is more like a museum than a salesroom. Here you'll find shells, rocks, skulls, artifacts and specimens from all over the world. Unlike a museum, if Maas has it, you can look, touch and buy (almost every item). "If you are interested in an unusual shopping experience, please come visit us. We don't usually have sales, but we definitely offer garden advice."

Directions: From Houston, take I-45 to NASA Rd One and travel east to Hwy 146 in Seabrook. Cross at the light and continue to the water, which is Todville. Take a left on Todville and follow the signs to Maas. Parking is just off Pine Gulley Rd.

Specialty Nurseries

Houston Palm Tree
20420 Gulf Fwy (I-45)
Webster, Texas 77598
281.338.2658
Hours: Mon–Sat 8–7, Sun 8–6

In business for almost 50 years, family-owned and operated Houston Palm Tree has been the source for 36 varieties of indoor and outdoor palms ranging from 1-gallon pots to huge B&B. Driving south toward Galveston, Houston Palm Tree covers 10 acres just past the Bay Area Blvd.

exit. The abundance in quantity and variety of palms is astounding. The regal Canary Island date palm is available here, up to 200-gallon. Other palms include the Medjool date, the Mediterranean fan, pygmy date, queen and an assortment of such high-quality indoor palms as raphis, areca, fishtail and pony tail. The knowledgeable staff will send home a care sheet with the purchase of a new palm, but also this nursery can deliver and plant a newly purchased tree, however far away that may be! Houston Palm accepts all competitors' coupons and will meet their prices.

Garden Furnishings

The Chair King
19801 Gulf Freeway
Webster, Texas 77598
281.557.0884
www.chairking.com
Hours: Tues, Wed, Fri 10–6, Mon, Thurs, Sat 10–8, Sun 12–6 (all stores)
See complete listing on page 118.

Orange (Orange County)

Specialty Nurseries

Doan's Nursery, Inc.
19024 Hwy 62 S
Orange, Texas 77630
409.735.8004
Hours: Mon–Sat 8–6, Sun 10–5

Although damaged by hurricane Ike, Doan's is, indeed, flourishing. Founded in 1978 by Tien and Lanthao Doan, this nursery boasts 20 greenhouses and some of the most amazing specimen plants we have seen! It's just brimming with huge sago palms, braided gardenia standards and hibiscus, to name a few of the plants we coveted. You will find cacti, lots of color, hanging baskets, tropicals and much, much more. And, the prices are most reasonable. This is well worth a visit.

Directions: Doan's is west of Orange, about 4.0 miles south of I-10.

Garden Furnishings

The Garden Store at Shangri La Botanical Gardens and Nature Center
2111 West Park Ave
Orange, Texas 77630
409.670.0805

At The Garden Store, you will find a good selection of books, a number of which are "how to" books. In keeping with Shangri La's philosophy, the store offers recycled glass hummingbird feeders and vases and other garden ornaments. There are also gardening tools, gloves and aprons. For Shangri La's complete listing, see page 100.

Pearland/Alvin (Brazoria County)

Specialty Nurseries

Payne's in the Grass Daylily Farm
2137 Melanie Ln
Pearland, Texas 77581
281.485.3821
www.paynesinthegrassdaylilyfarm.com
Hours: Thurs–Sun 9–5 during blooming time; by appointment at other times

As Paula and Leon Payne explain, "Our business evolved from our love of daylilies, and we take special interest in hybridizing. We offer many of the latest cultivars and our own introductions as well as those for the beginning collector or casual gardener. Visitors are welcome!" At least once a year during the blooming season the Paynes hold an "Open Garden" where they make a slide presentation. Wonderful pictures or slides are available by mail. Check out the website to see some of the 800 lily cultivars grown here. Call for directions.

Shimek Gardens
3122 County Rd 237
Alvin, Texas 77511
281.331.4395
http://users.hal-pc.org/~neshimek
Hours: By appointment

Shimek Gardens was a 2008 A.H.S. National Convention Tour Garden and boasts 800 named daylilies plus thousands of seedlings. Here you will also find hundreds of other plants, including roses, hibiscus, jatropha, bauhinia, ginger and plumeria. Harvey and Nell Shimek are obviously serious collectors! Quotes Nell, "When one of our many visitors commented that we couldn't possibly want for another daylily, I just laughed and replied that my want-list of daylilies was probably longer than his!" The best time to buy overstock is October through February. Garden advice is freely offered, and visitors are welcome to come and celebrate the daylilies. Call for directions. Don't miss this nursery's open gardens!

Garden Centers

The Arbor Gate
15635 FM 2920
Tomball, Texas 77377
www.arborgate.com
281.351.8851
Hours: Mon 12–6, Tues–Sat 9–6, Sun 9–5

With all the activity at Arbor Gate on a pretty spring Saturday, we were truly sorry we didn't have all day to take everything in. We met owner Beverly Welch out visiting with customers and friends in the nursery and aiming each to his or her desired destination. Looking for the day's Rose Society lecture, a special perennial, a cheerful garden gnome needing a home, or possibly organic soil amendments? And the list only gets better! Since 1996 Arbor Gate has kept Houston area gardeners in the know. Specializing in Texas natives, perennials, heirloom roses, herbs, and "hard-to-find, but not hard-to-grow" plants, this nursery has something for everyone. Just walking around is an adventure in garden art and wayward metal garden chickens, pecking at the beautifully maintained all-organic landscape. The gift shop is filled to overflowing with seeds, small tools, organic remedies for plant dilemmas and creative knickknacks. A true wealth of knowledge is waiting behind the counter in the form of very friendly staff to answer questions and guide gardeners. An abundance of pots are out front, surrounded by fountains and one-of-a-kind arbors of all sizes. We just loved wandering from greenhouse to greenhouse to see what was blooming and would inspire us to do some afternoon planting. The lecture series is not to miss!
Directions: The Arbor Gate is a few miles west of Hwy 249 or just east of Telge Rd.

Spring Nursery & Landscape
25252 FM 2978
Tomball, Texas 77357
281.357.1800
www.springnurseryandlandscape.net
Hours: Mon–Fri 9–6, Sat 9–5

The soothing sound of water provides a welcoming ambiance at Spring Nursery. Owned by Steve Garceau and Kelly Hammon for over 12 years, this complete garden center carries everything from 4-inch annuals and perennials to 200-gallon trees. We were particularly impressed with the stock of large palms. You will find pavestone, fountains, statuary, birdbaths, lavabos and Garden Iron Art. A number of additional services are provided: landscape installation and design, irrigation installation and repair, grounds management, and lawn and bed care. As they say at Spring Nursery, "Our goal is 100% customer satisfaction. It always has been and always will be." Check the informative website for information on seminars.
Directions: The nursery is located north of Tomball between FM 2920 and FM 1488.

Specialty Nurseries

Spring Creek Daylily Garden
25150 Gosling
Spring, Texas 77389
281.351.8827
Hours: By appointment

Mary and Eddie Gage's half-acre of daylilies includes some 1,500 different varieties! Of course, not all are in the couple's free catalog, but "every year we eliminate some and add others." With four registered varieties of their own, they are continuing to hybridize, and they enjoy sharing both their wares and their storehouse of knowledge with other plant lovers. The upcoming catalog will include lots of new items and can be ordered by phone or by e-mail (mary@springcreekdaylily.com).

Garden Furnishings

The Chair King
20407 Hwy 59 N
Humble, Texas 77338
281.446.8509
www.chairking.com
Hours: Tues, Wed, Fri 10–6, Mon, Thurs, Sat 10–8, Sun 12–6 (all stores)

See complete listing on page 118.

Cunningham Living
18700 Carrot St
Spring, Texas 77379
800.833.5998
www.cunninghamliving.com
Hours: Mon–Fri 10–6, Sat 9–4

There's much more here than the gas grills, lights and logs and kitchen equipment the company has been selling for 50 years. Cunningham Living offers practical and decorative items for outdoor living from an entire ready-built kitchen to old-fashioned wall hung bottle openers. (Remember them?) There are bars, attractive gas fire pits, barbeque grills, unobtrusive wall-mounted electric heaters, outdoor ice chests, handsome patio torches, etc. The newest feature of the website is a link to "Kitchenator," which allows customers to design their own outdoor kitchens.

Garden Accents
14907 Treichel Rd
Tomball, Texas 77375
713.351.4804
www.gardenaccentsinc.com
Hours: Mon–Fri 8–5 or later; Sat & Sun call to verify

Bob Folger is what makes Garden Accents especially memorable. He creates a beautiful rock waterfall, then makes a mold of the waterfall and casts the piece in concrete. His products are sold all over Texas. Homeowners can call the factory for the nearest dealer or come to the factory, where you'll find products not in the brochures. A visit to Garden Accents is an experience! Bob collects all sorts of concrete fountains and ornaments from his travels, but once he gets them, he doesn't always want to let them go. Through the years he has accumulated numerous items that are not for sale. In spite of that frustration, people leave with the trunk full. His wife Jeannine reports, "Bob adds his unique touch even to the business hours, and he is usually there seven days a week until dark." She jokes, "Fortunately for me, he is afraid of the dark! It's still best if you call first. Advice is given...sometimes without being asked!"

Directions: From the intersection of 2920 and 249 in Tomball, go 1.0 mile west on 2920 to Treichel Rd.

5
Coastal Bend

Coastal Bend

Corpus Christi is the major market center within this long, narrow region that extends from Port Lavaca to the tip of Padre Island. The cities of Victoria and Kingsville also fall within the maritime influence of the bays and cordgrass marshes that host rich marine life and serve as wintering grounds for numerous species of water birds. Coastal tall grasses, morning glories, sea ox-eyes and beach evening primroses color the landscape here.

The grasslands northeast of Corpus look similar to those of the upper coastal prairies, but the weather and soil conditions are harsher along this part of the coast. Corpus Christi can expect an average of only 30.2 inches of rain each year, which is about the same as Fort Worth, just to put things in perspective. The Coastal Bend is not only more arid than the Beaumont/Houston area, but also the soil contains layers of highly alkaline caliche (calcium carbonate) within the gray gumbo clay. The growing season lasts 309 days, and the January mean minimum temperature is 46°. Freezing temperatures are rare, but they occur often enough to discourage gardeners from planting some of the tropical foliage that thrives further south in the Valley.

The woods, tidal flats and brush of the **Aransas National Wildlife Refuge** provide an ideal habitat for birds and people who enjoy watching them. Grasslands, live oak and red bay thickets ringed by brackish tidal marshes provide the perfect haven for about 400 species of birds and animals. Best-known as the wintering grounds for whooping cranes, this refuge has counted more bird species than any other refuge in the country. For human visitors there's a 16-mile paved road, a Wildlife Interpretive Center, 40 feet observation tower and several miles of walking trails.

The area around Rockport is noted for its sculptural live oaks, shaped by wind and salt spray to appear as if pruned by a Japanese gardener. The biggest live oak in the state grows in **Goose Island State Park**. This 1,000-year-old tree has a circumference of 35 feet, a crown spread of 90 feet and is 44 feet in height! Activities at the park include nature study, wildlife observation and photography, and excellent birding. Spring migration guided bird tours are held in April each year.

Wind-blown sand up to 60-feet-deep covers the counties south of Corpus Christi. Here, grasses, prickly pears, the ubiquitous mesquites, and about two people per square mile occupy the land. Nature trails at **Padre Island National Seashore** offer access to the complicated ecosystems of sand dunes with their sea oats, soilbind morning glories and beach panic grass. Inland, the **Welder Wildlife Refuge** is a biological crossroads between coastal prairies and South Texas brushland.

Hosts of native and imported plants are available to area gardeners, but the choices are far fewer than in Houston. Such lovely natives trees as huisache and retama (the bane of ranchers) are becoming available to the nursery trade and prized in home gardens. In addition to frequent droughts, gardeners here struggle with two big problems: maintaining enough organic material in the soil to neutralize its alkalinity and draining standing water from flat lawns and planting beds after hurricane-force rains.

Corpus Christi Botanical Gardens & Nature Center and the **Xeriscape Learning Center and Design Garden** at the Museum of Science and History provide design inspiration. In Victoria's Riverside Park, gardeners will find **The Texas Zoo** and **Victoria Memorial Rose Garden**.

Public Gardens and Nature Preserves to Visit

Corpus Christi (Nueces County)

Corpus Christi Botanical Gardens & Nature Center
8545 South Staples St
Corpus Christi, Texas 78413
361.852.2100
www.stxbot.org
Hours: Tues–Sun 9–5
Admission: $5 (adults), $4 (seniors, active military & students with I.D.), $2 (children 5–12);
free (children under 5)

Blessed with a lovely 180-acre site on Oso Creek, this organization is up and running! Since 1999 it has added a Hibiscus Garden, Water Garden, Arid Garden and Hummingbird Garden. Construction projects have also included widening and resurfacing the Bird and Butterfly Trail; adding 500 feet to the Wetlands Awareness Boardwalk; and creating an earthen levee in the large wetlands to help maintain water levels. Its greenhouse is home to the Don Larkin Memorial Orchid collection, which is among the largest in the southwest with 2,100 orchids. The four-winged Exhibit House is surrounded by plumeria. The Sensory Garden focuses on sight, sound, touch and mobility enhancements. The Bird and Butterfly Trail leads to panoramic views from the Birding Tower. The Visitors Center houses a gift shop and gallery. Nearby, you'll also find water-wise display beds. For children, there's a self-guided tour that identifies animal tracks and native plants in a treasure hunt format and near the picnic area, a 60-bed children's garden area. The facility hosts seminars, workshops and ecology-oriented group tours.

Directions: From the downtown bayfront area, take Crosstown Expressway (Texas Hwy 286) to South Padre Island Dr, Hwy 358). Exit Staples St and turn right (south). Watch for green signs. Cross Oso Creek to entrance.

Xeriscape Learning Center and Design Garden
Museum of Science and History
1900 North Chaparral
Corpus Christi, Texas 78401
361.826.4650
www.ccmuseum.org
Hours: Daily dawn to dusk

The Xeriscape Learning Center and Design Garden on the museum's west side shows just how colorful a water-wise garden can be! About 100 species of native and adapted plants

(LISTING CONTINUED ON THE NEXT PAGE)

(CONTINUED)

bloom and grow at this outdoor learning center. The scale of the garden is just right for small city lots, and city officials are hoping people will want to copy its example. Exhibits demonstrate how to conserve water by properly planting, irrigating and mulching. Between the museum and the convention center, you'll also find a lovely recirculating fountain. A smaller version of this water feature would make a lovely addition to any home garden. A new gazebo exhibit includes text panels about harvesting rainwater and where to find the hardiest plants in Texas.

Directions: The Center is located just north of the city center near the waterfront.

Rockport (Aransas County)

Hummingbird Demonstration Garden and Wetlands Pond
404 Broadway (Rockport-Fulton Chamber of Commerce)
Rockport, Texas 78382
800.242.0071
Hours: Daily dawn to dusk
Admission: free

In early September, tens of thousands of hummingbirds (predominantly Ruby-throated) pass through Rockport. This small garden is designed to give homeowners ideas for plantings that attract hummingbirds and butterflies. Colorful stands of firecracker bush, cape honeysuckle, hummingbird bush, Mexican bush sage and other salvias provide the nectar that keeps these fascinating creatures returning every year. A new boardwalk extends into an immense patch of trumpet creeper (one of the vines with flowers that attract hummingbirds), ending at a willow grove and wet slough. The wetland demonstration pond was built to show the value of wetlands as a natural resource. Visit the Chamber of Commerce at the address listed above (across the street from the Rockport Harbor) to see its native plant garden and obtain information about the Connie Hager Bird Sanctuary, the annual Hummer/Bird Celebration (held in September) and various boat and bus tours that provide close-up views of coastal terrain and wildlife.

Directions: The hummingbird garden is located in a public rest area on the east side of Business Hwy 35 N, less than 0.5 miles north of downtown Rockport.

Sinton (San Patricio County)

Welder Wildlife Refuge
P.O. Box 1400
Sinton, Texas 78387
361.364.2643
Hours: Guided tours Thurs 3–5; groups by appointment
Admission: free

The Welder Wildlife Foundation is a non-profit institution dedicated to wildlife research and education. The two-hour bus tour offers an overview of the sixteen different plant communities that foster 1,300 native species within 7,800 acres. Its diverse topography and habitats make the refuge a treasure-trove for resident wildlife. The Foundation's property is but a small part of a sprawling ranch that has been owned by the same family since it was established as a Spanish land grant. The land has never been under cultivation. Pristine woodlands border the Aransas River, and former river channels form temporary lakes and marshes on the south end of the property. A biological crossroads, the landscape is part coastal in appearance, while other areas more resemble the native brushlands of the Rio Grande Plain. The tour also includes a visit to the Foundation headquarters and a discussion of the organization's objectives.

Directions: The Refuge is located on the east side of the Missouri Pacific railroad tracks on Hwy 77 approximately 7.4 miles northeast of Sinton.

Victoria (Victoria County)

The Texas Zoo
110 Memorial Dr
Victoria, Texas 77901
361.573.7681
www.texaszoo.org
Hours: Daily 9–5 (Front gates and some buildings close at 4:30); closed Thanksgiving Day, Christmas Eve and Christmas Day
Admission: $4.50 (ages 13–64); $3.50 (3–12); $3 (seniors 65 up); free (childern under 3)

Dedicated to the conservation, protection and preservation of Texas animal species, this zoo is also doing a wonderful job with a natural setting beside the Guadalupe River. Signage is provided to identify plants, and the plants are matched to the needs of the animals. The Butterfly Garden includes the Mexican milkweed that Monarchs love. The Bird Garden is filled with such shrubs as yaupon holly and American beautyberry, and columbine grows under the canopy of large pecans and oaks. Gardeners will also find joy in Victoria's Rose Gardens in Riverside Park.

Directions: From Hwy 87, travel south of the business district to Hwy 59. Turn left on Stayton St and follow the signs.

Coastal Bend Resources

Corpus Christi / Bishop / Port Aransas (Nueces County)

Garden Centers

Fox Tree & Landscape Nursery
5902 South Staples St
Corpus Christi, Texas 78413
361.992.6928
Hours: Mon–Sat 8–7, Sun 9–6

(LISTING CONTINUED ON THE NEXT PAGE)

(CONTINUED)

With 26 acres of nursery stock and greenhouses at the Staples St location, Fox's is the largest nursery in South Texas. It carries just about anything you could want. The big eye-opener, however, is the vast, not to mention fantastic, selection of weather-resistant, brightly colored pots from Mexico, China, Malaysia and India, which come in every size and shape. There is also a fabulous selection of fountains, ranging from classical to very modern in style. And to top it all off, there is furniture...rustic, funky and absolutely delightful. This is a visual treat! More than 50% of the trees and shrubs are Texas natives, and most of the seasonal color is grown on the premises. You'll also find landscaping materials from bulk soils to rock. The "back 40" is a forest of specimen-size trees, and the company has equipment with which to move and plant them. (The tree service arm of the business will also remove dead or damaged trees when needed.) There is a designer on staff, and the company offers landscaping and irrigation services.

Gill Landscape Nursery
2810 Airline Rd
Corpus Christi, Texas 78414
361.992.9674

4441 South Alameda
Corpus Christi, Texas 78412
361.993.4796
www.gillnursery.com
Hours: Mon–Sat 8–6, Sun 10–6

"Friendliest nursery in town! We have the best selection of native plants and Texas Certified Nursery Professionals and Master Certified Professionals to answer questions regarding plant problems or landscape techniques. Industry reps tell us we have the cleanest facility and healthiest plants of any place they sell to," proudly claims James Gill. The company also provides landscape design services. Special orders are welcome, as well as phone orders and in-town delivery service. You'll find a complete line of shrubs, tropicals, annuals and perennials, as well as garden supplies and gifts and an abundance of containers. Its selection of perennials is outstanding. "To sum it up," says Gill, "Quality plants, helpful and knowledgeable staff." The store on Airline Rd offers a pre-Christmas clearance on shrubs and holds seminars in February, May, June and October. Gill's on Alameda is the smaller of the two. It's located in an old gas station, and it specializes in blooming color and "fast-stop shopping."

Turner's Gardenland
6503 South Padre Island Dr
Corpus Christi, Texas 78412
361.991.9002 or 800.662.3467
www.turnersgardenland.com
Hours: Mon–Sat 9–6, Sun 10–6

There are few nurseries where you can buy patented plants that were actually developed there, but this is where landscape architect Ted L. Turner, Sr. cultivated a dwarf variegated pittosporum that is popular throughout the South, along with seven colorful new varieties of oleander. Ted grew up in the nursery trade with parents whose passion was propagating orchids. He founded Gardenland in '72 with his wife Elaine, who is a Texas Certified Nursery Professional and the first woman to serve as chair of the Texas Association of Nurserymen (now the TNLA). Their son Ted, Jr. left a career at NASA to join the company that year, and his wife Sherrie, also a Certified Nursery Professional, is now the company's general manager and buyer. His brother runs the landscaping division. Together this family has grown Turner's Gardenland into one of South Texas' most respected nurseries and landscape companies.

Ted Jr. told us that he believes the nursery's strengths are its highly knowledgeable staff (10 Certified, 2 Master Certified Professionals) and the wide variety of plants the nursery carries (30–40 varieties of palms, numerous types of hibiscus, and of course the largest selection of oleanders in the state.) With its large inventory of indoor and outdoor plants, Turner's continues to grow and serve its customers with gift ideas, garden supplies and expert advice.

Directions: Turner's is on the south access road of SPID between Airline and Nile.

Specialty Nurseries

Bishop Greenhouses
702 Hwy 77 Bypass
Bishop, Texas 78343
361.584.3139
Hours: Mon–Sat 9–5:30; Sun 9–5:30 (Feb–May)

Bruce and Johanna Schubert propagate and grow most of the plants they sell from their four greenhouses and two shadehouses on this half-acre site. You'll find such colorful tropicals as royal poinciana, passion vine and angel's trumpet here, alongside palms and ferns. They cater to the locals' preference for showy roses and crepe myrtles, and they grow lots of culinary herbs and native perennials. The seasonal color here draws customers from a wide area that includes Corpus Christi and Kingsville.

Garden Furnishings

Cita
129 North Alister St
Port Aransas, Texas 78373
361.749.2711
Hours: Mon–Sat 10–6; Sun 12–5 (during summer)

Most of the delectable merchandise at this interior design-oriented store is for resort homes. It carries tiki bars, antique and new cola coolers and wood bars and barstools from around the world. You'll also find fabulous pots, planters, lanterns, hammocks and sculptural items for accessorizing gardens, patios and balconies.

Corpus Christi Botanical Gardens
8545 South Staples St
Corpus Christi, Texas 78413
361.852.2100
Hours: Tues–Sun 9–5

The shop at the Corpus Christi Botanical Gardens carries "a little bit of everything." The turnover is great, so you never know what treasures await you. You will find books, wind chimes and birdhouses and feeders. This gift shop even carries a variety of plants — annuals, perennials, shrubs and trees. For the garden's complete listing, see page 135.

Patio & Interiors
4130 South Padre Island Dr
Corpus Christi, Texas 78411
361.853.8493
www.patioandinteriors.com
Hours: Mon–Sat 9:30–5:30

Wind and salt spray play havoc with outdoor furnishings in this climate where resort-style living is what its all about! Fortunately, Yvonne and Art Babbitt have 30 years of experience selecting lawn and patio products they know will endure. Their shop is filled with dining tables, seating groups, barstools and hammocks, plus an array of colorful art and accessories. What they don't have in stock, they can order in hundreds of styles and fabric choices from numerous manufacturers, including Seaside Casual, which makes heavy-duty vinyl-wood Adirondack furniture. Customer service is the vital component of Patio & Interiors' business. Delivery and setup are available. "It's not uncommon for us to furnish beach properties for customers who live in other states and other countries," says Yvonne. "Sometimes we never even get to meet them. Everything can be done on-line now."

Pipe Creations
946 Cora Lee Ln
Corpus Christi, Texas 78418
361.939.9731
www.pipecreations.com
Hours: Mon–Sat 10–5:30

Everything you can order on-line is available in the retail store here. Family-owned and operated since 1980, this company manufactures premier quality custom PVC patio furniture and other outdoor products. It never rusts or needs refinishing. The cushion fabrics, also made in America, feature a tight weave for long wear. Umbrellas can be made to match any of the fabrics. There are several styles of chairs, rockers, recliners, loungers, swings, love seats, as well as tables and serving carts available. Grande chairs, sofas and love seats and chaise lounges are designed for people who weigh 250 pounds or more. There is also a new line of beach chairs and accessories. Owner Ed Stacey is the designer, and he will attempt to custom-make anything you can't find in the catalog.

Directions: From Corpus Christi, take the Waldron Rd exit off SPID in Flour Bluff. Turn left (north). Turn right on Fawn and go 1 block to Cora Lee.

Cuero (De Witt County)

Specialty Nurseries

Texas Homestead Nursery
6145 South Hwy 183
Cuero, Texas 77954
361.275.3537
Hours: Tues–Sat 10–5

Sandy Dukes explained that she had a degree in horticulture she hadn't put to use, and her husband Wes is "a creative guy who can design and build anything." Both love the outdoors, so in 1996 they decided to start a nursery and landscape business from their home on property that had been in the family for over 100 years. The soils around Cuero vary from sandy or gravelly loams to black clay and caliche. The plant palette is limited. Coastal humidity makes it difficult to use the native plants that thrive toward San Antonio, and periodic freezes make it risky to plant many of the species that are happy in Corpus Christi. So, Sandy's nursery specializes in only the native and adapted trees, shrubs, roses, and perennials that are proven winners there. Their colorful display garden, a 19th century building they moved to the site, and her husband's attractive stonework combine to create a comforting rustic charm here.

Rockport (Aransas County)

Garden Centers

Adams Nursery
1515 Hwy 35 S
Rockport, Texas 78382
361.729.7111
Hours: Mon–Sat 9–5, Sun 10–5 (spring); Mon–Fri 9–5, Sat 9–1 (fall)

At Adams Nursery you will find three Texas Certified Nursery Professionals who offer advice on dealing with soil conditions, climate and water supply in the area. Says Thelma Adams, "We work with each customer who needs help to make their plantings successful. We love to share our many years of experience (even bad gardening days and stories.) We've helped gardeners from age 3 to 102, and we feel honored when these same people share their knowledge with us." You'll find tools, books and gifts, as well as a large variety of plant material. This tidy little garden center offers lots of seasonal color, butterfly and hummingbird-attracting plants along with some water plants and tropicals. And the company definitely carries bulk vegetable seed! "We feel our clientele appreciates the service we give, as well as the quality of our stock," she adds. Adams Nursery normally has sales of some sort throughout the year.

Specialty Nurseries

Bloomers
1703 Hwy 35 S
Rockport, Texas 78374
361.729.6603
Hours: Mon–Sat 8–5:30

Tropical plants are the primary focus here. There are palms of all kinds, including the distinctive traveler's palm, bougainvilleas of every color, hibiscus, birds of paradise....You'll also find specialized fertilizers for the various plants, plus cantera stone fountains and Balinese coconut palm containers.

Portland (San Patricio County)

Garden Centers

Greens & Things
9707 FM 1079
Portland, Texas 78374
361.528.2209

801 Moore Ave
Portland, Texas 78374
361.777.3758
Hours: Tues–Fri 9–6, Sat 9–4, Sun 11–4 (spring)

Just across Corpus Christi Bay, Helen Gonzales and her daughter Jo Ann Vasquez have created connected businesses in separate locations, drawing upon the best skills of each. Helen is the "green thumb plant lady" whose greenhouse is overflowing with 25 varieties of succulents, 10 varieties of ferns, 7 varieties of hoya and every begonia that can be grown in the area. And that's just for starters. Jo Ann is the designer in the family, and she runs the small, conveniently located garden center (Moore Ave.) where customers can find all the shrubs and small trees suitable for the area, including several varieties of petite oleander, crepe myrtles, bottle brush and Knock Out roses. There are soil conditioners and pest controls (more organic than not) and a good selection of containers and fountains, too. Her husband David does the landscape installation. The name may say "greens", but color is the star here!

Victoria (Victoria County)

Garden Centers

Four Seasons Garden Center
1209 East Salem Rd
Victoria, Texas 77904
361.575.8807
Hours: Mon–Sat 8:30–6, Sun 10–6

Customers agree that Four Seasons is a delightful destination for visiting and shopping. The park-like atmosphere, with an arbor and luxuriant year-round display beds is indeed inviting! Established in 1984, Four Seasons carries a large selection of natives and hard-to-find heirloom plants. This nursery carries antique roses from Brenham, and offers a vast selection of trees, shrubs, herbs, vegetables, bedding plants, large specimen plants and everything for the water garden. There are large cypress trees and plumerias, which are propagated on-site. You'll also find a full line of soils, including the nursery's own potting soil, pest controls, fertilizers and quality hand tools from Maine. The gift shop has books, and cut trees are available at Christmas. Owner John Fossati, who holds a degree in horticulture from A&M told us, "We provide friendly service and offer beautifully displayed plants. We also design and install gardens. Four Seasons is more than just a nursery." Wheelchairs access may be difficult on the gravel paths, but plants are cheerfully brought to customer when necessary.

Renken's Nursery
2701 Salem Rd
Victoria, Texas 77904
361.576.5657
Hours: Mon–Sat 8:30–5:30, Sun 10–5 (fall and spring)

Dina Poland started this nursery in 1985 with a business degree and a passion for landscape design and construction. Self-taught, she quickly became knowledgeable about the plants that grow in the area. "Bring me a leaf and I can identify it, she says. "I pick the plants, and every one in the garden is my baby." There's a good selection of shrubs and lots of perennials, as well as handsome large containers. The landscape crew will plant the large trees you buy here.
Directions: Turn off Loop 463 at Salem Rd.

Specialty Nurseries

Earthworks
102 East Airline Rd
Victoria, Texas 77901
361.573.3836
www.earthworksnursery.net
Hours: Mon–Sat 8–5:30

Earthworks, an all-natural nursery, began 16 years ago as a small "mom and pop" place. Laurie and Mark Garretson (and lots of happy customers) soon discovered they were the "different" ones in the garden business. Times have changed. Laurie is now the garden editor of the *Victoria Advocate,* and her word counts in the region. "Our great-grandparents were all natural/organic gardeners and farmers," she observes. "They had no choice. Chemicals were not yet available." Noting that "food was better tasting and better for you" at that time, she

(LISTING CONTINUED ON THE NEXT PAGE)

goes on to say, "Many people today want instant gratification in all areas of their lives. For some, finding bugs on prized tomatoes calls for an instant kill from a chemical insecticide. They are not considering that they are not only breathing that chemical, but also that it is absorbed into the skin of the vegetable and then ingested."

Earthworks is as interested in educating the public about the many benefits of organic gardening and most natural methods of pest and disease control as in selling plants, but the plants here are beautiful as well as healthy. At least 50% are Texas natives. Her first love is herbs, so you'll find them in abundance. There are also lots of shade-tolerant species since the site is nestled under a luxuriant tree canopy. (There's even a hammock here.) Many informative events are scheduled throughout the year. The resident macaw, Murphy, has become something of a celebrity, himself. You'll love this place.

Gulf Coast Floral
1207 Salem Rd
Victoria, Texas 77904
361.573.3356

Hours: Mon–Sat 9–6, Sun 12–5 (closed Sundays in summer)

Owner Michael Zeplin began growing orchids while still a child. He got his first greenhouse before he was in high school. Orchids, his first love, occupy a 3,000-square-foot greenhouse today. His specialty is cattleyas, but other genera are well represented. He told us that he can afford to sell blooming-size cattleya for only $15 because his stock is so extensive. Although it's not a florist shop, Michael will sell cut orchids to clients for corsages and party decorations. The three other equally large greenhouses on the property are filled with potted plants for all seasons, most of which are grown on site. You'll find geraniums, hibiscus, coleus, hydrangeas, impatiens (single, double and New Guinea), wax and angel wing begonias, garden mums and more. There's also a large selection of hanging baskets throughout the year. The Christmas season is especially festive with six- to ten-inch pots of every variety of poinsettias. He makes hanging baskets of red poinsettias and Christmas cactus. The company has recently gotten into landscaping, growing trees and shrubs in a sunny part of the site and shade-loving plants under the tree canopy. Michael's enthusiasm seems to know no bounds.

**6
Valley**

Valley

A chain of town — Brownsville, Harlingen, Pharr, McAllen, Mission and Edinburg — hug the lower Rio Grande River as it makes its way to the Gulf of Mexico. In addition to very mild winters, deep, fertile soil and water available for irrigation have made the Valley famous for citrus and winter vegetable crops. Homeowners grow palms, rubber trees, philodendrons and scores of other "houseplants" in their gardens and resign themselves to the killing frosts that come along every few years. Within a few months they'll be pruning their lush vegetation with machetes!

The Valley is not a valley at all, but rather the delta and floodplain of the lower Rio Grande River. Its native plants and animals are more typical of Mexico than of any other part of Texas. However, little native vegetation remains; the land is much too valuable for row crops. Our only native palm, *Sabal texana*, can be found mainly in residential gardens and city parks. In the few places where virgin countryside exists, native trees as such anaqua, Texas ebony and Mexican ash offer hospitality to rare birds. Cats such as ocelot and jaguarundi still stalk their prey.

Nature trails at **Bentsen-Rio Grande Valley State Park** provide insight to the ecology of the region. Located on the river 5.0 miles southwest of Mission in Hidalgo County, this 535-acre park is made up of subtropical resaca woodlands (low-lying former river channels now partially filled with silt) and brushland filled with thickets of thorny shrubs and small trees. The resaca banks support luxuriant stands of cedar elms, anaqua, ebony, ash and very large Mexican lead trees. One trail goes through the wilderness; the other leads to the river. Plants and animals here represent the northernmost extension of the Mexican subtropics.

The **Santa Ana National Wildlife Refuge** south of Alamo is another place that provides opportunity to experience the region's extraordinary habitats. Often called the "Gem of the National Refuge System," this 2000-acre tract of subtropical forest and native brushlands clasps the bank of the Rio Grande. There are guided walks throughout the year and printed guides to all the trails, one of which is paved and completely accessible. You can visit a Spanish moss forest where cedar elm, sugar hackberry, Rio Grande ash, Texas persimmon and a host of other native trees thrive. A 2-mile trail loops down to the river. In winter an accessible tram provides a bird's eye view of the scenery.

The **Hugh Ramsey Nature Park** on the east side of Harlingen provides a gateway to the World Birding Center network. Texas ebony woodlands dominate this 55-acre park. On the west side of town, the **Harlingen Thicket** (an upland thorn forest) provides another important reservoir of nature in a rapidly growing part of Texas. Volunteers are helping to restore both to their former beauty, planting native trees, shrubs and flowering plants that support varied wildlife. A new visitors' center at Hugh Ramsey Nature Park includes an observation tower and enclosed viewing areas.

It takes a great deal of water to keep lawns green in the Valley during the hot, windy summer months, so many of the area's native trees actually struggle in irrigated residential landscapes. (Choice native trees such as retama, guayacan, anaqua, Mexican poinciana and Texas ebony are commonly planted and prized for their flowers.) Both the soil and the water are highly alkaline, so gardeners find it necessary to maintain the soil with continuous additions of compost, which also serves to improve the texture of heavy river soils. Because standing water can be a problem during heavy rains, many homeowners also contend with difficult drainage.

Such an abundance of exotic species thrive in the region that the homeowner's biggest problem may be in achieving a cohesive design plan. Valley gardens are typically a riot of colors. With bananas, bougainvillea, allamandas, oleanders and plumarias part of the plant palette, how could they not be? A visit to one of the region's garden centers will introduce you to plants unimaginable in the rest of the state. Pothos, the world's most hard-to-kill houseplant, is actually grown as a lawn substitute here!

The Gladys Porter Zoo in Brownsville is the closest thing to a tropical botanical garden that exists in Texas. Other botanical treasures include Brownsville's **Sabal Palm Audubon Center, Quinta Mazatlan** in McAllen and **Valley Nature Center** in Weslaco.

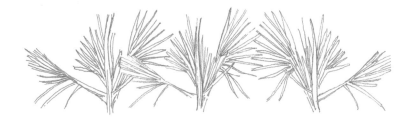

Public Gardens and Nature Preserves to Visit

Brownsville (Cameron County)

Gladys Porter Zoo
500 Ringgold St
Brownsville, Texas 78520
956.546.2177 (recording); 956.546.7187 (education office)
www.gpz.org
Hours: Daily 9–5; extended summer hours until dusk
Admission: $9 (adults); $7.50 (seniors over 65); $6 (children 2–13); free (children under 2)

All animals live in open exhibits, completely surrounded by naturally flowing waterways and a botanical wonderland here. Over 375 species of tropical and semi-tropical plants bloom year-round in environments that make every attempt to replicate the animals' native habitats in Africa, Asia, Indo-Australia and Tropical America. Among the botanical treasures are a cactus and succulent garden and a rare Hong Kong orchid tree, which no longer exists in the wild. Other gorgeous blooming plants are royal poinciana, silk floss tree and lots of bougainvillea. Strollers, wheelchairs and wagons are available for rent.
Directions: The zoo is located off Hwy 77/83 at 6th and Ringgold.

Sabal Palm Audubon Center and Sanctuary
FM 1419
Brownsville, Texas 78523
956.541.8034
http://tx.audubon.org/Sabal.html
(LISTING CONTINUED ON THE NEXT PAGE)

(CONTINUED)

Hours: Daily 9–5; closed Thanksgiving Day, Christmas Day and New Year's Day. For safety reasons Sabal Palm Sanctuary may be closed to the public during inclement weather.

Admission: $5 (adults), $3 (children 7–18), $2 (children under 1)

Cradled in a bend of the Rio Grande, this National Audubon Society property is a remnant of a grove of Texas sabal palms and Texas ebony trees that once extended 80 miles upriver. One 0.5 mile loop trail explores how people traditionally used the plants native to this area. A second 0.5-mile trail takes you into a "jungle" of plant, animal and bird species, many of which reach their northernmost limit here and occur nowhere else in the United States. The trails are self-guided, but you can borrow or buy trail maps in the Center, which also contains educational displays, a wildlife viewing area and small gift shop. *Note: As went were about to go to press, Audubon Society members and local landowners were fighting the Department of Homeland Security, which had announced plans to erect the border fence just north of the bird sanctuary. This will effectively separate this natural treasure from the rest of the country and possibly force its closure. If it remains open, see the website or call (Mon-Fri 9-5) for directions.*

McAllen/Weslaco (Hidalgo County)

Quinta Mazatlan
600 Sunset Ave
McAllen, Texas 78503
956.688.3370
www.quintamazatlan.com
Hours: Tues–Sat 8–5; open Thursdays until dark
Admission: $2 (adults), $1 (seniors 65 and over and children 5 to 12), free (children 4 and under)

Lush tropical gardens and native woodland surround this handsome Spanish Revival hacienda, built in 1935 by Jason Matthews, a composer, writer and adventurer, and his wife Marcia. Now owned by the McAllen Parks and Recreation Department, Quinta Mazatlan serves as a conference and events center. Visitors are invited to enjoy the grounds of this oasis, which includes new trails winding through 15 acres of birding habitat. The gardens have been enriched with native plants as living examples of what any backyard birder can achieve. The outlying wild Tamaulipan thorn forest now has water features and feeding stations to attract species found no place in the country other than the Rio Grande Valley. Black-bellied whistling ducks nest in the palm trees around the patio. Green jays, chachalacas and buff-bellied hummingbirds frequent the site, and a native butterfly garden teems with activity. Quinta Mazatlan offers organized programs that include natural history tours and native plant walks.

Directions: Take Expressway 83 to 10th St exit. Travel south on 10th St and turn east on Sunset Dr. Proceed to Quinta Mazatlan at the end of the street. Parking available outside the big brown gates.

Valley Nature Center
301 South Border Ave
Weslaco, Texas 78599
956.969.2475
www.valleynaturecenter.org
Hours: Tues–Fri 9–5, Sat 8–5, Sun 1–5
Admission: $3 (adults), $2.50 (seniors 55 and over), $1 (children under 12)

This 6-acre park hosts a wide array of the Lower Rio Grande Valley's native plants and animals. In an on-going effort to enhance the plant diversity of this nature center, many of its species have been transplanted from sites that were slated for development. The purpose here is not only to protect local plant species diversity, but also to make a diverse food and habitat available for resident and migratory wildlife. Its trails take visitors to three cactus gardens, butterfly gardens and several small ponds. There is a native plant nursery on site at this superb natural retreat. Native plant rescue and public education will remain as the Center's primary missions.

Valley Resources

Brownsville / Harlingen / Los Fresnos / San Benito (Cameron County)

Garden Centers

Gentry's Garden Center & Flower Shop
4580 North Expressway
Brownsville, Texas 78526
956.350.9805
Hours: Mon–Sat 9–5, Sun 12–4

As owner Joe Flores noted, "Since my surname means flowers in Spanish, it makes sense that I should be drawn into this industry." Opened in 1987, Gentry's carries a full line of trees, shrubs, palms, bedding plants and, of course, tropicals. Some of the most popular tropicals include bird of paradise, heliconias and banana trees, among others. You will find fertilizers and some organics as well as concrete fountains and statuary. Gentry's offers landscape design and installation services, most notably for residences and small businesses where "the personal touch" is truly appreciated. There is also a full-line florist on site.

Grimsell Seed Company
213 West Monroe Ave
Harlingen, Texas 78550
956.423.0370
Hours: Mon–Sat 8–5:30, Sun 10:30–2:30

"An oasis amidst the asphalt," Grimsell Seed Company was founded in 1915 by Frank Grimsell. Today his grandson, Donald Giffen, owns and manages the store. Located in downtown Harlingen, its large adjacent garden projects a feeling far different from one's image of a seed store! Grimsell's has prospered over the years because its well-educated personnel strive to offer the highest level of service and customer attention possible.

(LISTING CONTINUED ON THE NEXT PAGE)

(CONTINUED)

The company carries a large and varied selection of plant materials (from natives to tropicals) as well as tools, drip irrigation equipment, and pest management supplies. Says Donald Giffen," Customers come from all over the four-county area because of our good service and friendly atmosphere. The 'big calling cards' are our huge inventory of fertilizers formulated for us and sold under the Grimsell label and our vast inventory of garden seeds (package and bulk.)" The long-time motto of Grimsell Seed Company is "Grimsell's has it!" Skilled staff members offer advice on plants, plant diseases and maladies, insecticides and anything garden related. The store boasts the tallest freestanding flagpole in Texas!

My Nursery
2178 West US Hwy 77
San Benito, Texas 78586
956.361.0035
www.mynurseryonline.com
Hours: Mon–Fri 8–6, Sat 8–5, Sun 11–5 (closes at 5 weekdays in winter)

Fernando A. Russek says, "Our garden center is your best resource for your planting needs. We not only offer topsoil, mulch and fertilizers but a variety of beautiful plants, trees and palms. If you don't find the plant or tree you're looking for, we can order it for you." Since there are 20,000 plants in this four-acre wholesale/retail garden center. The specialty here is large trees up to nine-inch caliper. There are many natives to be found, including mesquite, ebony, wild olive, mountain laurel and Anachacho orchid, plus lots of big palms. You'll find citrus trees, of course, but also guava, avocado, mango, loquat, papaya and several other fruit trees. My Nursery also carries native shrubs, ferns and other shade plants, water plants and quite a few Texas perennials. The company does design and landscape installation, so it stocks a good supply of stone mulches and soil amendments.

Stuart Place Nursery
7701 West Business Hwy 83
Harlingen, Texas 78552
956.428.4439
Hours: Mon–Sat 8–5, Sun 12–5

Native trees, shrubs, cacti and grasses are in a very special category at this full-range garden center. As Ernie Shofner, who bought Stuart Place three years ago, says, "In addition to native and adapted plants suitable for area landscapes, we carry lots of cycads, palms and exotic tropicals you couldn't find elsewhere." You will also find everything from containers, statuary, books and wall ornaments to pest management and soil amendment supplies. The friendly staff is always available for advice and assistance.

Tony's Nursery
895 East Los Ebanos Blvd
Brownsville, Texas 78520
956.541.5322
Hours: Mon–Sat 8–5:30, Sun 9–4:30

In business for 26 years, Tony's is a small, but very nice retail nursery that offers trees, shrubs and tropicals. We noticed especially attractive hanging baskets and bedding plants. The nursery also carries gypsum soil conditioners. There are no sales, but Tony's prices are always competitive.

Specialty Nurseries

Rivers End Nursery and Farm
P.O. Box 1729
Los Fresnos, Texas 78566
956.233.4792
www.riversendnursery.com
Hours: Fri & Sat 10–5 or by appointment

Ed and Kathy Pechacek (pronounced paycheck) developed this unique nursery over the last 18 years. It started with a vision of enjoying delicious tropical fruits from around the world and introducing these trees and fruits to homeowners in the Valley. The couple's fruit trees, flowering trees, exotic palms and several varieties of bamboo are available online through the website. Plant descriptions are followed by the minimum temperatures the plants can tolerate before damage will occur. Most can be grown outdoors only in the southernmost tip of Texas, but many would make wonderful houseplants in sunny garden rooms and greenhouses throughout the state. This nursery offers two-hour walking tours of the orchard. (Call for times, directions and reservations.) Fresh eggs and seasonal fruits are almost always available for purchase.

While the company is not certified organic, the Pechaceks do sell organic supplies and soil amendments. They especially recommend BioWash 1227, a non-toxic, biodegradable plant wash that they spray in their own orchard and greenhouses and use to wash fruit after it has been picked. "Because our grandchildren like to taste all the fruits they find in the orchard, we don't want to use anything toxic. Regular use of this plant wash makes it sooo much easier to keep things healthy," says Kathy.

McAllen/Mission/Pharr/Weslaco (Hidalgo County)

Garden Centers

Mid Valley Garden & Pond Supply
1800 E. Hwy 83
Weslaco, Texas 78596
956 973.1998 or 877.225.3052 (toll free)
www.midvalley-gardenandpond.com
Hours: Mon–Fri 8:30–5:30, Sat 8:30–5

The specialty at Mid Valley is pondscaping, and the creative display area is sure to convince you that you absolutely must have a pond! Everything you need is here...from fish and water

(LISTING CONTINUED ON THE NEXT PAGE)

(CONTINUED)

plants and grasses to pond liners, pumps, filtration supplies and pond art. Mid Valley is, however, also a complete landscaping company carrying a wide selection of trees, shrubs, vines, tropicals and cacti. If the truth be known, our favorite aspect of this exceptional nursery was wandering the exotic paths lined with monstera, clerodendrums, heliconias, thorny kapok trees and a spiny gru-gru palm. There are huge Hong Kong orchid trees, bougainvillea trees, cacti, bromeliads and a vast collection of coastal palm trees. Some of the brick walkways and step-downs are not wheelchair/stroller accessible. And, don't forget the giant wind chimes and the patio furniture ranging from whimsical to Victorian. Owner Paul Crerar has created an atmosphere that has often been compared to a Hawaiian paradise, and a visit to Mid Valley is always a delight.

Shary Acres Landscaping and Irrigation
3421 North Shary Rd
Mission, Texas 78572
956.581.7783
www.sharyacres.com
Hours: Mon–Fri 9–5, Sat seasonal

As the new owner of this longstanding, traditional nursery, Dorian Madrigal plans to "continue the rich tradition of quality, consistency and excellent customer service" that Shary Acres has offered for 30 years. The inventory includes native and hard-to-find plants, trees and shrubs. Among the services available are landscape design and construction, sprinkler systems, tree trimming, lawn maintenance and repairs. As they say at Shary Acres, "We are a one stop shop." The knowledgeable staff is prepared to assist regarding special problems with your garden or lawn....The Plant Doctor is in! Dorian's column with information, moneysaving tips and advice appears monthly on the nursery's web site.

Valley Garden Center
701 East Hwy 83
McAllen, Texas 78501
956.682.9411
www.valleygardencenter.com
Hours: Mon–Sat 8:30–6, Sun 12–5

Andy Guidry, an original owner since 1977, and Jon Klement, an owner since 1985, are at the helm at Valley Garden Center today. There are four departments: The Garden Center Store and the irrigation, landscaping and maintenance departments, which operate under the name Southern Landscapes. The business, which started with a staff of 18, now boasts over 110 employees devoted to serving the public in every area. Valley Garden Center does indeed have everything, from a large selection of plant materials and water gardening supplies to pottery, books, tools, and even hummingbird and songbird supplies. It also carries unusual and common citrus fruit trees, packaged and bulk seeds and a good selection of native shrubs and trees. As we were told, "Our stock is maintained year-round, not just during fall and spring planting seasons." With a staff that includes one Master Certified and two Certified Nursery Professionals, as well as a licensed Irrigator, you can be assured of "the most complete and professional level of services and materials for all of your outdoor needs."

Waugh's Nursery & Fruit Ranch
5012 North Jackson Rd
Pharr, Texas 78577
956.686.5591
Hours: Mon–Sat 8:30–6, Sun 1–5

"Fifty-eight years in business means we must be doing something right!" comments Ceciele Waugh Beamsley. "What makes us special is our friendly staff. We know and care about plants and gardening and want to help others understand and enjoy them as well." Although Waugh's is a complete garden center, its specialties are such tropicals as heliconias, bauhinias, bougainvillea, hibiscus, plumeria, etc. The company also offers an outstanding selection of both culinary and medicinal herbs. Advice is always available to customers, and Ceciele is still hosting her KURV radio program to keep you informed.

Garden Furnishings

Arte en Cantera
2900 North McColl Rd
McAllen, Texas 78501
956.682.1623
www.arteencantera.com
Hours: Mon–Fri 8–5

Since our last visit, Arte en Cantera has added its own local manufacturing facility, which ensures maximum efficiency in meeting customers' demands. Products include columns, fireplaces, fountains, molding, balustrades, flooring, pool coping and signs and entries. You can choose from the following materials: cantera in 12 colors, limestone in six colors and travertine marble. These custom pieces, which are hand-carved by expert in-house craftsmen, are truly works of art and are elegant as well as functional. Owner Richard Azubell says, "We have been in business for over 15 years, and we are committed to turning out each product exactly as ordered." Installation and delivery services are available, and each piece carries a one-year guarantee.

Raymondville (Willacy County)

Specialty Nurseries

Caldwell Jungle Nursery
P.O. Box 537
Raymondville, Texas 78580
956.689.3432

(LISTING CONTINUED ON THE NEXT PAGE)

(CONTINUED)

Hours: Mon–Fri 9–5, Sat 9–12

As you sift through the enormous inventory at Caldwell Jungle, you will find a wealth of tropicals...palms of all kinds, several varieties of ficus, bird of paradise, crotons, bougainvilleas, plumbago and oleander. There are also several kinds of cacti as well as an assortment of heat-tolerant ground covers and hedge materials.

Directions: The nursery is located 1.5 miles west of Raymondville on Hwy 186 W. Call if you need further directions.

Rio Grande City (Starr County)

Specialty Nurseries

Rancho Lomitas Nursery
P.O. Box 442
Rio Grande City, Texas 78582
956.486.2576
www.rancholomitas.com
Hours: Daily, by appointment

Since Benito and Toni Trevino purchased one hundred seventy-seven acres of Tamaulipan brushland near Rio Grande City in 1986, they have created quite a business in native plants suitable for South Texas. As a result of native landscaping, this is the perfect place for bird and butterfly watching as well as photographing nature. In addition, there are four beautifully landscaped RV parks with hook-ups, and tours are offered October–May on "the many uses of natives." Toni is happy to share her "cooking with natives" recipes featuring such treats as mesquite cookies and prickly pear cobbler. The web site offers a wealth of information, including an extensive plant list. Whether you are looking for native shade trees, hedges or bird and butterfly attractors, Benito is just the man you need! Be sure and call ahead for reservations, directions and driving conditions.

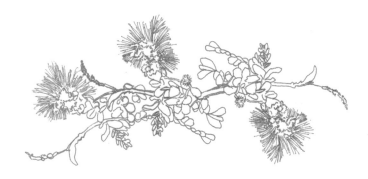

7

Rio Grande Plain

Rio Grande Plain

I nland from the Gulf of Mexico, the landscape quickly becomes harsh. Population centers are few and far between in this large, arid region that was once open grassland. San Antonio, Laredo and Del Rio serve as its major market areas. The land is primarily used for grazing, but several small farming communities occur along the Rio Grande or in the northern portion of the region along the Nueces and its several tributaries. The Atascosa and Frio Rivers converge with the Nueces at Three Rivers in Live Oak County, and then the latter continues to Corpus Christi Bay. No river flows through the southern half of the region between the Nueces and Rio Grande.

South Texas is cattle country. It was here that Texas longhorns evolved from wild cattle abandoned by Mexican ranchers when Texas won its independence and the Rio Grande became the boundary between the two countries. The region has been described as a place where every living thing bites, stings or otherwise punctures the skin! Its climate is subtropical and subject to occasional hard freezes. There's rarely more than 25 inches of rainfall each year, but when rain comes, it's downpours produce a colorful show of cactus blossoms. The moisture also brings life to such wildflowers as prickly poppies and the beautiful gray shrub, cenizo, which is also called a "barometer plant" because it flowers only during periods of high humidity.

The Rio Grande Plain is dotted with mesquite and huisache trees and an assortment of fierce shrubs. Cross fencing and the elimination of fire allowed trees and chaparral to muscle out much of the natural grass. This takeover has not only eliminated grass, but has dried up numerous little streams. However, the brush is a lively plant community, rich in berries and fruits. The legumes — mimosas, acacias, locusts, paloverdes and mesquites — "fix" nitrogen in the soil and bear seeds in pods. The thorn-bearing plants provide protection for small mammals and food for numerous birds and animals.

Choke Canyon State Park, west of Three Rivers, is located on the 26,000-acre Choke Canyon Reservoir where Native Americans crossed the Frio River Valley more than 10,000 years ago following bison and mammoth. A wide variety of wildlife inhabits the dense thickets of mesquite and blackbush acacia. Among the attractions for naturalists are 2.0 miles of hiking trails, a mile-long bird trail with feeders and a wildlife educational center that offers educational programs. **Falcon State Park** on the southern end of Falcon Reservoir provides trails into ruggedly beautiful brushlands where, mesquite, huisache, wild olive, ebony, cactus and native grasses cover gently rolling hills. One popular hiking/nature trail features signs detailing the plant life.

A thriving nursery industry has developed west of San Antonio in the fertile sandy loam soil of the Medina River. The beautiful canyons in Uvalde County were formed by four spring-fed rivers flowing off the Balcones Escarpment onto the Rio Grande Plain. Here, bees utilize the fragrant blooms of guajillo (*Acacia berlandieri*) to make the highly prized Uvalde honey. Further south, the area around Carrizo Springs and Crystal City is known as the Winter Garden and famous for its vegetables, especially spinach. Crops are irrigated by underground water drawn from the Carrizo Springs.

San Antonio sits at the northern edge of the Rio Grande Plain. The eastern section of the city juts into the Central Blacklands and Savannas region, and its northwest neighborhoods are rapidly growing into the adjacent Hill Country. **The San Antonio Botanical Garden** celebrates the city's biological diversity with plant materials drawn from all three regions. Several acres are devoted to native Texas plantings. Another botanical treasure is the **River Walk**, which is lined with lush semi-tropical plants that could thrive only in the protected environment of a sunken waterway.

Within Bexar County alone there are nine distinct soil types, ranging from black clay to acidic sand. San Antonio gardeners are well-advised to test their soils and understand the topography before assuming that "anything grows." Gardeners may also want to peruse the nearby garden resources in Boerne (listed under The Hill Country), as well as Seguin and Marion (listed under Central Blacklands and Savannas).

Public Gardens and Nature Preserves to Visit

San Antonio Metropolitan Area (Bexar County)

McNay Art Museum
6000 North New Braunfels Ave
San Antonio, Texas 78209
210.824.5368
www.mcnayart.org
Hours: Grounds: Daily 7–6, 7–7 (Daylight Savings Time). Museum: Sun 12–5, Tues, Wed & Fri 10–4, Thurs 10–9; Sat 10–5; closed New Year's Day, July 4th, Thanksgiving and Christmas Day. Admission: $8 (adults), $5 (students with I.D., seniors 65+ and active military).

This museum's building and grounds are as vibrant as the art on display within. Built in the 1920s by Marion Koogler McNay, the Spanish Colonial-style residence sits on an exquisite 23-acre site. Originally built in the form of a horseshoe, the two-story house wraps around a central courtyard with a reflecting pool built in the shape of the rose window of the Mission San Jose. The original tile remains, including a large peacock wall fresco and the Don Quixote story told in individual tiles. During her lifetime Mrs. McNay was so fond of the courtyard that she directed visitors through a rear drive so that they could enter the house through the open court. Although it was enclosed by the addition of new galleries in the early 70s, the courtyard remains the museum's focal point. Today it's filled with palms, bougainvillea, ferns, night-blooming jasmine and pots of blooming plants and adorned with sculptures by Barbara Hepworth, Renoir, Charles Umlauf and Ana Hyatt Huntington. Water lilies and goldfish enliven the pool. (Because the courtyard is enclosed, museum admission is required. However, the entire museum is free the first Sunday of every month and on Thursdays from 4-9.)

The impressive Marcia and Otto Koehler Fountain commands the entrance to the museum, and the grounds, which include a Japanese-style garden, are maintained in a way

(LISTING CONTINUED ON THE NEXT PAGE)

(CONTINUED)

that would make the museum's founder proud. The landscape of the new outdoor sculpture garden beside the Jane & Arthur Stieren Center for Exhibitions is a minimalist jewel. (And, like the remainder of the grounds, it's open free to the public).

San Antonio Botanical Gardens
555 Funston Place
San Antonio, Texas 78209
210.207.3250
www.sabot.org
Hours: Daily 9–5; closed Thanksgiving, Christmas Day and New Year's Day; Carriage House Bistro: Tues–Sun 11–2.
Admission: $7 (adults), $5 (seniors 65+, active military personnel, retirees, and reservists with current ID), $5 (students), $4 (children 3–13)

Located on a hill near Fort Sam Houston, the 33-acre site is ideal for demonstrating every style of gardening, and San Antonio's mild climate is conducive to particularly luxuriant plant displays. Allow lots of time to stroll! A trail map leads you through a connected series of gardens that begin with an appealing fountain and arbor. Paths wind through a series of intimate garden rooms, including fragrant, highly tactile raised beds for the blind. Then an opening in a massive rock wall leads into the Lucile Halsell Conservatory, a complex of bermed, earth-sheltered limestone and glass greenhouses. Organized around a central outdoor courtyard and pond, the conservatory nurtures all manner of tropical and desert plants. From here you'll enter a 15-acre expanse of native Texas gardens representing the vegetation of Piney Woods, Hill Country and South Texas Plains, plus a marvelous cactus garden. Other paths encircle a lake and take you to four thematic formal gardens that display roses, herbs, perennials and plants of the Bible. All paths lead back to the entrance and then out to the historic Sullivan Carriage House, which houses a fine gift shop, a tearoom and lecture hall.
Directions: From I-35, exit on New Braunfels Ave and travel north to Funston. Turn right on Funston.

Schultz House
514 Hemisfair Park
San Antonio, Texas 78205
210.229.9161
Hours: Daily dawn to dusk; gift shop: Tues–Sat 10–4
Admission: free

One of the few remaining examples of German-Texas domestic architecture in downtown San Antonio, this 1893 home is now a gift shop operated by Bexar County Master Gardeners. Surrounding the home is a period garden of the late 1800s and demonstration gardens of native and adapted plants, lovingly tended by Master Gardeners. This garden is just a short stroll from the beautiful Paseo del Rio (River Walk), which has become a botanical paradise in the last few years, and a few blocks from the King William Historic District.
Directions: the Schultz House is located just north of the Federal Courthouse.

Steves Homestead
509 King William St
San Antonio, Texas
210.224.6163
Hours: Daily dawn to dusk; call for house tour hours
Admission: Grounds free; house tour $2

The only property in the King William Historic District that's open regularly to the public, this Italian Villa-style home is representative of the eclectic Victorian architecture favored by San Antonio's successful merchant class. The garden's planting beds and a fountain from the Philadelphia Centennial Exposition of 1876 are original to the house and typical of the period. The entire neighborhood warrants exploration on foot. Colorful plantings literally spill out from the iron fences that surround the sturdily built limestone cottages and mansions of this restored enclave. You can pick up a brochure for a walking tour at the Steves Homestead or at the headquarters of the San Antonio Conservation Society (107 King William St, across from the gazebo in King William Park).

Directions: The Steves Homestead is about 0.5 miles south of the River Walk and Hemisfair grounds.

Rio Grande Plain Resources

Carrizo Springs (Dimmit County)

Specialty Nurseries

Dixondale Farms
2007 Hwy 83
Carrizo Springs, Texas 78834
877.367.1015
www.dixondalefarms.com
Hours: By appointment only

This fourth generation, family-owned business is the largest and oldest producer of onion plants in the country. According to Bruce Frasier, "If you haven't planted your onion transplants by the end of January, it is probably too late for this year. But if you're planning for next year, our little onion factory in South Texas has the freshest starter plants and best advice."

Castroville (Medina County)

Specialty Nurseries

Medina Valley Greenhouses
1151 CR 477 (Old River Rd)
Castroville, Texas 78009
830.931.2298
www.castroville.com/mvgreenhouses

Hours: Daily 9–5 except Christmas, New Years and Thanksgiving

The motto at Medina Valley Greenhouses is "Everything from Cactus to Orchids," and the place is sometimes described as "a schoolteacher's hobby that got out of hand." Over the years, Mary and Ellis Burges enlivened their vacation travels by seeking out beautiful and unusual plants for their collection. Mrs. Burges, a Texas Certified Nursery Professional, received a special award for her long-time support of xeriscape, and native plants are a specialty, along with other species adapted to the local semi-arid conditions. These range from shrubs to full-sized trees and include both perennials and self-seeding annuals as well as herbs. The greenhouse itself is set into the side of a hill to protect it from cold winter winds, and one room is devoted to cactus, euphorbias, aloes and other desert plants. Because of a recent flood, the orchids and other tropicals have been moved to higher ground. Mrs. Burges is ready to give expert advice to the shopper. "People keep coming back to see what else we have added. The prices are so reasonable that items are rarely marked down," she says.

Directions: Medina Valley Greenhouses is located just northwest of Castroville on the scenic Old River Rd, which is an extension of Mexico St. Once you get to the river, the road curves to the left. The sign is small, but look for it on the left side of the road.

Del Rio (Val Verde County)

Specialty Nurseries

Bowers Cactus Nursery
101 Clouse
Del Rio, Texas 78840
830.775.5692

Hours: By appointment only

Although he has sold the tree farm (see next listing), George Bowers maintains a huge inventory of ocotillo and many other cacti suitable for use on the Rio Grande Plain and West Texas.

JW Tree Farm
101½ Clouse
Del Rio, Texas 78840
830.775.4181 (office) or 830.313.1223 (mobile)
www.jwtreefarm.com
Hours: Mon–Sat 8:30–5:30

Since April 2008, John and Barbara Flippo have owned the former Bowers Tree Farm. "We plan to continue to serve Del Rio and the surrounding area with the finest trees and landscaping services," they maintain. The largest tree farm in Southwest Texas, this nursery has been growing trees for wholesale and retail customers for over 25 years. It carries an enormous inventory of Monterrey oak/Mexican white oak (*Quercus polymorpha*) ranging from 1-inch to 7-inch caliper. These trees are not susceptible to oak wilt, even when planted in the same area as affected live oaks. It's a rapidly growing tree that is drought-tolerant, adapts well to acid or alkaline soils, and has proven to be highly disease and pest resistant. The farm also grows Texas red oaks and live oaks and has added such popular small trees and shrubs as crepe myrtle, Texas mountain laurel, Mexican plum, bottlebrush, oleander, red yucca and even some seasonal color to its inventory. They do landscaping and will plant the trees they sell.

Laredo (Webb County)

Garden Centers

Yardart Garden Center
2517 East Del Mar Blvd.
Laredo, Texas 78045
956.726.3796
Hours: Mon–Sat 8:30–5:30, Sun 10:30–3:30

In the years since Tony Barrera opened this lovely garden center in 1976, he has seen lots of other independent nurseries close. He credits his success in the face of competition from "big box stores" to the good prices he can offer because he grows much of what he sells. There's also the fact that he and his staff know which plants thrive in Laredo and how to improve the soil. Then there's the popular Paradiso restaurant on the property, which draws new customers into the acre of colorful plants and fountains here. Barrera notes that while Laredo's winter temperatures are a bit cooler than in The Valley, as the climate is warming he is able to use more and more tropical plants in his landscape designs, and notes that his greenhouse is constantly brimming with palms and other tropicals. The nursery carries a complete line of garden supplies, as well as lots of pots, fountains and art for the garden. Watch for a new website and seminars soon to follow.

New Braunfels (Comal County)

Garden Centers

Maldonado Landscape & Irrigation, Ltd.
120 East Zipp Rd
New Braunfels, Texas 78130
830.625.1020
www.maldonadonursery.net

(LISTING CONTINUED ON THE NEXT PAGE)

(CONTINUED)

Hours: Mon–Sat 8–5

This tidy nursery was opened by Jorge Maldonado in 1982 and is devoted primarily to native trees and shrubs, most of which are grown on site. Not only is there a large quantity of everything, but we spotted some exceptionally large trees and shrubs. Maldonado's also carries bedding plants, Mexican pots and chimeneas. This company is well equipped to serve the landscape and irrigation needs of the area.

Directions: From I-35 S, Exit 187 (Hwy 725 to McQueeny), 3.0 miles east to Zipp Rd. It's on the corner.

The Plant Haus
956 North Walnut
New Braunfels, Texas 78130
830.629.2401

Hours: Mon–Sat 8–6 (Mar–Oct), Mon–Sat 8–5 (Nov–Feb); Sun 10–4 (Mar–Dec)

As Weston Pacharzina told us, "If you see it and like it, you better take it now, because it won't be here later!" This bright, airy nursery, which opened 31 years ago, offers many plants native to the area. Of course, The Plant Haus carries ornamental trees and shrubs, annuals and perennials of all kinds, plus bulbs, hanging baskets, bonsai, cacti, tropicals, vegetable starts and seeds. Most of the hanging baskets and bedding plants are grown on-site, and we were pleased to see such reasonable prices. You can also find materials for walks, patios and retaining walls, as well as soil and soil amendments, pest management supplies, and garden tools. There are lots of birdbaths and fountains from which to choose, and overstock sales on plant materials are held periodically.

Directions: From I-35, take Hwy 46 W; it's located 1.5 miles on the right.

Specialty Nurseries

Schumacher's Hill Country Gardens, Inc.
588 FM 1863
New Braunfels, Texas 78132
830.620.5149 or 830.629.2603
www.hillcountrygardens.com

Hours: Tues–Sat 10–4

This is still our favorite place to shop for native plants in Texas. It is a pretty site, and the sales staff is extremely knowledgeable. The goal of Schumacher's Hill Country Gardens has always been "to introduce and provide exceptional quality landscape material, with special emphasis on native perennials and plants for xeriscaping and naturalizing." The labeling the company has developed gives naturalist gardeners easy-to-read information on plant size, sun and water requirements, bloom time and color. Chip Schumacher comments, "We feel that we have grown the widest selection of plants for landscaping in the state." Schumacher's often has sales in fall and winter and holds seasonal seminars. And if you're buying more than the family car can hold, the firm offers delivery within the Austin-San Antonio corridor. *Directions: The nursery is located west of New Braunfels off of Hwy 46 toward Boerne, Texas. (Take Loop 357 off I-35 to get to Hwy 46 without getting into town traffic.)*

Thai-T Nursery
1403 Hwy 46 S
New Braunfels, Texas 78130
830.625.4685
Hours: Mon–Sat 7:30–5

Fred and Gay Schultz opened Thai-T Nursery in 1994 and, as Fred told us, "It's really Gay's nursery. She just lets me work here." That having been said, we were treated to a most informative tour by Fred. When asked to meet Gay, his reply was, "She's over there playing in the dirt." And there was Gay in front of a large pile of soil, potting a multitude of starts. Most of the plant material is grown on-site, and we were really taken with the shrubs, perennials, gorgeous verbena, unusual bleeding heart, as well as 'Centennial' and 'Tuscarora' crepe myrtles and hardy dwarf gardenias, which we couldn't resist purchasing. We were also interested in the Kaffir lime and lemon grass, both of which are used in Thai cooking. Thai-T Nursery is truly a "hands on" operation with very healthy plants and even better prices. Do, however, bring cash or a checkbook...no credit cards accepted.

Garden Furnishings

Gruene Gardens
1632 Hunter Rd
New Braunfels, Texas 78130
830.625.8816
Hours: Daily 10–5

You might miss Gruene Gardens if you don't know that it is behind The Dancing Bear Gift Shop, and you don't want to miss this one if you are in the market for unusual pots and urns. In this intimate, shaded area, complete with signs, yard art and doves, you will find a surprise around every corner. The pots and urns, which are from Guadalajara, come in all shapes, sizes and colors and are certainly some of the largest and most attractive we have seen. The tall bamboo ones really caught our eye. The plants offered are predominately native perennials and herbs. Owners Beth Fuselier and Oscar Duenas have created a whimsical atmosphere in which to display their impressive wares.

Ornamental Iron Works
1308 Gruene Rd
New Braunfels, Texas 78130
830.624.3511
www.oiw-ornamentaliron.net
Hours: Mon–Thurs 10:30–5:30, Fri 10:30–6, Sat 10–7, Sun 1–6 (spring); open until 6 on weekdays and 7 on Saturday in summer; closed Monday in fall and winter.

Angie Hernandez finds all of her wrought iron from suppliers in Mexico. What you will find at her shop is a wild and wonderful array of iron benches, trellises, arbors, plant stands, yard art

(LISTING CONTINUED ON THE NEXT PAGE)

(CONTINUED)

(big butterflies, hummingbirds and dragonflies on stakes) and even iron birdhouses, which she says birds actually use to nest. There are also 3-foot and 5-foot fence sections and matching gates, powder-finished to look like antiques. And, most of the low-fired Mexican pots she stocks are sealed on the inside to prevent cracking in winter. She also carries lots of hand-painted Talavera containers.

Pleasanton (Atascosa County)

Garden Centers

Virginia Twins Garden Market
1402 West Oakland Rd
Pleasanton, Texas 78064
830.569.2054
Hours: Mon–Sat 9–6, Sun 10–4

The first question we asked was about this garden center's name... Well, it's owned by twins, Catie Blaha and Kristen Heider, and they grew up in Leesburg, Virginia. But they've become good Texas gals here in the "Home of the Cowboy," as Pleasanton is known. And, having run their father's nursery back east, they really "dig" the business they began here six years ago. Their nursery carries only Texas-grown trees, shrubs, annuals and perennials along with some tropicals from Florida. It's all-organic; Lady Bug is their premier line of soil amendments and pest controls. Kristin is the designer, and Catie is in charge of landscape installation. They offer lots of nice pottery, fountains and decorative ironwork, and these energetic twins have recently added a floral shop.

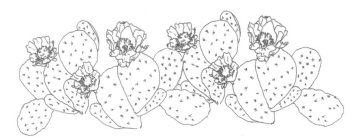

San Antonio Metropolitan Area (Bexar County)

Garden Centers

Burns Nursery and Landscape
13893 East Hwy 87
Adkins, Texas 78101
210.649.4377
www.burnsnurseryandlandscape.com
Hours: Mon–Fri 9–6, Sat 8–5, Sun 9–3. Closed Mondays in winter.

This complete wholesale/retail garden center was founded in 2003 by Travis Heath Burns with the idea of revolutionizing the retail nursery business. The concept was to allow the customer to experience several design scenarios in a relaxing setting. There are meandering granite pathways that lead into shade gardens, patios and a Southwest native plant display. You'll find everything from water garden plants and products to bulk materials, landscape lighting, tools, pottery and Garden-Ville products. The specialty is native Texas plants, with a large selection of perennials, shrubs and trees. You'll also find a lot of seasonal color and many mixed-plant container arrangements here.

Fanick's Garden Center Inc.
1025 Holmgreen Rd
San Antonio, Texas 78220
210.648.1303
www.fanicks.com
Hours: Daily 8:30–5

Opened in 1939 on this site by Eddie Fanick, the nursery has become an institution in San Antonio and a Texas treasure. Starting with just iris and morning glory seeds, Mr. Fanick developed thirteen different trees, including 'Fan-Tex' ash, 'Fan-Stil' Pear and 'Texas Blue Giant' fig. John Fanick phlox was named for Mr. Fanick's son, who followed him at the helm of this nursery and continued to enhance its reputation in Texas horticulture circles. Today, Fanick's is in the capable hands of his grandsons, Mark and Mike Fanick, as well as several granddaughters who also work here. There is such a huge inventory of trees and shrubs on this ten-acre property that is feels more like an arboretum than a nursery. For example, there are eight different varieties of cypress trees. Eight greenhouses are in full use, and plans are underway to start a "self-pick" orchard. The Pot House holds a huge assortment of containers, and the Gift Shop offers such excellent products as Altas gloves and Felco pruners, as well as potting benches, wind chimes, and western-theme gifts from Regal and Windy Wings. Don't miss the new Pond House, which contains several ponds, fountains, statuary and all the equipment and supplies you need to build and maintain a water garden.
Directions: From I-10 take the W.W. White exit. Go south to the sixth traffic light and turn left on Holmgreen Rd.

The Garden Center
10682 Bandera Rd
San Antonio, Texas 78250
210.647.7900
www.thegardencenter.com
Hours: Daily 9–6

It all started in 1968 when Gerald Harrell became a registered Landscape Architect in Texas and started his own company in Houston. However, the lure of the Hill Country compelled him move to San Antonio and open a nursery in 1985. It has been at this location since 1995, and Gerald's son Wayne, who has been involved (off and on) most of his life, began managing the nursery in 2002. As a Certified Master Nursery Professional, Wayne is most interested in sustainable gardening, drought-tolerant plants, water conservation and organic gardening. When we visited, this tidy garden center was brimming with color and lots of hanging baskets, and we spotted three greenhouses in which perennials, fruit trees and roses are grown. All other plant material is supplied by Texas growers. There is a huge selection of trees, and a tree planting service (with a one-year guarantee) is available, as well as an in-house design division headed by Scott Lunt. The Garden Center provides a pleasant shopping experience with a knowledgeable staff ready to assist.

Milberger Landscape
3920 North Loop 1604 E
San Antonio, Texas 78247
210.497.3760
www.milbergernursery.com
Hours: Mon–Sat 9–6, Sun 10–6

As always, we love the "feel" of Milberger's, with its weathered wooden buildings and large spreading oak trees. Sinatra singing in the background, the resident rooster strutting, the water features gurgling and color, color everywhere! Charles Martelli, the manager, told us: "Milberger's retail nursery specializes in providing the community with the very best available in plants, garden supplies and related services, and professional advice is readily available from a friendly, well trained staff on all aspects of plant culture." We found an abundance of trees, shrubs, turf grass, groundcovers, hanging baskets, specimen tropicals, topiary and color ... a real depth of plant material. We were impressed with the good selection of pottery, as well. Milberger's is a "Water Garden Exellence" retailer. The company carries pond kits, pond plants and installation expertise.

This well-stocked garden center provides all of the aids needed for keeping your garden at peak performance as well as providing gift items of special seasonal interest, books, tools and a large assortment of seeds and bulbs. The landscape management department provides turf management, tree and shrub maintenance, chemical programs and irrigation. Milberger's interior foliage department offers consultation, installation, maintenance, leasing, short term rental, seasonal color, florals and silks. The company holds sales throughout the year, and the San Antonio Farmers Market is held at the nursery on Saturdays and Sundays from May through December. According to Mr. Martelli, "We take the same pride in all of our landscape operations regardless of the size of the project. We are just as particular with a small residential renovation as we are with a vast commercial landscape such as Fiesta Texas." To receive Milberger's free monthly newsletter, sign up on-line at www.PlantAnswers.com or call the nursery.

Directions: Take the Bulverde Rd exit off 1602. The nursery is on the SE corner.

Rainbow Gardens
8516 Bandera Rd
San Antonio, Texas 78250
210.680.2394

2585 Thousand Oaks
San Antonio, Texas 78232
210.494.6131
www.rainbowgardens.biz
Hours: Mon–Sat 9–6, Sun 10–6 (both stores)

We first visited the Bandera Rd location of this nursery and found it to be every bit as colorful as the name suggests. Rainbow Gardens provides a very pleasant shopping atmosphere, complete with encyclopedic descriptive signage for all the plants. The meandering paths are built around large old oak trees, and rest spots are provided throughout the five acres of trees, shrubs, annuals and perennials. There are squirrels, rabbits and pet cats along with a koi pond that delights all ages. And even better, free popsicles during the summer months! The inventory here is extensive. You will find a large variety of plant materials, fountains and statuary, books, furniture, pots and much, much more. We were especially impressed with the excellent water plants and the unusual perennials, many of which are native to the Edwards plateau. In the spring, you'll find over 100 varieties of herbs and display pots of herbs and perennials for customers to "sniff and pinch." Although the Thousand Oaks location is not blessed with large shade trees, this store offers the same depth of quality plant material with an even greater selection of natives. Owner Frank Kirby is proud to say, "Rainbow Gardens is devoted to selling quality merchandise at competitive prices. We specialize in customer service, emphasizing a friendly staff and knowledgeable sales personnel." The nurseries offer perennial and shrub sales, spring specials and occasional speakers in the spring.

Schulz Nursery
3700 Broadway
San Antonio, Texas 78212
210.804.0600
www.schulznursery.net
Hours: Daily 9–6

This is a new store for Schulz Nursery, which is an institution in Marion. Its inventory leans more toward shade plants suitable for the gardens of the established San Antonio neighborhoods nearby. But the quantity and quality of plant materials for which Schulz is renown are in place here! See page 187 for the complete listing.

Shades of Green
334 West Sunset Rd
San Antonio, Texas 78209
210.824.3772
www.shadesofgreensa.com
Hours: Mon–Sat 9–5, Sun 10–4

This is a must, an absolute delight! With it boardwalks and brick paths, this complete garden center displays its wares in a way that gives customers ideas and inspiration. The first all-organic nursery in the area, Shades of Green is involved in environmental issues from wildlife backyard habitats to zero-tolerance for pesticides. Bob Webster and Roberta Churchin, who founded the nursery, have once again resumed ownership, and Bob is well known in the area for Saturday and Sunday shows on KTSA radio. The plants are very healthy; the garden-related items are unusual; the garden tools are of the highest quality. It's just a comforting place to be. Shades of Green is known for its large selection of antique roses and herbs, and we were especially taken with the fabulous houseplants and the greenhouse filled with tropicals and cacti. The knowledgeable staff is friendly and helpful, assisting with design decisions and teaching the public how to replace dependence on toxic chemicals with beneficial insects and other organic pest control measures. Handouts are available, as well as a newsletter, and the nursery offers seminars on Saturday mornings in the spring and fall.
Directions: Turn west off of Broadway onto Sunset.

Specialty Nurseries

The Antique Rose Emporium
7561 East Evans Rd
San Antonio, Texas 78226
210.651.4565
www.antiqueroseemporium.com
Hours: Mon–Sat 9–5:30, Sun 11–5:30

Same company, totally different look! In and around the old adobe-style buildings here you'll not only find a breathtaking array of roses clambering up pergolas and gracing display beds, but also lots of native trees, shrubs and colorful perennials for sale. The nursery also stocks herbs, pots and giftware. Manager Robbi Will says, "Antique Rose Emporium is a hidden-away garden that's close to the city, but tucked in the hills. Take a deep breath and know you've left your cares behind. Some people say they find it spiritual experience. Bring a picnic lunch and enjoy the moment. This isn't the kind of place you just dash in to pick up something you need for your garden." There are all kinds of organic supplies, and you will find everything here from plants to garden art.

Directions: From Loop 1604, exit at Nacogdoches, turn north outside loop. Go 1.5 miles and take a left on Evans. It's 1.0 mile on the right.

Casa Verde Landscaping
5405 Broadway
San Antonio, Texas 78209
210.826.2923
Hours: Mon–Sat 9–5

This shady boutique nursery, owned by Walter Baker, Jr., provides a delightful shopping experience with lovely water features, handsome pots and statuary surrounding a wrought iron gazebo. Although not every level is wheelchair accessible, the charming displays are clearly visible. The plants were a happy combination of various trees, shrubs, tropicals and loads of color. Under the guidance of Tanya Siddeque and Daniel Vasquez, this eight-year-old nursery offers custom container gardens, landscaping, sprinklers and lighting. You will find wrought iron tables, chairs, chandeliers and other garden accessories as well as soil and plant care products. And, of course, Lily will be there to welcome you…she's the yellow lab who has been at Casa Verde since "puppyhood."

Greens & Blooms
1550 East Borgfeld Rd
San Antonio, Texas 78260
830.980.4441
Hours: Mon–Fri 8–5, Sat 9–5, Sun 10–3

With its attractive white stucco buildings, big trees and running creek, this nursery/landscape company projects a garden-like atmosphere. Lattice fences screen off the four greenhouses that hold the company's trove of tropical plants. It's replete with really lovely pottery, hanging baskets and specimen plants, including the largest sego palm (planted in a 300 gallon container) that we've ever seen for sale! Bob and Anna Jones opened this retail store 16 years ago, but Bob has been designing gardens for over 30 years. (His landscape designs have been featured in *Southern Living*.)

Directions: From Hwy 281, just south of Bulverde, turn west from the light at Borgfeld. It's on the left, about 1.0 mile from 281.

Nature's Herb Farm
7193 Old Talley Rd #7
San Antonio, Texas 78253
210.688.9421
Hours: Mon–Sat 9–4 (spring and fall only)

With its eleven greenhouses and two big shade areas, Nature's Herb Farm offers a huge selection of potted culinary herbs, as well as edible flowers, peppers, vegetable starts and native plants. "We farm naturally; we're 100% organic, and we work hard to produce high quality plants," says owner Mary Dunford. The farm has been in business for more than 33 years and has become a major supplier for other nurseries, landscape companies and grocery stores. She still welcomes retail customers to this beautiful setting in spring and fall. New concrete walkways make wheelchair and stroller access more comfortable now.

Directions: Take 1604 to 471 S and go 4.0 miles to a big white fireworks stand. Turn on right Old Talley Rd and look for the company's sign leading into a wide dirt road.

Garden Furnishings

The Chair King
5219 de Zavala Rd
San Antonio, Texas 78249
210.690.1338

6931 San Pedro Ave
San Antonio, Texas 78216
210.979.8930

8348 Agora Pkwy
Selma, Texas 78154
210.566.5340
www.chairking.com
Hours: Tues, Wed, Fri 10–6, Mon, Thurs, Sat 10–8, Sun 12–6 (all stores)

See complete listing on page 118.

Greenhouse Mall
11255 Huebner Rd
San Antonio, Texas 78230
210.558.1818
www.greenhousemall.com
Hours: Mon–Sat 10–6, Sun 12–6 (all locations)

This retail store is the second location of the big indoor-outdoor Greenhouse Mall on Hwy 620 west of Austin. There is no outdoor showroom here, but the collection of furnishings is very upscale. See complete listing on page 212.

Garden Gate at San Antonio Botanical Gardens
555 Funston Place
San Antonio, Texas 78209
210.829.1227

The Garden Gate at the San Antonio Botanical Gardens is a charming place to shop for tools, gloves, seeds, books and garden ornaments such as wind chimes, birdhouses and feeders. For the garden's complete listing, see page 158.

Home & Patio
1047 N. E. Loop 410
San Antonio, Texas 78216
210.828.2807
www.homeandpatio.com
Hours: Mon–Sat 10–5:30

Forty-one years ago, Home & Patio was established as the nation's first all- outdoor venue. Today this well stocked, casual patio store is run by second and third generation Kelleys, Roger and Judy Kelley, and son Adam. The furniture lines they carry include Lane Venture, Woodard, Meadowcraft, Telescope, Mallin and Windom. The Kelleys travel to six markets a year to hand-select special items to make a complete casual living atmosphere. You will find hammocks, umbrellas, statuary, outdoor clocks and thermometers, wall sculptures and signs. There is a large selection of replacement cushions (Nan bought some) and an array of outdoor dinnerware, from whimsical to handsome and all unbreakable! (Pat couldn't resist). In addition, this company does a big business in special orders. Home & Patio boasts a very large selection of fountains, and along with these are good choices in fountain pumps and spray heads. According to Roger the store becomes a total Christmas store during the Yule season...the largest display in San Antonio. As Adam says, "We believe in straight talk and fair prices. At Home & Patio, you will get true value for your dollar!" *Directions: Exit Nacogdoches from Loop 410. It's next to the Crown Plaza Hotel.*

Texas Backroads Furniture
7006 Clear Valley Dr
San Antonio, Texas 78242
210.673.5657
www.texas-backroads.com
Hours: By appointment only

"We offer a wide range of custom, rustic/Western-style furniture built from reclaimed woods, from chairs and garden benches to tables of all sizes and styles," says Bill Groppel. "Photos on the website are just examples of our custom work and illustrate the types of furniture and accessories that we can construct. We have been building custom furniture from old barnwood and other reclaimed woods since 1996. The lumber comes from a variety of sources, some with quite an interesting story. From antique, longleaf yellow pine found on the old firing range at Fort Sam Houston in San Antonio to cypress from the banks of the Cypress Creek in Comfort, each piece is virtually one of a kind. Our Alamo Adirondack Chair is similar in design to the original Adirondack chair, but not quite. Actually, it is a whole lot more comfortable, with a Texas flair."

Three Rivers (Live Oak County)

Garden Centers

Curry's Nursery
1604 Hwy 281 N
Three Rivers, Texas 78071
361.786.9921
Hours: Mon–Sat 8–6, Sun 12–5 (open later in summer)

Wayne and Terry Curry have been in this business for 22 years and haven't lost their senses of humor. "With our difficult soils, if it grows, it's a good thing. If it grows too much, keep it in a pot," advises Terry. "We're half way between Corpus Christi and San Antonio, so we get the best and worst of both in terms of weather (hurricanes in summer and occasional freezes in winter)." Such native and highly adaptable species as cenizo, Texas mountain laurel, esperanza (aka yellowbells), butterfly weed and Mexican olive are the mainstays of their nursery and landscaping business. "We can get such brush plants as huisache and retama as well, but they are hard-sells because they are so common here. They are actually very nice garden trees," she notes. The couple encourage the use of organic soil amendments and beneficial insects for pest control. They carry tools, bulk and bagged mulches, and compost, and they freely offer their good advice.

8

**Central Blacklands
& Savannas**

Central Blacklands & Savannas

The metropolitan areas of Waco, Temple and Bryan/College Station are the largest market areas in this region that also encompasses such charming small towns as Brenham and Seguin. The southern portion of the region is sparsely dotted with small farming communities in the midst of fertile farmland favored by early German immigrants to Texas. Clay soils (blackland prairie) and sandy-soils (post oak savanna) occur in bands throughout this south-central region of the state.

Technically, a savanna is grassland with scattered trees; in Central Texas, the post oak savannas are transition zones between dense pine and hardwood forests of East Texas and open prairie grassland to the west. This area is an extension of the Central Hardwoods region of the United States. Before settlement, these park-like meadows were almost entirely covered with an evenly spaced tree canopy. Settlers loved the post oak savanna; its trees supplied timber for houses and barns, and its grass easily submitted to the plow.

Like the Trinity Blacklands, the blackland prairies of Central Texas originally hosted tall grasses and heavily wooded riverbottoms. The entire region has been so altered by the elimination of prairie fires and the conversion to agriculture that it's hard to tell blackland prairie from savanna until you look at the color of the soil. (Hint: savanna soils are lighter.) Once the most prosperous farmland in Texas, this region has more recently turned to ranching. Little remains of the original character of Central Texas. Today's farmers and ranchers accept as a given that they must spend money to root out the briars and mesquites that invaded after the natural grasses were removed.

The Brazos River flows through the center of the region. Before it was dammed, the river flooded regularly, depositing deep alluvial soil across a wide area. Numerous old channels can still be seen from an airplane. These bottomlands provide a rich environment for a wide range of native shade trees — elms, ashes, pecans, soapberry and a variety of oaks (bur, red, chinquapin). Such flowering trees as Texas redbud, Mexican plum and rusty blackhaw viburnum bloom in the understory. Wildflowers blanket these gently rolling meadows in spring. Here and there, post oak woodlands are still punctuated by ponds and streams with dense stands of yaupon, dogwood, hawthorn, elm and hackberry. Gardening can be tricky in post oak country. A water-impervious "black clay pan" may underlie the soil's loamy surface layers. Dryer than the Piney Woods, the region's annual rainfall ranges from 40-inches in eastern counties down to 32-inches in counties to the west.

Two isolated features of Central Texas are unique. The "lost pines" that grow in **Bastrop State Park** are not lost at all; the trees are merely isolated from the main body of East Texas pines by approximately 100 miles of post oak savanna because a pocket of sandy acidic soil met their conditions for survival. **Palmetto State Park** on the San Marcos River south of Luling is truly a strange place. Orchids, hibiscus, ferns and wild iris combine with palm-like dwarf palmettos to create an environment that could pass for jungle. "Mud boils" caused by gases rising up from under the swampy ground burp and sigh, and colorful butterflies flit through the thick vegetation. The park is named for the tropical dwarf sabal palm found here. Diverse flora abounds throughout this unusual botanical area in which the ranges of eastern and western species merge. The San Marcos River runs through the park, which also incorporates a four-acre oxbow lake. Artesian wells produce distinctive, sulfur-laden water. There is a mile-long interpretive trail and two miles of hiking trails through this park.

The dry sandy soils of the post oak savanna are especially good for growing melons and sweet potatoes. The soil is also hospitable to such wildflowers as wild phlox and bluebells, both of which were shipped to England in the early 19th century, hybridized, and returned to us as prized garden species! There's probably no better place for viewing spring wildflowers than the back roads of Washington County, in the heart of post oak country. Southwest of Brenham at Round Top, the fantasy landscape at **McAshan Gardens at Festival Hill** is well worth visiting for inspiration.

Nature Trails in heavily wooded **Mother Neff State Park** west of Moody wind past ancient riverbottom oaks and elms, native pecans and old cedars. The terrain is a mix of prairie land and rugged limestone hills overlooking the rich bottomland of the Leon River, which is also shaded by pecans, cottonwood and sycamore. You'll also discover ravines and rock cliffs with a rich array of vegetation. The park is vibrant with wildflowers in spring. **Cameron Park** and the **Sculpture Garden at The Art Center** in Waco (the old Cameron family summer home) offer spectacular vistas of the wooded plain where the Brazos and Bosque Rivers converge.

With summer irrigation, Central Texas gardeners can grow a very wide range of plants. The **Horticultural Gardens of Texas A&M University** is the only public botanical garden that showcases the region's plants. The campus of **Temple College** is being developed into a colorful landscape of native plants by Reid Lewis, who is a well-respected member of the Native Plant Society.

Public Gardens and Nature Preserves to Visit

College Station (Brazos County)

Horticultural Gardens of Texas A&M University
Hensel Dr
College Station, Texas 77840
979.845.3658
http://aggie-horticulture.tamu.edu/gardens
Hours: Daily dawn to dusk
Admission: free

The 8.3-acre Horticultural Gardens at Texas A&M University are student managed and maintained. The collection consists of over 2,500 specimens in 30 different planting areas, ranging from bog and wetlands to desert southwest. The colorful trial beds change frequently, as different plants are tested for hardiness and resistance to pests and diseases. This is an official test site for the statewide Texas Superstar™ program, which has introduced numerous popular plants to the trade. The Gardens focus on water conservation and provide learning

(LISTING CONTINUED ON THE NEXT PAGE)

(CONTINUED)

opportunities for home gardeners and horticultural professionals alike. An all-terrain path winds through the facility, with seating every 100 feet. There is a shaded patio for people who prefer to sit and relax. The native habitat and lots of birdfeeders make this a pleasant place for bird watching, as well.

Directions: From Texas Ave, turn west onto University Dr. Take a right onto College Ave and the first right onto Hensel Dr. Go past 2 stop signs. The garden is on the left.

Temple (Bell County)

Temple College
S First St @ Loop 363
Temple, Texas 76501
254.298.8992
Hours: Daily dawn to dusk

The entire 100-acre campus is a work in progress as it becomes a model sustainable landscape and classroom for students and the community. Reid Lewis, who served for ten years on the board of the Native Plant Society of Texas, is in charge of the grounds here. Over 100 species of trees and a wide spectrum of native and hardy adaptable plants are already in place. While great strides have been made, Lewis expects the project will require another twenty years of dedicated work. He takes inspiration from his friend, the late Benny J. Simpson, the renown horticulturist whose 40-year career at the Texas A&M Research and Extension Center in Dallas introduced Texans to the magnificence of their state's native flora. This will be a project to watch.

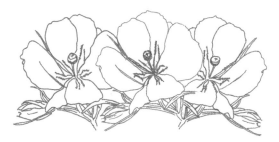

Round Top (Fayette County)

McAshan Gardens of Festival Hill
248 Jaster Rd
Round Top, Texas 78954
979.249.3129
www.festivalhill.org
Hours: Daily dawn to dusk
Admission: free

More than a mecca for music, the International Festival-Institute is a wonderful, improbable landscape! James Dick's earliest vision for this place included planting more than 18,000 trees on his 200-acre utopia. Now, the site is emerging as a vast romantic landscape painting as eclectic as the Institute's cast of international musicians. It includes lakes, picnic areas and jogging trails. Stonemason Jack Finke has turned "reject" stone salvaged from a quarry near Georgetown into a massive "Roman bridge" and waterfall that spills into a duck pond. The site's handsome structures, walls and other robust "follies" recall Celtic, Roman, Moorish and medieval European architecture. Beautiful old statuary and benches are skillfully woven into the fabric of the site, and the mother-daughter culinary team of Madalene Hill and Gwen Barclay contributed their herb collection. Colorful perennials and roses are combined with fragrant, edible plants in four Mediterranean herb gardens. Organic in feel and still germinating in the artists' imagination, this landscape will continue to progress. "Nature is a great teacher," James has been quoted as saying. "That everything is interconnected is her greatest lesson." Accessibility is difficult on the gravel paths.

Directions: Round Top is about half way between Austin and Houston on Texas Hwy 237 off US 290.

Waco (McLennan County)

Cameron Park
Cameron Park Dr
Waco, Texas 76707
254.750.5996 or 800.922.6386 (Waco Tourist Information Center)
Hours: 6 am–midnight
Admission: free

Filled with twisting roads and ancient trees, this large urban park is an under-appreciated Texas treasure. Located just a few blocks west of boring old I-35 you'll discover dramatic cliffs and scenic overlooks high above the confluence of the Brazos and Bosque Rivers, a wildflower preserve (Miss Nellie's Pretty Place) and Proctor Springs. Another unexpected pleasure is the new Cameron Park Zoo, a 53-acre natural habitat, which occupies the east end of the park. Hiking trails crisscross the park's 416 acres where you'll find lots of scenic spots for picnics. Request a trail map from the Tourist Information Center at the numbers listed above or stop by (it's located on the east side of the freeway at the entrance to Fort Fisher.) You'll pass Indian Spring Park and Waco's answer to the Brooklyn Bridge on your way to Cameron Park. If you have time, stop and take a look at the old suspension bridge.

Directions: From I-35, take Exit 335B and travel west on University Parks Dr, which turns into Cameron Park Dr.

Nell Pape Gardens
1901 North 5th St
Waco, Texas 76708
254.753.2032 or 254.752.2667 (Nell Pape Garden Center)
Hours: Daily dawn to dusk
Admission: free

A winding brick walk invites a stroll through five acres of elegant gardens between two historic homes built during the pre-Civil War era when cotton plantations fueled Waco's economy. A recent work of garden art by landscape architects Hal Stringer and J. Robert Anderson, the garden was designed to evoke the graciousness of the Old South. Its rolling lawns are shaded by giant live oaks, and its walkways lead to a lily pond, fountain and handsome double gazebo. Planting beds are filled with old-fashioned flowers, fragrant herbs and vegetables useful to 19th-century cooking.

Directions: The house and gardens are located just south of the Cameron Park Zoo. (N 5th street is parallel to University Parks Dr)

Sculpture Garden at Art Center of Waco
1300 College Dr
Waco, Texas 76708
254.752.4371
www.artcenterwaco.org
Hours: Daily dawn to dusk; Art Center: Tues–Sat 10–5, Sun 1–5
Admission: free

Once the William Cameron family's summer home, the Art Center now occupies two and a half acres between Cameron Park and McLennan Community College. Sculpture and nature mix here in a garden that was designed to take advantage of a breathtaking view of the river valley below. A walk through the serene natural settings of both the upper and lower trails introduces you to 25 works of art, primarily by Texas sculptors. There's a playful spirit to many of the works, and the pieces are carefully placed to surprise and delight visitors. "The Waco Door" a 22 feet tall monolith by internationally renowned Waco native Robert Wilson, is the garden's signature piece. Landscape architect Hal Stringer laid out the grounds of both the Art Center and the beautifully wooded college campus next door.

Directions: From I-35 traveling north, take Exit 338 (traveling south take Exit 339) onto Lake Shore Dr. Turn left into McLennan Community College. On campus, take the second left (Highland Dr) and then the first left (Scottish Trail). There is no direct connection from within Cameron Park up to the Art Center, but you can cross a bridge over the Brazos from Herring St and turn left onto Lake Shore Dr.

Central Blacklands & Savannas Resources

Bastrop/Elgin (Bastrop County)

Garden Centers

Bloomers Garden Center
507 Hwy 95 N
Elgin, Texas 78621
512.281.2020
www.bloomerselgin.com
Hours: Mon–Fri 8:30–6, Sat 8:30–5, Sun 1–5

This little nursery is home to native Texas plants, organic gardening supplies, a great selection of herbs, perennials, antique roses, ornamental grasses and much more. Locally owned and operated, Bloomers has been providing quality nursery stock to Elgin and surrounding communities since 1987. Its "gardening guru", Marcus Young, keeps locals informed on a Saturday morning radio show. "We can help you select the perfect shade or ornamental trees or shrubs that will compliment your landscape. Seasonal fruit trees, berry vines, vegetable starts (many of these we grow ourselves) are just a few of the plants we carry." You'll also find handsome pottery, water gardening supplies and beautiful koi for your water garden. There is landscape stone — limestone suitable for patios or drystack walls, as well as moss boulders. There's lots of seasonal color.

Directions: From Austin, take Hwy 290 E to Elgin. Turn left at the first traffic light, which is Hwy 95 N. It's about 0.5 miles, on the right.

Specialty Nurseries

Kimas Tejas Nursery
962 Hwy 71 E
Bastrop, Texas 78602
512.303.4769
www.texasgrown.com
Hours: Tues–Sat 9–5:30

Owner Kim Bridges has spent 13 years building this business. A charming, family-oriented nursery, it carries a lot of native plants and a few well-adapted shrubs, perennials and tropical plants from local growers. The specialty here, however, is herbs and vegetables, and Kim is committed to helping people learn how easy it is to grow food for a family in a small space. It is *totally* organic here. This is one of the few places you'll find certified organic herbs. She devotes a lot of time to one-on-one education on the "how-to" of organic gardening methods. The nursery carries all the bulk mulch, soil amendments and other products you'll need. "People garden for many different reasons. You may garden for better tasting food. Others may garden for cut flowers for the dinner table. For whatever reason, you need to garden," says Kim, "it is one of those things in this world that gives you a place in time."

Directions: Stay on Hwy 71 through town. The nursery is about 4.0 miles outside of town on the road to Smithville, on the left side of the highway.

Brenham (Washington County)

Garden Centers

Discount Trees
10050 Hwy 36 N
Brenham, Texas 77833
979.836.7225
Hours: Tues–Sat 9–5

Discount Trees, owned by John and Verna Lammers, certainly lives up to its name. With 80% of the trees grown on site and many of them native, this nursery has shade trees, small ornamental trees (including hard-to-find Anachacho orchid, parsley hawthorn, weeping yaupon to name only three of more than 30) and fruit and nut trees ranging in size from 7 gallon to 95 gallon. What we hadn't expected to find was the array of shrubs, desert plants, tropicals, ground covers, herbs, ornamental grasses and perennials. It was nice to see such old favorites as mock orange and winter honeysuckle. In addition, you will find a good selection of organic products, compost and informative books by Texas garden writers. The friendly atmosphere and the helpful signage ensure a pleasant shopping experience, although wheelchair/stroller access is difficult.

Directions: Discount Trees is located 7.0 miles north of Brenham on the right side of Hwy 36.

Plants 'N Things
3900 Hwy 36 S
Brenham, Texas 77833
979.836.471
Hours: Mon–Fri 8–5:30, Sat 8–5; Sun 11–5 (spring)

We found this complete garden center very tidy and brimming with color when we visited, and the attractive pond at the entrance provided a welcoming touch. The nursery has been owned and operated by the Stolz family since 1990. You will find lots of bedding plants and shrubs and trees galore, as well as mulches and soils.

Specialty Nurseries

The Antique Rose Emporium
9300 Lueckemeyer Rd
Brenham, Texas 77833
979.836.5548 or 800.441.0002
www.antiqueroseemporium.com
Hours: Mon–Sat 9–5:30, Sun 11:30–5:30

The Antique Rose Emporium is one of our "Texas Treasures." We've always thoroughly enjoyed our visits. The eight-acre display garden is located on an old homestead where in the early '80s Mike and Jean Shoup restored an 1850s salt box house, a turn-of-the-century Victorian home and an 1855 stone kitchen. They beautifully landscaped the grounds with old-fashioned cottage garden perennials, herbs and of course, lots of colorful old roses. Today you'll find whimsical touches such as the bottle tree and a purple picket fence, plus several comfortable seating areas. "Most of our roses were 'rustled' from cemeteries and abandoned home sites. These roses are garden-friendly; they retain the characteristics of fragrance, drought tolerance, disease resistance and diversity of form. You plant them with perennials and companion plants," says Mike. In addition to roses, the nursery here sells many of these "companions" — flowering trees and shrubs, seeds, bulbs, herbs, and a wide variety of hardy perennials. You'll also find organic supplies and hard-to-find composted sheep manure.

Last year (2007) many unflattering comments were posted on the Texas Gardening Forum of gardenweb.com concerning the lack of maintenance and sorry state of the roses. Mike made this response on June 15: "I agree! The comments that I have read regarding the condition of our Brenham display gardens with respect to weeds and inventory are not unfounded. As beautiful as the gardens were in April, I regret that I must agree that they look unkempt now. Thank you for making me acutely aware. I must remember to look at my gardens as if I'm seeing them for the first time everyday I visit them. I got too complacent and the gardens suffered. Customer feedback, both positive and negative, is always appreciated. (Granted, I like the positive better!)" He didn't blame the extremely wet weather, which was especially hard on plants selected for drought tolerance! We call that "classy" and suggest that folks give this place another try! The Antique Rose Emporium holds an Open House every weekend in April and a Fall Festival the first weekend in November. Not all areas are wheelchair/stroller-friendly, but most of the garden walks are flat. There are weddings in this charming nursery almost every weekend.

Directions: From Brenham, take Hwy 105 E and turn left (north) on Hwy 50. It's about 9.0 miles from this intersection and the site is well marked.

Ellison's Greenhouses, Inc.
2107 East Stone St
Brenham, Texas 77833
979.836.6011
www.ellisonsgreenhouses.com
Hours: Mon–Fri 8–6, Sat 9–5, Sun 10–5

This will certainly be the only nursery you visit in Texas that boasts a US Post Office! Besides that claim to fame, Ellison Greenhouses is one of the top wholesale greenhouse operations in the state. Retail customers will always find something blooming. The "house specials" are Easter lilies, hydrangeas and poinsettias, and there are also some trees and shrubs, vegetables and herbs and a nice array of colorful hanging baskets. Guided tours of the greenhouses are by appointment, and the large gift shop is brimming with everything from frames and jewelry to home accessories and antiques. The highlight of the year at Ellison's is the Poinsettia Celebration, which has been a tradition since 1990 and is held the weekend before Thanksgiving. There are Christmas cacti, Norfolk pines, cyclamen, kalanchoes, mums and over 80,000 multicolor poinsettia varieties ranging in size from three inches to six feet. Also featured at this spectacular event are fun activities, mini-seminars and visits with garden design experts and growers.
Directions: From Hwy 290, take Hwy 577 north. Take a left on East Stone St.

Bryan / College Station (Brazos County)

Garden Centers

Heirloom Gardens
12900 Old Wellborn Rd
College Station, Texas 77845
979.695.2944
www.heirloomgardenexperts.com
Hours: Mon–Sat 9–6, Sun 10–4

Heirloom Gardens carries a wide selection of herbs, vegetables, flowering plants, bedding plants, trees and shrubs, and will special-order any plants not in stock. "Our goal is to help you find the right plant for that problem spot in your landscape, and to make your landscape an extension of your interior living space," says owner Bryan Kotrla. "Our inventory is hand-picked for growing conditions in the Brazos Valley." You'll find aquatic plants and all the fish and supplies for your water garden. You don't have one? This company's landscaping division will install and maintain one that meets your needs. Bryan is a Master Certified Nursery Professional whose background is in environmental science, and his staff is highly qualified and knowledgeable. "We carry the highest quality lawn and garden supplies, including organic products and fertilizer and we offer weekly classes in spring to keep our customers aware of the latest and best gardening techniques," he notes. There is a nice floral and gift department here, as well.

(LISTING CONTINUED ON THE NEXT PAGE)

(CONTINUED)

Directions: From Hwy 6, exit at Rock Prairie and continue west past the railroad tracks. Take an immediate left. It's the 3rd building on the right.

Producers Lawn & Garden Center
1800 North Texas Ave
Bryan, Texas 77803
979.778.6000
www.producerscooperative.com
Hours: Mon–Sat 7:30–5:30

Producers Cooperative Association has a fancy new building and a bright, airy department for the garden supplies and tools. The outdoor gardening section is smaller than the old place across the street, but there is still a good selection of adapted and native shrubs and trees and, especially in spring, lots of herbs, vegetable starts, annuals and perennials available. There are two Master Certified Nursery Professionals on board, and manager Michael Vader, who holds a degree in horticulture from TAMU, prides himself on customer service. "We are here to solve problems, and we often special-order things for customers," he says. The garden center is one of the sponsors of Dr. Doug Welsh's Friday morning TV programs. Producers has developed its own fertilizers, and while it carries a wide range of products, there are many organic products on the shelves. You will find an excellent selection of books, and in the garden accessories department, Henri statuary, lots of terra cotta containers, tools, garden benches and swings. Students will find a nice selection of houseplants in the fall.

Columbus (Colorado County)

Specialty Nurseries

Midway Water Gardens
1156 Santa Anna Rd
Columbus, Texas 78934
979.732.6129
www.midwaywatergardens.com
Hours: Daily 8–dusk

Dustin Machinsky lives on the site, hence his long hours! There's a lot to take care of here with pond displays, fish and 120 varieties of water lilies (including the giant 'Victoria' cultivar) and a sizable collection of lotus. He stocks 150 varieties of bog plants, including 'Black Magic' and 'Black Princess' taro, dwarf cattails, variegated sweet flag, white, purple and blue pickerel rush and red-stem sagittaria. (He has been told it's the largest selection of bog plants in the state and customers marvel at his good prices.) He does not stock or sell invasive plants. There are all kinds of supplies to be found — liners, pumps, filters, landscape rock, statuary and pond conditioners. His company designs and installs water features within 50 miles.

Directions: Midway Water Gardens is indeed midway between Columbus and La Grange off Hwy 71. Two miles southeast of Ellinger (which is actually in Fayette County), turn south on Kallus Beyer Rd. Follow the signs.

Giddings (Lee County)

Specialty Nurseries

Yucca Do
P.O .Box 1039
Giddings, Texas 78942
979.542.8811
www.yuccado.com

This nationally known online nursery occasionally invites serious gardeners and garden groups to visit. Peruse the website to view the state's most extensive collection of rare plants from all over the world!

Hallettsville / Shiner (Lavaca County)

Garden Centers

Janak Brothers Nursery
2604 Hwy 90 Alternate E
Shiner, Texas 77984
361.594.4321
Hours: Mon–Sat 8–5, Sun 11–4 (spring only)

At Janak Brothers Nursery, you will find a wide variety of plants, some of them most unusual. The third-generation nursery carries everything that grows in the area — native trees, fruit trees (including three varieties of hardy jujube), native and adapted shrubs, perennials, herbs and vegetables, seed and cacti. You'll also find a full line of soil, soil amendments, and pest control supplies. The company is getting much more into organics now that young Chad Janak is running the nursery. His father, Patrick, is occupied fulltime with the landscaping end of the business. The gift shop offers many kinds of terra cotta pots and baskets among other things. Garden advice is free.

Jo's Green Hut & Nursery
1898 US Hwy 90A W
Hallettsville, Texas 77964
361.798.2209
Hours: Mon–Fri 8:30–5:30, Sat 8:30–12:30

When Jo Kutac was ready to retire, Katie Steffek (who had worked for Jo for several years) and her husband Ronnie decided to buy the nursery and move it to their own property. So now this good hometown garden center continues serving local residents, as well as lots of folks from Houston, San Antonio and Austin who have weekend places in this pretty area of German and Czech farming communities. "We still specialize in individual attention to our customers, whom we also consider our friends," says Katie. The nursery carries a wide selection of plant materials, including numerous trees in various size containers and lots of seasonal color. You'll also find materials for walks and patios, soils, pest management supplies, pots and concrete statuary. Ronnie Steffek has established a good reputation in the landscape installation end of the business.

Huntsville (Walker County)

Garden Centers

Stewarts Garden Center, Inc.
194 I-45 S
Huntsville, Texas 77340
936.295.5282 or 800.976.1707
Hours: Mon–Sat 8–5:30, Sun 12–4

Kim Stewart, fresh out of college, opened this boutique garden center 24 years ago, and Stewarts has become a delightful shopping experience. Kim is a Texas Certified Master Garden Professional, and, with several Texas Certified Garden Professionals on staff, you will receive knowledgeable help in selecting trees shrubs, bedding plants, perennials, tropicals, herbs and roses, both Jackson Perkins and antique. As Kim says, "We use only the best growers and make sure that every plant is suitable for our area." Monthly seminars are held, and the staff is committed to educating the public on the advantages of organic gardening. The large gift shop features every-thing from furniture and statuary to candles and gourmet foods. Christmas is an especially big time at Stewarts, with enticing gifts, seasonal plants and parties adding enjoyment to the season.

Specialty Nurseries

The Plant Environment
1809 Normal Park Dr
Huntsville, Texas 77340
936.291.0542
Hours: Mon–Sat 9–6, Sun 9–5

Hidden away in a Huntsville neighborhood in a heavily wooded natural setting, this nursery is crammed full of surprises. It is owned by Clyde Lavelle, who has been a Texas Certified Nurseryman and plant consultant for 30 years. His specialty is unusual shade-tolerant plants. We found, for example, Japanese jack-in-the pulpit, yellow shrimp plant, blue-eyed grass, bear's britches and thryalis *(Galphimia glauca),* but there are thousands of treasures waiting to be discovered here. The site is not easily wheelchair/stroller accessible. *Directions: The nursery is located just east of I-45 at the corner of 19th St and Normal Park Dr.*

Martindale (Caldwell County)

Specialty Nurseries

C & J Greenhouses
404 Greenhouse Rd
Martindale, Texas 78655
512.357.6153
Hours: Mon–Sat 9–5:30, Sun 11–5

Mike Johnson's 35 greenhouses are brimming with color year around, and his retail clientele comes from as far away as Houston to take advantage of his good prices and high-quality plants. His establishment, which is 0.25 mile from front to back (all under cover), grows about 12,000 geraniums in spring, 4,000 mums for fall and 10,000 poinsettias. The fern baskets are always popular here, and the good selection of vegetables, perennials and flowering shrubs ensures that there will be something to please every variety of gardener.

Directions: From I-35 exit Hwy 80 in San Marcos and continue 5.0-6.0 miles south to Martindale. Turn left at CR 142 and right on Greenhouse Rd. From I-10, take Hwy 80 N to Martindale.

Navasota (Grimes County)

Garden Centers

Martha's Bloomers
8101 Hwy 6 Bypass
Navasota, Texas 77868
936.825.7400 or 936.870.3277 (Café M. Bloomers)
www.MarthasBloomers.com
Hours: Mon–Sat 9–6, Sun 11–5; Café M Bloomers open Tues–Sun 11–3 (desserts until 4)

This nursery's website is one the best. Here, you will you find complete information on everything from butterfly gardens and mulching to shade shrubs and deer-resistant plants. There is also a photo gallery with enticing pictures of all aspects of the establishment. That having been said, the only thing better is a leisurely visit to this destination nursery, which can easily last the better part of a day. You can attend one of the many seminars the nursery offers, have a delicious lunch at Café M. Bloomers and shop to your heart's content. The plants, which include natives, perennials, shrubs, trees, herbs and vines, are displayed in a large greenhouse or in lovely garden settings. There is a vast collection of antiques, garden books, stained glass and unusual gift items for the home and garden. The charming floral shop, Petal 'n Bloomers, is replete with gorgeous herb and European hand-tied bouquets, silk arrangements and other gift ideas. And don't miss the pottery shop. It is certainly no surprise that *Southern Living* selected Martha's Bloomers as one of the top 50 garden shops in the country!

Round Top/Schulenburg (Fayette County)

Garden Centers

The Garden Company
217 Kessler Ave
Schulenburg, Texas 78956
(979) 743.4648
www.thegardencompanytexas.com
Hours: Fri 9–5:30, Sat 9–5, Sun 11–4; open until 6 every day in spring

This little garden center owned by Stevie Smith is an absolute delight to visit. You'll encounter friendly, knowledgeable personnel, which is always a big plus. Stevie and her husband

(LISTING CONTINUED ON THE NEXT PAGE)

(CONTINUED)

Jeff, who runs the landscape construction end of the business, began this venture 1998. They bought the retail part of a grower's company and moved across the street to an old farmhouse on two acres. They proceeded to paint it a putty color with lime green trim and surrounded it with colorful, carefully manicured display gardens. They carry all kinds of plants, but concentrate on natives and other xeriscape plants that work well in the area. There's lots of seasonal color, some houseplants and all-organic mulches, soil amendments and pest management supplies here, as well. The gift and accessory shop is eclectic and decidedly upscale. Stevie does all the design work for the store and for their landscape clientele, which not only includes local people, but also families from Houston, Austin and San Antonio who own weekend retreats. Their work is renown for charming mixed-flower container gardens and handsome disappearing fountains and naturalistic waterscapes made of local sandstone. *Directions: Take the Schulenburg exit off I-10. The nursery is less than a mile from the Interstate on the right at the first light.*

Treeland
2530 Finke Rd
Round Top, Texas 78954
979.249.3414
Hours: Mon–Sat 8–5, Sun 1–5

Owned by BJ Finke, Treeland has been in the family for over 30 years. It offers an extensive assortment of trees, of course, but there's much more than the name suggests at this complete garden center. You'll find lots of shrubs as well as ferns, vegetables, herbs, perennials and roses, which are grown on site. There are hanging baskets, especially Boston ferns, as well as autumn and lace ferns in abundance and lots of tropicals. Landscape installation is also available. BJ's father, Jack Finke, creates handsome stone furniture and fountains, which are on display. It's not totally wheelchair/stroller accessible, but the very friendly staff is happy to bring plants to you.

Directions: Exit from Hwy 290 at Carmine and take Hwy 458 S. Turn right on Hwy 237 and right again on Hills Rd, then left on Finke Rd.

Seguin/Marion (Guadalupe County)

Garden Centers

Maldonado Nursery Landscape & Irrigation, Inc.
3911 Hwy 90 W
Seguin, Texas 78155
830.372.3879
Hours: Mon–Fri 8–5:30, Sat 8–4; Sun 9–3 (spring)

Having been in the landscape business for some years, Juan Maldonado opened this retail nursery six years ago, and continued expansion is planned for this 16-acre site. Today there is a very large shade house, and you will find trees, shrubs, grasses, color, tropicals and sub tropicals. Maldonado's provides landscape and irrigation services for local residents.

Schulz Nursery
100 West Huebinger
Marion, Texas 78124
830.914.2384

1722 Steffens
Seguin, Texas 78124
830.303.1720
www.schulznursery.net
Hours: Daily 9–6

Now in its 50th year of business, Schulz Nursery in Marion has 12 greenhouses, a lovely wooded shade house, an attractive gift shop and provides a very knowledgeable staff of Nursery Professionals. Today, Larry Walker (retired publisher of the San Antonio Express News) is at the helm and, along with Steve and Amanda Spalten (who had run the Marion nursery for 12 years), are carrying on the Schulz commitment to quality. They have built a new facility at Seguin, which houses a complete garden center, plus The Texas Plant Ranch, with numerous greenhouses, where the company will be growing lots of seasonal color for their own use and for wholesale customers. They have also opened a San Antonio branch (see page 167).

As well as a complete stock of plant material, this nursery offers soils, seriously organic-oriented pest management supplies, tools, garden books, furniture and gifts. Schulz is known for trees and shrubs that grow in alkaline soil: crepe myrtles, hollies, nandina, cedar elm, Sierra oak, bur oak, live oak and loquat, to name a few. Bougainvilleas are a specialty here, and perennials are coming on strong. We were particularly impressed with a large greenhouse brimming with begonias, bromeliads, cacti, succulents, tropicals and orchids. Schulz Nursery holds regular seminars on turf care, herbs, roses, African violets, hummingbirds and purple martins. As Steve told us when we met him ten years ago, "This is a great place to bring your family!" And it still is.

Directions: From I-10, take Hwy 465 N into Marion; Huebinger is a cross-street. The Seguin location is easily accessed off I-10. Take the 123 Bypass exit south to the intersection of Hwy 90. Turn left and turn immediately into the nursery. From I-35 at New Braunfels, take Hwy 46 S to I-10 and go east (less than 5.0 miles) to the 123 Bypass exit.

Specialty Nurseries

The Green Gate
990 South 123 By-Pass
Sequin, Texas 78155
830.372.4060
Hours: Mon–Sat 8–5:30, Sun 9–5

The Green Gate, owned by Joe Tocquignys, boasts a number of greenhouses, but only two of them are open to the public. In them, you will find a vast array of annuals and perennials. This nursery also propagates its poinsettias, bedding plants and geraniums, which not only ensures good quality, but also lower prices. Although the company doesn't advertise, a loyal customer base continues to shop here.
Directions: Take 610 S off I-10 and continue south about 4.0 miles on 123 By-Pass.

Water Garden Gems, Inc.
3136 Bolton Rd
Marion, Texas 78124
210.659.5841 or 800.682.6098
www.watergardengems.com
Hours: Mon–Sat 9–5:30 (daylight saving time), Mon–Sat 9–5 (standard time); Sun 11–4; Closed New Year, Christmas, Easter and Thanksgiving

Founded in 1990 by Burton Nichols, Water Garden Gems has become the largest full-service water garden center in South Central United States. There are over 100 ponds onsite, ten of which are fully landscaped and truly inspiring. The other ponds are water lily and bog plant selling ponds. We could have spent hours going from one tank to another in the 3,000 sq. ft. indoor Koi facility. Fabulous fish! You will also find statuary, wind chimes, benches and absolutely everything in the way of pond supplies. The staff at Water Garden Gems is very helpful and knowledgeable, and you will certainly enjoy your visit to this attractive water garden center.
Directions: From I-10, take Exit 595 (Zuehl Rd). The water garden abuts the north side of the freeway beside the access road. It's very visible from the highway.

Temple / Salado (Bell County)

Garden Centers

Cen-Tex Nursery
3220 FM 2086
Temple, Texas 76501
254.773.5191
Hours: Mon–Sat 8–5:30

"We offer a country atmosphere, away from the hustle and bustle of the city, yet we're a pleasant drive away. We try to provide as much personal attention as possible to make our customers feel important," comments Alvin D. Simcik, owner and Texas Master Certified Nurseryman. The plants you'll find here are recommended and proven for the area; the owners specialize in natives and stock as many as possible. He adds, "People have really enjoyed it because they can look all they want and, when ready to purchase, be helped by one of us." The nursery carries everything needed for planting and maintaining a landscape, plus it offers landscape design and a fertilization program for lawns. The staff mails a newsletter and presents programs to various service organizations. The nursery's gravel surfaces may be difficult for wheelchairs and strollers.

Directions: Take Exit 304 off I-35 and turn east. Go on Loop 363 about 2.0 miles. At the blinking light, turn left on FM 438, go about 0.9 miles and turn right on FM 2086.

Earthscapes
5317 Loop 205
Temple, Texas 76502
254.773.4668
Hours: Tues–Sat 9–5:30, Sun 1–5

This nursery is owned and operated by Mike and Kay Lynch, both talented landscape architects (Nan's classmates at TAMU), who are committed to the highest quality in every-thing they offer to the public. Earthscapes is an elegant garden center with attractively designed planting displays outdoors and a 12,000-square-foot tropical greenhouse. The wonderfully fragrant indoor showroom is housed in an architecturally attractive building, and the decks, arbors, fountains and even the parking area are all designed to provide inspiration for homeowners. In addition to landscape plants, you'll find herbs, garden and nature gift items, and an extensive Christmas shop here. Specialties include topiary (indoor and outdoor) and a wide array of annuals, perennials and native plants. Earthscapes offers expert advice, great plants and more — a gardener's paradise in Central Texas!

Directions: Take I-35 to W Loop 363 and exit to FM 2305 W. Take the first right to Loop 205. (One block off FM 2305.)

Lonesome Pine Nursery
3120 East Adams
Temple, Texas 76501
254.791.0884 or 254.773.1042
Hours: Daily 9–5, 11–5 Sun (seasonal)

As owner, Jeanette Holtman told us, "Henry and I have had this nursery for 13 years, and we are still remodeling it." Lonesome Pine carries trees, shrubs, tropicals, annuals, lots of hanging baskets and perennials, some of which are grown on site. There are fountains, birdbaths, wind chimes and some furniture. Design help is always available.

Tem-Bel Nursery & Landscaping
5300 South General Bruce Dr (I-35)
Temple, Texas 76502
254.778.5651
Hours: Mon–Fri 9–5:30, Sat 9–5

Since 1967 Tem-Bel has offered a large variety of plants that do well in the area. Janet and David Lockwood, who is a Landscape Architect, bought this 1.5-acre nursery in 1984. As David comments, "Our sales staff is knowledgeable, and the plants are well tended year-round."

(LISTING CONTINUED ON THE NEXT PAGE)

(CONTINUED)

In addition to trees, shrubs, tropicals and a beautiful selection of bedding plants, you'll find Knock Out roses, eight varieties of Encore azaleas and such accessories as pottery, birdbaths and feeders. They also carry a good selection of organic products. The company provides design and construction services, including walks and drainage, as well as plant installation. Watch for specials in the Saturday newspaper. We enjoyed our visit with Janet at this tidy, colorful nursery. *Directions: Take the Loop 363 exit on the south side of Temple and follow the southbound access road almost to Midway.*

Garden Furnishings

Accents of Salado
3366 FM 2484
Salado, Texas 76571
877.947.5938
www.accentsofsalado.com
Hours: Mon–Sat 10–3; Showroom closed Dec 24–Jan 31

"The beauty of things imperfect, fresh and simple" is the tag line on this company's website. Everything available on the website is available in the huge showroom. Accents of Salado specializes in Mediterranean-style accessories, and if you click on Old World Tuscan Gardens, you'll discover all kinds of containers and planters, window baskets, plant stands and candle sconces. Other "pages" of the online catalog offer gorgeous dinnerware and accessories for elegant outdoor entertaining. There are pictures of gardens that will make your mouth water! *Directions: From I-35, take Exit 286. Go west 0.25 miles. The showroom is on the right.*

Waco (McLennan County)

Garden Centers

Berrera's Nursery and Landscape Company
201 Sun Valley Dr
Hewitt, Texas 76643
254.666.9806
Hours: Mon–Sat 8:30–5:30

Nick Barrera, who was previously in the landscape business, bought this old nursery ten years ago. He and wife, Diane, have turned it into a thriving, attractive, complete garden center. As one customer told us, "They have the best plants and the best prices anywhere!" Diane commented. "I won't sell a plant I wouldn't buy for myself. I've been known to send trucks back." You will find everything from trees, shrubs, seasonal color, hanging baskets, St.

Augustine and Bermuda to landscape materials, rocks, pavers, bulk materials and fertilizers. They also offer very reasonable tree and sod installation services. Despite a very windy day and an overloaded car, Pat couldn't resist buying two gorgeous hanging baskets!

Directions: Exit at Hwy 2063 (Sun Valley Dr) off I-35, just south of Waco.

GreenLife Nursery
1312 North New Rd
Waco, Texas 76710
254.776.2400

Hours: Mon–Sat 8:30–6, Sun 12:30–5 (spring and summer); Mon–Sat 8:30–5:30 (fall and winter

Brett Boyd has owned GreenLife Nursery for 25 years, and wife Debby joined the company about 12 years ago. As she says, "We just love what we are doing." And, it shows. This tidy, complete garden center carries trees, shrubs, tropicals, bulbs, vegetable plants, hanging baskets, house plants and boasts of "Waco's largest selection of annuals and perennials." You will also find Nature's Guide organic products, mulches and fertilizers as well as garden art, statuary, bird baths and decorative clay pots.

Directions: This nursery is on the corner of Bosque and New Rd.

Speegleville Nursery
6610 North State Hwy 6
Waco, Texas 76712
254.848.7155

Hours: Mon–Sat 8–5, Sun 11–5

Since it opened in 2001, owner Larry Cathey has been busy building this new nursery and landscaping company into a one-stop resource for gardeners. You'll find good seasonal color and lots of tropicals here. In addition to a complete palette of plant materials, including some very large trees (200- and 300-gallon) and an excellent selection of grasses, the company stocks mulches, compost, gravel, boulders and building rock. The landscape division of this wholesale/retail nursery will deliver and plant the trees it sells. It designs and installs ponds and sells the fish and plants to complete the project.

Storm's Nursery & Gifts
9605 China Spring Rd
Waco, Texas 76708
254.836.0022

Hours: Mon–Fri 8–6, Sat 8–5, Sun 10–5 (spring and summer); Mon–Fri 8–5:30, Sat 8–5, Sunday 10–5 (fall and winter)

The first thing we noticed upon finding this complete garden center was the selection of very large trees. After visiting with owners Bobby Storm, a Texas Certified Nursery Professional, and wife Brenda, we discovered that Storm's also carries shrubs, bedding plants, a lot of natives, on root roses such as Earth Kind and Knock Out and bulk and package vegetable seeds. Having been in business for 12 years, this nursery boasts a very knowledgeable staff.

Directions: From downtown Waco, go northwest on 19th St (Hwy 1637), which becomes China Spring Rd.

Westview Nursery & Landscape Company
1136 North Valley Mills Dr
Waco, Texas 76710
254.772.7890

10000 Woodway Dr
Waco, Texas 76712
254.776.2334
Hours: Mon–Sat 8:30–5:30, Sun 12–5 (Valley Mills); Mon–Sat 9–5:30, Sun 12–5 (Woodway)

Four generations of the family have been active in this landscape design company/garden center during its 50-year history. Now headed by landscape architect Eugene Houck, Westview is known as "the place you can get answers" and has been voted yet again Waco's #1 Nursery and Landscape Co. You'll find a lot of everything here. There's always a big selection of trees (shade and fruit), and good choices in shrubs, seasonal color, herbs, ground covers, seeds and indoor plants. Shoppers will tell you, "Westview has the best stock in town." The plants are healthy, and the knowledgeable staff is there to lend support. Estimates, planning and consultation services are free. For your walks and walls, there are rocks, gravel and timbers. Finishing touches include fountains, statuary, trellises, arbors, birdhouses and feeders. You'll also find good books and tools here. Westview provides a fertilizer service (four times per year). Large ads appear in the Waco paper informing customers of sales.

Specialty Nurseries

Bonnie's Greenhouse
5198 Orchard Ln
Waco, Texas 76705
254.799.7909
Hours: Mon–Sat 8:30–6

Judging by the neighborhood, we thought perhaps we were lost, but, after a few twists and turns, we found Bonnie's. And what a treat we had in store! Sandra Killough, the current owner, bubbles with enthusiasm, and the large staff was busy with customers and cuttings. Bonnie's was started 27 years ago to sell daylilies and iris, but today this enterprise offers antique and garden roses, herbs, native Texas perennials, annuals, and grasses. You will discover some very hard-to-find heirloom plants and affordable 4-inch pots of such things as hardy begonia, ferns and perennial hibiscus. There are all kinds of vines, as well as plants for attracting butterflies. The guinea hens that stroll the property (paid employees, who earn their keep by devouring bugs) add to the charm of Bonnie's Greenhouse. The site is only partially accessible for wheelchairs and strollers. This place is a serious gardener's dream.
Directions: From I-35 north of downtown, take Hwy 84 E to 340 Loop. Turn right (south) and take a left (east) on Orchard Ln.

Colors of Texas
804 N. Lacy Dr
Waco, Texas 76705
254.799.8634
Hours: Mon–Sat 8–5, open Sun 8–5 in spring.

Colors of Texas has been in business for 13 years, and when we visited owners Danny and Renée Davis were planning to expand this already large wholesale/retail nursery. With

16 greenhouses and 16 shade houses, they specialize in hanging baskets, seasonal color and ground covers in great quantities! Retail customers must buy entire flats of a single variety, but the prices are great, and the color choices are spectacular. Wheelchair access will be difficult.

Directions: Take the Crest exit off I-35 and go west on Crest. Turn right (north) on Hwy 77. It's on the left, so you'll have to go past the greenhouses and make a U-turn.

Organic + Nursery
10568 North River Crossing
Waco, Texas 76712
254.848.2103
Hours: Mon–Fri 8:30–5:30, Sat 8:30–4

During the growing season, native trees, shrubs and perennials, herbs and vegetable starts share space with the organic supplies and soil amendments at this nursery. When we stopped by in March the plant stock had not yet arrived, but we enjoyed our visit with owner Larry Walker and were most impressed with his inventory of bulk composts and mulches as well as organic supplies. These include Rabbit Hill, Master Grow, Nature's Guide and Garden-Ville. Even if you are not in the market for plants, this is a place that's well worth visiting to learn all about the benefits of organic growing.

Directions: From Hwy 6, 12.0 miles west of I-35, turn right on North River Crossing (Hwy 185).

Robinson's Greenhouse
628 North Robinson Dr
Robinson, Texas 76706
254.662.0311
Hours: Mon–Sat 8–5, open Sun 12–5 in spring

Robinson's Greenhouse is owned by the same people who own Berrera's Nursery in Hewitt. Its ten greenhouses are brimming with seasonal color and over 15 varieties of hanging baskets including verbena, petunias, begonias and Boston fern.

Directions: From I-35 south of Waco, exit Hwy 6 and go east. Turn south on Hwy 77 (Robinson Dr).

Garden Furnishings

Furniture Center Casual Shop
7407 Woodway
Waco, Texas 76712
254.772.7090
www.furniturecenterwaco.com
Hours: Mon & Thurs 9–8; Tues, Wed, Fri & Sat 9–6

This company is family-owned and operated by Mary Brewer and her son Robert, and it features a very good selection of furniture and accessories for the patio and garden. According to Robert Brewer, "We've been in business since 1961, and people know about our 'fair mark-up' policy and our 'almost anywhere' delivery policy. Our patio furniture lines include, Mallin, Woodard, Cast Classics, Meadowcraft, Lane Venture, Hanamint and Treasure Garden. We have environmental friendly furniture by Envirowood, which is made of recycled plastic that looks like wood. We specialize in quality outdoor furnishings that give you many years of service in our rough Texas climate." You will also find Hatteras hammocks, patio umbrellas, fountains, statuary and much more. Replacement cushions are available in your choice of fabrics by special order.

9

Hill Country

Hill Country

What Texans commonly call "Hill Country" incorporates two distinct physiographic regions — the eastern portion of the Edwards Plateau and the Llano Uplift (also called the Central Mineral Region). I-35 as it passes through Austin and San Marcos roughly marks the eastern boundary of the Edwards Plateau. Kerrville and Fredericksburg are at its center.

This geologically interesting region is replete with rocky cliffs, springs and sparkling streams. Its meadows and roadsides provide a perfect habitat for wildflowers. Bluebonnets, Indian paintbrush, winecups and lemon mint literally carpet the skimpy soils in spring. Some of the most scenic drives in the state are FM 337 between Leakey and Vanderpool, FM 187 north of Vanderpool (the route to **Lost Maples State Natural Area**) and Devil's Backbone (Hwy 32) from south of Wimberley to near Blanco. Hill Country vistas along these and other back roads define the Texas Hill Country.

Now ranging from 1,500 to 3,000 feet above sea level, the Edwards Plateau was, for millions of years, the bottom of a shallow sea. The ocean floor kept sinking as sediments accumulated to depths of up to two miles and morphed into limestone. Because limestone holds water like a sponge, water bubbles out of springs all along the Balcones fault at the eastern edge of the Edwards Plateau. Over the eons, underground water has slowly dissolved the limestone, forming thousands of caves throughout the region.

Highway cuts merely scratch the surface of these deep limestone formations. A unique feature of the Edwards Plateau is the stair-step appearance of the hills. Alternating deposits of soft rock (marl) and solid limestone caused the phenomenon; marl layers erode more readily than the limestone. From the air, the hills resemble contour maps. From the ground, the grasses and other plant life that grows more abundantly in the marl appear as green bands purposefully planted across the hillsides.

Soils in the Central Mineral Region around Llano are sandy and granitic. If you've never been there, you'll be surprised to find that the 70-mile-wide Llano Uplift is not a mountain, but rather a basin surrounded by rough hills. The "uplift" occurred millions of years ago when molten rock forced up from inside the earth cooled to form a blister on the surface. The surface rock that later covered the "uplift" eroded, exposing stone that contains such minerals as gold, silver and gemstones (in insufficient quantity to mine). **Enchanted Rock State Natural Area** is the best known of the numerous bald granite domes that occur throughout the region. The area's grasses were especially tall and vigorous before overgrazing allowed the colonization of mesquite, whitebrush and shorter grasses.

The Colorado River cuts through the Llano Uplift on its way to the Gulf of Mexico. This formerly flood-prone river has been dammed in its entirety; four of its lakes lie within the Llano Uplift. The dams provide electricity and city water supplies, but the lakes inundated thousands of acres of valuable wooded bottomlands. The Pedernales, Guadalupe, Medina, Sabinal, and Frio Rivers rise out of springs in the western edges of the region. Some of the state's best peaches, apples, grapes, pecans and walnuts are produced in the valleys of these clear streams.

Many of the Hill Country's native trees and shrubs, such as the sycamore-leafed styrax, can be found nowhere else on earth. A surprising number of the natives are evergreen — live oaks, junipers (erroneously called cedars), Texas mountain laurel, evergreen sumac and agarito. Ferns and wildflowers indigenous to the region can be found growing in the tiniest crevices. Stands of big-toothed maples and bald cypress are hardy remnants of bygone epochs.

The scrubbier live oaks of the Hill Country appear to be a different species from the big moss-laden live oaks of the Gulf Coast, but the only difference is environment. Likewise, bald cypress trees growing beside Hill Country streams are the same species as the ones in Eastern swamps, but here the trees rarely need to develop "knees" for support. However, the shallow soil and lesser rainfall of the Edwards Plateau have forced adaptations that actually resulted in several new species. The cedars (*Juniperus ashei*) are thought to be a cross between Eastern red cedar and Western red cedar. Buckeyes, persimmons and mulberries of the Hill Country are all quite different from their eastern cousins.

Because Austin is perched at the eastern edge of the Hill Country, the plants growing beside the hiking trails at **McKinney Falls State Park** east of the city are quite different from the vegetation you'll find at **Wild Basin Wilderness** on the city's west side. Both preserves offer ponds, waterfalls and boundless scenic beauty, but McKinney Falls is in a transition zone between Blackland Prairie and Hill Country while Wild Basin is on an escarpment where woodlands meet short grass prairie. Its 227 tranquil acres are covered with wildflowers and a wide variety of Hill Country trees and shrubs.

Out Hamilton Pool Rd off Hwy 71, **Westcave Preserve** is a grassland savanna with wild-flower meadows and stands of juniper/live oak woodlands. The collapsed roof of a huge limestone cave caused its most interesting feature. Here, a canopy of cypress trees has created a gorgeous natural terrarium. (It's only open for guided tours.) Plan to picnic at nearby **Hamilton Pool**, which is now a beautifully maintained Travis County Park. Here, a 50 feet waterfall spills into an incredible natural grotto where you'll discover lush ferns and other plant life at the water's edge.

Northwest of Austin into the Hill Country, you'll find another water feature at **Colorado Bend State Park**. Gorman Falls is a "living and growing" waterfall. Here, water from a spring fed creek flows over a 60 feet cliff, depositing minerals that create travertine formations. These formations and associated lush vegetation are exceptionally scenic. Small natural dams have formed quiet clear-water pools. Located between Lampasas and San Saba, this park remains a pristine wilderness. There is a guided tour to the falls on Saturdays, and it is also accessible by a day-use hiking trail.

Although the Pedernales River is the focal point at **Pedernales Falls State Park** near Johnson City, other areas interest nature lovers. Well-marked trails pass through hills dotted with oak and juniper woodlands and provide access to more-heavily-wooded areas of pecan, elm, sycamore, walnut, and hackberry in the major drainage ways. Ash, buttonbush, and cypress grow on the terrace adjacent to the river. Formed by the flow of water over tilted, layered limestone, the falls can be viewed from a scenic overlook at the north end of the park where the river drops about 50 feet.

On the Guadalupe River at the boundary between Comal and Kendall Counties, **Guadalupe River State Park** is another picturesque area to explore landscaping ideas for Hill Country sites. On its winding path, the river courses over four natural rapids. Two steep limestone bluffs reflect its awesome erosive power. Bottomland trees include sycamore, elm, basswood, pecan, walnut, persimmon, willow and hackberry. In the uplands away from the river, the limestone terrain is typical of the Edwards Plateau. One area of virgin Ashe juniper woodland provides the perfect nesting habitat for the rare golden-cheeked warbler.

The adjacent **Honey Creek State Natural Area**, once a 2300-acre ranch, was acquired from the Texas Nature Conservancy in 1985 and opened for two-hour guided interpretive tours that introduce history, geology, flora, and fauna along two miles of nature trails. Ashe juniper, live oak, agarita, and Texas persimmon dominate the dry, rocky hills, and a few grasses find enough soil in the cracks to persist. Juniper and baccharis are being removed from the upland flats. Stands of native grasses are increasing. Down in the creek's canyon, you'll notice cedar elm and old cedar trees, as well as the abrupt appearance of Spanish oak, pecan, walnut and Mexican buckeye. Where the terrain levels out, the dominant species are sycamore and bald cypress.

Lost Maples State Natural Area covers over 2,000 scenic acres in Bandera and Real Counties on the Sabinal River. Its name and fame come from a large, isolated stand of bigtooth maple, which produces spectacular fall foliage. Its steep, rugged limestone canyons, springs, plateau grasslands, wooded slopes and clear streams also make this a prime example of Hill Country landscape year around.

The rich palette of plants and naturally occurring rock for paths and walls make garden design in the region particularly interesting, provided that the gardener accepts alkaline soil as a given. There was so little topsoil at my hilltop home in Austin that I had to use a jack-hammer to make planting holes in solid limestone! Once fractured, however, the soil drained well, unlike the black clay soil to the east. With the increased availability of indigenous plants, gardeners here are creating a truly distinctive regional garden style.

In terms of regional style, the **Lady Bird Johnson Wildflower Center** should be first on your list, not only for the native plant materials, but also for its beautiful use of native limestone in both buildings and gardens. Although its focus is more traditional, **Zilker Botanical Gardens** showcases the region's gardening possibilities while also promoting sustainable gardening practices.

Public Gardens and Nature Preserves to Visit

Austin Metropolitan Area (Travis County)

Austin Nature and Science Center & Austin Nature Preserves
301 Nature Center Dr
Austin, Texas 78746
512.327.8180 (Austin Nature and Science Center)
www.ci.austin.tx.us/cepreserves
Hours: Daily dawn to dusk; some preserves in the system open by appointment only
Admission: free

The Austin Nature and Science Center's mission is to promote knowledge, awareness and appreciation of the Central Texas natural environment and its connection to other world ecosystems. As a "living museum," its efforts are focused on interpretive exhibits, programs, collections and trails. The Center offers a wide variety of educational opportunities for children such as elementary school programs, high adventure activities and camps.

Zilker Preserve (on the same site) features a meadow-edged creek, streamside habitats and a high cliff with shallow caves. Foot trails are accessed from Barton Springs Rd under the Loop 1 bridge. The Parks and Recreation Department operates and maintains the Austin Nature Preserves system. Many of these preserves are open to the public. See the website for addition information.

Directions: To visit the Austin Nature and Science Center and Zilker Preserve, turn north off of Barton Springs Rd at the west end of Zilker Park, west of Loop 1 (Mopac). Park under Mopac bridge.

Lady Bird Johnson Wildflower Center
4801 La Crosse Ave
Austin, Texas 78739
512.292.4100
www.wildflower.org
Hours: Tues–Sat 9–5:30, Sun 12–5:30; (Daily in April, 9–5:30); Wildflower Café Tues–Sat 10–4, Sun 1–4. Closed July 4th, Thanksgiving, Christmas and New Year's Day.
Admission: $7 (adults), $6 (seniors 60 years and older & students 13 years and older), $3 (children 5–12 years), free (members and children under 5)

This is a must-visit for every Texan! The plantings and water features here illustrate just how rich and varied a Hill Country landscape can be. But the Center's courtyard plantings and demonstration gardens are instructional for home gardeners from every region of the state. The planting beds here are on a scale that easily translates even to gardens of modest size. The Center's theme gardens and trails are beautifully designed. (Also see the description on page 16.)

One very interesting feature is the Center's rainwater collection system, which uses cisterns and aqueducts to collect and distribute by drip irrigation 250,000 gallons of water into the garden annually. (Although the entire complex consists strictly of Texas natives, the plants do need an occasional drink in the driest months.) The Wildflower Center's purpose is almost entirely education-oriented. Its Clearinghouse contains an extensive research library, database and slide collection of wildflower species. It has compiled lists of recommended species for every region and published bibliographies and fact sheets on numerous subjects, from how to plant a buffalo grass lawn to organizing a community wildflower project. Members partake in the workshops and classes, receive *Wildflower* magazine and take a 10% discount at Wild Ideas, the bookstore/gift shop. The Wildflower Center is now part of The University of Texas at Austin. A new Master Plan calls for enlarging the gardens. Soon to come are a Texas Arboretum and a wonderful Children's Garden.

Directions: Take Loop 1 (Mopac) south across the river, past Slaughter Ln. Turn left on La Crosse Blvd.

Umlauf Sculpture Garden
605 Robert E. Lee Rd
Austin, Texas 78704
512.445.5582
www.umlaufsculpture.org
(LISTING CONTINUED ON THE NEXT PAGE)

(CONTINUED)

Hours: Wed–Fri 10–4:30, Sat & Sun 1–4:30

Admission: $3.50 (adults), $2.50 (seniors), $1 (students), free (members and children under 6)

Charles Umlauf was already an acclaimed artist when he moved to Austin to teach life drawing and sculpture at the University of Texas in 1941. During his forty years of teaching, he produced works in bronze, stone, wood and terra cotta that brought him international fame. His subject matter was diverse, ranging from lyrical abstractions to detailed figurative pieces. Mothers and children are a recurring theme, as well as animals and mythological creatures. Working with a slim budget, landscape architect Aan Garrett-Coleman supervised a cleanup of the swampy site below the artist's home in the early '90s.

She formed a recirculating stream and waterfalls with donated rock, and preserved most of the existing trees as she manipulated the grades to open up vistas and lay out the garden's intertwining pathways. She supplemented the native flora with a "hodgepodge" of aspidistra, ferns, daylilies, iris, roses and liriope scrounged from various private gardens. Coleman recalls spending hours with the Umlaufs discussing the strategic placement of each piece to show at its best advantage. The result of her work is stunning! Plan to spend several hours exploring, yes, even touching, the expressive sculptures that animate this serene place. Both the museum and the garden are accessible to people with disabilities.

Directions: Turn south off Barton Springs Rd onto Robert E. Lee. There is limited free parking inside the museum gates. Additional free parking is available across from the museum, adjacent to the ball fields. (To use this additional parking on Saturdays and Sundays, tell the parking attendant that you are visiting the Museum. Pick up a parking pass inside the museum.)

Wild Basin Wilderness
805 South Capitol of Texas Hwy
Austin, Texas 78746
512.327.7622
www.wildbasin.org

Hours: Trails: Daily dawn to dusk, office: Mon–Fri 9–4:30, Sat & Sun 9–5

Admission: free

Seven visionary women who were members of a 1970s environmental group called "Now or Never" founded Wild Basin. Its 227 tranquil acres lie on an escarpment where woodlands meet grasslands. Two and a half miles of trails begin from the Environmental Education Center. Here you can obtain the book, *The Trails of Old Time Texas*. The Easy Access Trail has benches every 300 feet and no steep inclines. However, to fully experience the beauty, wear good walking shoes and explore it all. You'll be rewarded with ponds, a waterfall, wonderful scenic views, wildflowers and a wide variety of Hill Country trees and shrubs. The organization is membership supported, and guided tours are available.

Directions: Wild Basin is located on the east side of Loop 360, 1.5 miles north of Bee Caves Rd.

Zilker Botanical Gardens
2220 Barton Springs Rd
Austin, Texas 78746
512.477.8672
www.zilkergarden.com

Hours: Daily 7–7
Admission: free

The Zilker Botanical Gardens grew out of the cooperative efforts of several local garden clubs, whose members continue to use the Austin Area Garden Center's facilities for meetings, flower shows and plant sales. Started without any serious funding or cohesive master plan, the gardens have evolved into a remarkably lovely place. The site's spectacular topography on the south bank of the Colorado River is especially suited to depicting different habitats and displaying native and exotic plants. Highlights include a Japanese Garden literally carved out of a cliff by Isamu Taniguchi, who worked with no salary and no restrictions in his retirement years to create the most tranquil retreat in the city. "It is my desire for the peace of mankind which has endowed this man of old age the physical health and stamina to pile stone upon stone without a day's absence from the work for the last 18 months," he said at its completion in the late 1960s. He maintained his work of art until his death in 1992.

The Rose Garden's Gazebo remains one of Austin's most popular places for outdoor weddings. The Xeriscape Demonstration Garden and Douglas Blachly Butterfly Trail reflect the spirit of environmentally conscious Austinites. Zilker Garden Festival, the garden's annual spring fund-raiser, is a terrific place to find unusual plants from vendors throughout Texas. The Violet Crown Fountain, which can be seen from the garden center, attracts birds of all species and gives an illusion of coolness and beauty to this quiet corner of the garden. The Info Kiosk provides a detailed map of the grounds and notes of interest to visitors.

Directions: From downtown, cross the river on Congress Ave, turn left on Barton Springs Rd. The Garden Center is on the west end of Zilker Park, past Barton Springs pool.

Boerne (Kendall County)

Cibolo Nature Center
140 City Park Rd
Boerne, Texas 78006
830.249.4616
www.cibolo.org
Hours: Daily 8–dusk; Visitor Center: 9–5
Admission: free

In 1988 Carolyn Chipman Evans approached the City of Boerne urging them to restore disappearing marshland and create nature trails in 100 acres of the existing Boerne City Park. The city's cooperation and Carolyn's enthusiasm brought a rebirth to the land and a renaissance of public concern for conservation of Boerne's natural resources. The center embraces four distinct ecosystems: riparian forest, live oak savannah, tall-grass prairie and spring-fed marsh. Since its opening in 1990, the Cibolo Nature Center has provided education, research,

(LISTING CONTINUED ON THE NEXT PAGE)

(CONTINUED)

entertainment and outdoor activities for more than 100,000 visitors a year. It's located on what was once Herff Ranch, established in 1852 by pioneer surgeon Dr. Ferdinand Herff. Much of the original 10,000-acre ranch has been developed, but the Friends of the Cibolo Wilderness have purchased the original ranch homestead on acreage adjacent to the Cibolo Nature Center. The Visitor Center is located in a turn-of-the-century home donated and moved to this location. Talented volunteers renovated the structure, and kids are welcome to come inside to learn about nature through hands-on displays. A third structure, The Lende Learning Center, designed by award-winning Lake/Flato Architects, combines elements of nature with state-of-the-art technology.

Fredericksburg (Gillespie County)

Japanese Garden of Peace
National Museum of the Pacific War
340 East Main St
Fredericksburg, Texas 78624
830.997.4379
www.nimitz-museum.org/japanese_garden.htm
Hours: Daily 9–5 (Gates are open from 8:15 until about 4:30); Museum: until 8 pm on weekends in summer; closed Thanksgiving Day and Christmas Day.
Admission: free

A gift from the military leaders of Japan to the American people, this garden honors Fleet Admiral Chester W. Nimitz, a Texan who served as Commander in Chief in the Pacific for U.S. and Allied forces during World War II. It was designed in Japan and constructed by seven Japanese craftsmen working for two months in Texas in 1976. Its raked gravel represents the waves in the ocean and the clumps of stone and plants within the "ocean" represent the islands in the Pacific. The stream that surrounds the garden represents a single raindrop returning to the ocean. As you enter the garden you are transported to a replica of Admiral Togo's meditation study. The building was built in Japan, disassembled and shipped to Fredericksburg, where it was reassembled (without nails) by the same craftsmen. This serene garden stands in stark contract to the museum's battle exhibits. Adjacent to the garden is the Memorial Courtyard where cut limestone walls display plaques honoring the service of individuals, ships and units in the war in the Pacific.

Kerrville (Kerr County)

Riverside Nature Center
150 Lemos St
Kerrville, Texas 78028
830.257.4837
www.riversidenaturecenter.org
Hours: Gardens and trails: Daily dawn to dusk; Visitor Center: Mon–Fri 9–4,
Sat & Sun 10–3
Admission: free

Located only a few blocks from the downtown area on the Guadalupe River, this former farm has been transformed into an urban wildlife and native plant sanctuary. It features an arboretum with over 140 species of trees as well as cacti, glorious wildflowers, shrubs and native grasses. Meandering walking trails lead you through the Nature Center and down to the riverbank. The Visitors Center and many of the walks are wheelchair/stroller accessible. Sculptor Dean Mitchell created and donated the lyrical carved limestone sculpture that graces the garden beside the Nature Center.

Round Mountain (western Travis County)

Hamilton Pool
24300 Hamilton Pool Rd
Round Mountain, Texas 78663
512.264.2740 for daily updates
Hours: Daily 9–6, weather permitting. No entry after 5:30
Admission: $8 (per vehicle), $3 (pedestrian/bicyclist). Seniors age 62 and over are eligible for a Lone Star Pass, which provides free admission and discounts on camping fees. Veterans with 60% service related disabilities are also entitled to Lone Star Passes.

Hamilton Pool Preserve, a historic swimming hole, was designated a preserve by the Travis County Commissioner's Court in 1990. Formerly a privately owned and somewhat trashy "hippie" hangout, it is now well-maintained. Located 0.75 miles upstream from its confluence with the Pedernales River, Hamilton Creek spills out over limestone outcroppings to create a 50 feet waterfall as it plunges into the head of a beautiful natural grotto. The waterfall never completely dries up, but in dry times it does slow to a trickle. However, the pool's water level stays fairly constant. The preserve is home to the golden-cheeked warbler and several rare plant species including canyon mock orange, red bay (western-most colony of this eastern species) and chatter box orchid. Hamilton Pool Preserve is a part of the Balcones Canyonlands Preserve, a 30,428-acre system of endangered species habitats owned by Travis County, the City of Austin, The Nature Conservancy, the Lower Colorado River Authority, the Travis Audubon Society, as well as privately owned lands. For more information about BCP, log onto www.ci.austin.tx.us/water/wildland/bcp.htm to find out about the hike and lecture series.

Westcave Preserve
24814 Hamilton Pool Rd
Round Mountain, Texas 78663
830.825.3442
www.westcave.org

(LISTING CONTINUED ON THE NEXT PAGE)

(CONTINUED)

Hours: Sat and Sun only. Tours at 10, 12, 2 and 4. Thirty people per tour; no reservations accepted. Weekdays by reservation only.

Admission: Guided Canyon Tours: $5 (adults), $2 (children under 12) or $15 per family.

Two distinct ecosystems meet on the Preserve; its grasslands are scattered with wildflower meadows, ash junipers, oaks and cacti bordering a sheltered limestone canyon punctuated with rare plants and cypress trees. The highlight of the site is a 40 feet waterfall backed by caves, tumbling over fern-covered travertine columns into an emerald pool. The collapsed roof of a huge limestone cave created a gorgeous natural terrarium. Located adjacent to the Pedernales River in southwestern Travis County about 40 miles from downtown Austin, this 30-acre gem is managed by the non-profit Westcave Preserve Corporation. It offers an array of natural science educational programs for children and adults in the Warren Skaaren Environmental Learning Center, which opened in 2003. Designed by architect Robert Jackson, the building is a model of sustainable building with such features as ground-source heating and cooling, a solar energy panel and a rainwater harvesting system. Visitation to the Westcave Preserve canyon trail is by guided tour only to minimize the impact on this beautiful and fragile natural site. The trail is not wheelchair/stroller accessible.

Directions: *Take Hwy 71 to Hamilton Pool Rd. Hamilton Pool is about 13.0 miles from Hwy 71, and Westcave Preserve is 1.0 mile beyond.*

Hill Country Resources

Austin Metropolitan Area (Travis County)

Garden Centers

Barton Springs Nursery
3601 Bee Cave Rd
Austin, Texas 78746
512.328.6655

Hours: Mon–Sat 9–6, Sun 10–6

Barton Springs Nursery embodies the essence of the "Austin Hill Country" with the same rustic and relaxed atmosphere we have known and loved for years. This nursery established its fine reputation by specializing in native Texas and well-adapted plants before they became popular. And, it continues to do so. Now it lays claim to "the largest selection of perennials in the city of Austin and possibly Texas!" The retail area covers approximately 2.5 acres, and it's filled with beautiful display gardens and quiet sitting spaces. You will find all the plant materials that are well suited for Austin gardens, of course, but also tools, wonderful pots, books, soil and soil amendments, organic pest control supplies, gifts and accessories. A visit to Barton Springs is always a big treat!

Gardens
1818 West 35th St
Austin, Texas 78703
512.451.5490
www.gardens-austin.com
Hours: Mon–Sat 9–6, Sun 11–5

To give you some idea how special this place is, suffice it to say that it has been featured in *Metropolitan Home, Southern Accents, House and Gardens, House Beautiful* and the *New York Times* Home Design section. During its 26 years, Gardens has introduced Texans to more hard-to-find perennials and shrubs than even Nan can name. "We cater to customers who are intensely interested in gardening," says owner, Bill Bauer. Inside the garden shop, you'll discover imported seeds from Italy and garden books and magazine you can't find anywhere else. The upscale gift shop includes chic garden furniture and merchandise from around the world. You'll find elegant teak benches, Swedish rubber chairs, terra cotta pots from Italy and England, zinc fountains, large copper vessels, high quality garden tools and steel outdoor fire-pits. The knowledgeable staff includes botanists and horticulturists, as well as landscape architects and designers. The firm also provides installation and construction. Don't miss the summer sales at Gardens.

The Great Outdoors
2730 South Congress Ave
Austin, Texas 78704
512.448.2992
www.gonursery.com
Hours: Mon–Sat 9–6, Sun 10–6

Even on a warm September day, we found visiting The Great Outdoors with its majestic shade trees, meandering paths and lovely water features a most delightful experience. We happened upon one of the semi-annual pottery sales (Labor Day and Memorial Day.) And pots there were! Of every shape, size and color displayed throughout this very large nursery. We were especially drawn to the large glazed planters we had not seen elsewhere. The Great Outdoors is definitely a complete garden center that carries natives, annuals, perennials, trees, shrubs, tropicals and a large selection of gardening accessories, including Radius ergonomic gardening tools. While talking with manager Merrideth Jiles, we learned that all of the soil amendments and pest management control products are organic, with only a few carefully selected exceptions. You can even take a break and enjoy and cup of coffee or a sandwich at the Garden District Café, which overlooks the lovely garden area.

Green 'n Growing
601 West Pecan
Pflugerville, Texas 78660
512.251.3262
Hours: Mon–Sat 9–6, Sun 11–5, open until 7 weekdays in spring

Green 'n Growing, opened in 1975 and owned by Tim and Rhonda Pfluger, maintains real depth in natives and carries a wide selection of adapted trees (up to 25-gallon), shrubs, and seasonal plants. Since our last visit, the nursery had been expanded to include huge tanks of goldfish and water plants as well as water garden supplies. The owners stress organic gardening and use only a few herbicides. This nursery is aware of the importance of xeriscape plants and prides itself on the "unusual and hard-to-find." In addition, you will find tools,

(LISTING CONTINUED ON THE NEXT PAGE)

CH 9

(CONTINUED)

books, gifts, lots of pottery, arbors, fountains and wind chimes. Wheelchair/stroller accessibility is limited. As Rhonda Pfluger assured us, "We have a knowledgeable sales staff and healthy plants. There is a good selection all year, not just at peak season."

Directions: From I-35, exit at 1825. Go east for about 3.0 miles.

The Natural Gardener
8648 Old Bee Cave Rd
Austin, Texas 78735
512.288.6113
www.naturalgardeneraustin.com
Hours: Mon–Sat 8–5:30, Sun 10–5 (Nov–Jan); Mon–Sat 8–6, Sun 10–5 (Feb–Oct)

John Dromgoole has been dedicated to the organic technique of gardening for the past 37 years. As he can tell you, "In that time I have never lost a tree, shrub, lawn or garden because the organic did not meet certain standards. We have taught literally thousands of gardeners about organics. You, too, can garden organically and successfully." You'll find a great selection of plants, bulk soils and compost blends, seeds, books, tools, and organic soil amendments and pest control supplies here. And many display gardens have made this nursery a destination for gardeners: an herb display by Lucinda Hutson, a vegetable garden, a marvelous orchard, a butterfly garden, and more. "We will be glad to share our non-toxic approach. You, your neighbors, your pets and your children will all benefit the day you go organic," says John. There's no lack of advice available at this nursery! John hosts a weekly radio show on KLBJ 590 on Sat 9–11 a.m. and Sun 8–10 a.m. The company has sales periodically throughout the year. This is also the home of Lady Bug Natural Brand Products.

Directions: From MOPAC (Loop 1), exit Southwest Pkwy, go west 4.5 miles, turn left on Travis Cook Rd. After 0.5 miles, Travis Cook will dead-end into Old Bee Caves Rd. Turn right and take the first driveway to the right.

Pots & Plants
5902 Bee Cave Rd
Austin, Texas 78746
512.327.4564
Hours: Mon–Sat 9–6, Sun 10–5

Now, this is a nursery "with an attitude!" You'll know you have arrived when you see a flock of pink plastic flamingos, which, by the way, have been officially proclaimed "Fine Art" by the city of West Lake. The exception to the rule occurs during the month of August when the penguins appear in an effort to coax a little cool weather into the area. According to owner Pat Swanson, "The 'scout bird' usually arrives mid-February, a true harbinger of spring. The rest of the flock arrives about two weeks later." If a laugh is good for the soul, so is the shady, inviting atmosphere at Pots & Plants. (Most of the areas are wheelchair/stroller accessible.) You will find natives, antique roses, seasonal color, herbs, tropicals, handmade hanging baskets, topiaries, garden gifts, books, European hand tools, teak furniture and much more. The friendly, professional staff includes a degreed horticulturist, a licensed irrigator and several Texas Master Certified Professionals. Pots & Plants offers a wonderful Christmas Tree Program, which includes free delivery and, best of all, free haul-off after the holidays. Be sure to call ahead and get your name on the list! As you must have guessed, we were impressed and delighted with our visit to Pots & Plants!

Red Barn Garden Center
13858 Hwy 183 N
Austin, Texas 78750
512.335.8093

Hours: Mon–Sat 9–6, Sun 10–5; call for extended hours in spring.

We found Red Barn a welcoming neighborhood nursery in a park-like three-acre setting with lots of shade trees and wide pathways throughout. "We have a large selection of plants, good prices and a very knowledgeable staff with six Certified Texas Nurserymen," says owner Emily McDaniel. This garden center carries a great number of natives with an eye to more sustainable gardening, as well as many perennials from which to choose. We were particularly impressed with the depth of inventory that included several cultivars of tried and true Texas plants. There are, of course, tools, books, accessories, soil and soil amendments and organic pest management supplies. At Red Barn, you will find weekly sales and always friendly and professional advice.

Shoal Creek Nursery
2710 Hancock Dr
Austin, Texas 78731
512.458.5909

Hours: Daily 8:30–6; After Oct 8:30–5:30, Closed Thanksgiving day, Christmas Day and New Years day

We have loved Shoal Creek since it was just a converted gas station named Park Place. Three years ago, Mike and Veronica Sewell bought the nursery, changed the name, and it just keeps getting better and better! You will find a lot of native Texas plants, a huge selection of perennials, annuals, specimen trees, rare palms, cactus, herbs, and antique roses. Even on a hot summer day, the sound of gurgling fountains seems to cool the tropical display and the shade houses, which are filled with lush, healthy plants. The shaded back part of the property (much larger than it appears from the street) features a large and varied selection of trees, fountains and statuary as well as spectacular pottery in all sizes, shapes and colors. A new addition to the inventory is the handsome, high-quality outdoor wicker by North Cape International. We never fail to find something unexpected in the way of garden accessories here, and the nursery is now 85–90% organic Landscaping assistance and gardening advice are readily available from a knowledgeable staff. Always a pleasure!

Sledd Nursery
1211 West Lynn
Austin, Texas 78703
512.478.9977

Hours: Mon–Sat 8:30–5:30, Sun 10–5

Sledd's has "served three generations of great Austin gardeners!" The clientele is, of course, citywide, but the West Austin crowd is both "legion and loyal." As one customer said, "I go to the grocery store, the drug store, the cleaners, and then I stop at Sledd's " According to the owner, "Our employees have all been in the nursery business from many years. We not only carry the highest quality plants, but we also offer complete service. We assist in your selection; we deliver, pot or plant and are happy to answer questions and offer advice." On a recent visit, we were impressed with the large number of tropicals, which are featured in the fall and the early spring. Sledd's carries garden related products from pots and baskets to soil amendments, pest management supplies, tools and a few unusual pieces of furniture. Good "specials" are offered regularly.

Sunshine Landscape and Garden Center
2002 Hwy 620 S
Austin, Texas 78734
512.263.5275
www.sunshineaustin.com
Hours: Mon–Fri 8–6, Sat 8:30–6, Sun 10–5 (spring); Mon–Sat 8–5:30, Sun 11–4 (winter)

Sunshine Landscape and Garden Center certainly lives up to its well-earned reputation as "the place to go in the Lakeway area." This nursery, opened in 1976 by Daniel and Diane Carpenter, was purchased and relocated in 1998 by the present owners, Brett and Shelly Greer. Shaded by stately old trees, Sunshine was a riot of color when we visited and featured all of the standard seasonal offerings, as well as some "hard-to-find" plants. Fountains, statuary, stone benches and a delightful water feature completed this tranquil scene. You will find trees, shrubs, tropicals, seeds, lots of herbs and natives and bagged and bulk mulch. As Manager Mary Kay Pope, who is a degreed Horticulturist and TMCP, pointed out, "We also carry a lot of houseplants which most retail nurseries don't offer." As for the deer problem, you can try Liquid Fence or Scarecrow, an anti-animal motion activated sprinkler. The garden center's secret weapon is Leon, the Nursery Dog! Sunshine offers complete landscaping service including installation within 10 miles and delivery for a fee, as well rock work design and installation. You are sure to see something you "can't live without"...we did!
Directions: Sunshine is 3.0 miles north of Hwy 71, near Lohman's Crossing.

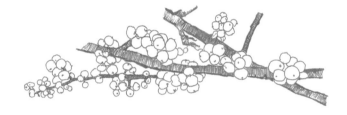

Specialty Nurseries

Big Red Sun
1102 East Cesar Chavez
Austin, Texas 78702
512.480.0688
www.bigredsun.com
Hours: Mon–Sat 9–6, Sun 11–5

Big Red Sun is all about design. It's sophisticated, eclectic and hip. You know you've arrived at someplace special when you see the display gardens in front of the bright blue house. The garden entry is through a sculptured concrete portal and the fencing is made of corrugated steel. Inside, the specialties are succulents (many of them winter hardy) and unusual, sculptural plants, including palms, clumping bamboo, yuccas and eucalyptus. We saw the largest ponytail palm in captivity when last we visited. There are handsome metal containers, colorful ceramic pots and shallow planting dishes mounted on simple pedestals and contemporary metal tripods. If you want to glimpse the aesthetic of this awesome nursery, go to the website, which wordlessly presents picture after picture of the company's design work. A picture *is* worth a thousand words! We owe a special debt of gratitude to Big Red Sun because the photograph on the cover of this book was taken in one of the gardens this company designed.

Breed & Company Garden Shop
718 West 29th
Austin, Texas 78705
512.474.6679
Hours: Mon–Sat 7:30–6, Thurs 7:30–8 p.m.

3663 Bee Cave Rd
Austin, Texas 78746
512.328.3960
Hours: Mon–Fri 7:30 7, Sat 8–6

Austin natives quip that "You can find anything except a size-four dress at Breed's!" Gifts and garden accessories abound, and there is certainly no problem finding tools and books at this combination hardware/housewares store and nursery. Even 10 years ago, this company was promoting xeriscaping, native plant materials and organic gardening. They still are. The seasonal color is always a draw, and you will find lots of annuals in four-inch pots and large native perennials. Breed's also carries grasses and wildflowers, trees and shrubs, natives, seeds, bonsai, cacti, tropicals and organically grown herbs and vegetables. As Barbara Jasper, manager of the original store told us, "Most of what we carry is the same at both stores, but the clientele is somewhat different, and we try to accommodate them. You will find larger pots and fountains and more topiary at the Bee Cave store and more seeds and herbs at this location." Regardless of which store you visit, rest assured that you will find something you "just have to have!"

The Emerald Garden
5700 Hwy 290 W
Austin, Texas 78735
512.288.5900
Hours: Mon–Sat 8–5, Sun 10–4

"We are Central Texas' water garden specialists, offering plants, pumps, filters, fiberglass ponds, rubber liners, fish, snails, tub gardens, pond chemicals, fish food, fountains, waterfalls and all kinds of decorative rock, from river gravel to boulders," says Jeff Yarbrough. You'll also find a bulk soil yard with over 20 different materials, as well as specimen trees and shrubs. The Emerald Garden holds a water lily show and sale in June, as well as seminars on ponds, herbs, perennials and soil amendments.

It's a Jungle
907 Kramer Ln
Austin, Texas 78758
512.837.1205
www.itsajungleaustin.com
Hours: Mon–Fri 10–6, Sat 9–5, Sun 12–5

Things have really changed since our last visit to It's a Jungle. It is, of course, still the "go to" place for orchid lovers. People come from everywhere in the state to find some of the 500–600 varieties of the orchids in Juanice Davis' collection from all over the world — *Phalaenopsis, Dendrobium, Cattaleya, Cymbidium, Oncidim*. In addition, she grows many varieties of bromeliads and other exotic plants, including the carnivorous ones. Her unusual baskets complement the plants and make perfect containers for her fabulous, custom gift

(LISTING CONTINUED ON THE NEXT PAGE)

arrangements. (Delivery in the Austin area is available.) There's an annual winter sale, and Davis travels to several orchid shows each year. "People who grow orchids can't stop," observes this charming former banker! Note that not all areas of the nursery are wheel-chair/stroller accessible.

Since we last visited Davis had turned the adjoining lot into a growing area for over 5,000 roses. Under the direction of Dicke Patterson, this has become a mecca for rosarians and for the rest of us who just love roses. There are some very unusual varieties. Nan quickly snapped up an evergreen climbing rose from Mexico that was blooming on the nursery's fence in February! Patterson and his employees seem to know everything about growing roses. They are training some of the climbers into wonderful, whimsical topiaries.

It's About Thyme
11726 Manchaca Rd
Austin, Texas 78748
512.280.1192
www.itsaboutthyme.com
Hours: Daily 8–6 daylight savings time, 8–5 otherwise

In business for 20 years in a rural area that's rapidly becoming urbanized, It's About Thyme specializes in medicinal, culinary and ornamental herbs. This nursery is definitely "herbs and more!" Owners Diane and Chris Winslow also carry annuals, perennials, shrubs, a good selection of antique roses, such trees as crepe myrtle and oaks, as well as water garden supplies. The gift shop offers herbal oils, dried herbs, vinegars, candles, soaps, pottery and books. Landscape design and installation are also part of the package of services available. Natives have always been favorites here, and items not displayed can be ordered. Although not all areas are wheelchair/stroller accessible, we were impressed with the three greenhouses filled with a variety of tropicals. We enjoyed being greeted by the resident collection of birds, which certainly enhance the bucolic atmosphere. We think you'll find it a most pleasant shopping experience!
Directions: From Austin, go out Manchaca Rd, past Slaughter Ln, almost to 1626.

Living Desert Cactus and Glass
12719 Hwy 71 W
Austin, Texas 78736
512.263.2428
Hours: Tues–Sat 10–6, Sun 11–4

Living Desert Cactus and Glass offers not only a wide selection of cacti, but also garden gifts and accessories such as pottery, wind chimes, birdhouses and feeders. As Darrell and Yvonna Dunten explain, "We specialize in the rugged, but romantic liveliness of the Southwest species of life, creating a flavor of sensual awareness." Texture, geometric designs, color and fragrances overwhelm in a nursery of desert landscapes. The store carries generic to artisan-designed vessels and crafts of Southwestern mythology as well as cacti and succulents of the world deserts. Living Desert Cactus Nursery also offers xeriscaping advice. While the nursery does not have a catalog, the Duntens are willing to ship merchandise to customers and are always happy to offer advice on xeriscaping. Some areas are not wheelchair/stroller accessible.
Directions: The nursery is located on Hwy 71, 1 block west of 2244 (Bee Cave Rd)

MBP Bonsai Studio and Pottery
601 Kay Ln
Pflugerville, Texas
512.989.5831
www.mbpbonsai.com
Hours: Tues–Sat 9–5, Sun 1–5

MBP Bonsai Studio has been in business for more than 26 years, and numerous bonsai enthusiasts have recommended this nursery to us. "It's our policy is to personally test every product before we offer it for sale," say Mike and Candy Hansen. Their online catalog includes plants, pots, tools and classes. The nursery is 100% organic, and the Aoki Brand fertilizer they use and sell is made from rape seed meal and especially formulated for bonsai. "Like all true organic fertilizers, it takes a little longer to produce results, but the wait is well worth it. Dark green foliage and short internodes are its hallmarks." MBP Bonsai Studio imports Yagimitsu and Ryuko brand tools directly from the factory in Japan, where they are made from high quality Japanese tool steel and, with reasonable care, they will last even the professional grower many years.

Ted's Trees, Ltd.
1118 Tillery St
Austin, Texas 78702
512.928.8733
www.tedstrees.com
Hours: Mon–Sat 8–5

Ted Lopez established this family-owned business in 1991 in an older residential neighborhood two miles east of downtown. Tucked behind an impressive entry, you'll find an equally impressive array of specimen-size trees that includes numerous natives and other adapted species. The company offers landscaping, irrigation and transplanting. Visit the website for photographs of the plants available and to get directions from your home.

Garden Furnishings

The Chair King
1201 Barbara Jordan Blvd.
Austin, Texas 78723
512.454.5464

13945 Hwy 183 N
Austin, Texas 78717
512.219.9978

2300 Lohman's Spur
Austin, Texas 78734
512.402.9707
www.chairking.com
See complete listing on page 118.

Churchill's Fireside & Patio
3300 Bee Caves Rd
Austin, Texas 78746
512.328.9356
www.churchillsaustin.com
Hours: Mon–Sat 10–6, Sun 12–5 (Oct–Jan)

For over 20 years, Dorothy and Ray Duhon have been "dedicated to creating beautiful spaces that function not only as an outdoor escape, but also as an extension of the home." Churchill's carries outdoor wicker, wrought iron, aluminum and cast aluminum by Casual Creations, Mallin, Summer Classics and Telescope and mosaic tables By KNF. You will find outdoor art, lighting, fire pits and rugs as well as wind chimes, weather vanes and lanterns. From umbrellas to candles, cushions to garden ornaments...they have it. The service is friendly, the prices competitive and the atmosphere relaxing.

Desert Dreams
10900 RR 2222
Austin, Texas 78738
512.231.0814

3715 RR 620 S
Austin, Texas 78738
512.266.4703
www.dd-austin.com
Hours: Mon–Sat 10–6, Sun 11–6

"Unlike many import stores that often feature products available in any border town mercado, we travel deep into the interior of Mexico, buying directly from local artisans who create works of beauty and character in much the same way their ancestors have done for centuries past," say Lee and Sylvia Reyes. "Each item at Desert Dreams represents the character and talent of the artisan who created it." You'll find vast quantities of Talavera and rustic Mexican clay pots, plus colorful glazed ceramic pots from Asia. There are also wide selections of wrought iron and blown glass accessories.

The Greenhouse Mall
9900 Ranch Rd 620 N
Austin, Texas 78726-2203
512.250.0000

12501 Hwy 71
Austin, Texas 78738
512.617.8888
www.greenhousemall.com
Hours: Mon–Sat 10–6, Sun 12–6 (all locations)

Opened over 30 years ago by Matt and Muriel Wiggers, The Greenhouse Mall initially sold only greenhouses and hydroponic plants. Today the Wiggers' daughter, Karen Galindo, is at the helm and has opened two new stores in the last few years. As she says, "I was practically born into the casual industry." Three years ago, an 8,000-square-foot showroom was added to the original location on 620, and the original 4,000-square-foot showroom is now used as a discount clearance center. This, in addition to the eight-acre outdoor display area provides a colorful, varied and vast array of casual furniture and accessories.

These high-end stores carry merchandise from such manufacturers as O. W. Lee, Laneventure, Gloster, Windham Castings, Kessler, Brown Jordan International, Olympia Lighting, TUUCI, Jensen Jarrah, Riverwood Casual, Treasure Garden and more. It is hard to believe that this furniture is really made for outdoor living! Galindo has become more interested in accessories in recent years, attending trade shows and adding such vendors as Alfresco Home, NDI and Vietri. You will find hammocks, umbrellas, replacement cushions, tableware and a large selection of fabrics for special orders. There are greenhouses, of course, as well as several sizes of DCS grills, which are available for propane or natural gas.

Lars Stanley — Architects & Artisans
1901 E.M. Franklin Ave
Austin, Texas 78723
512.445.0444
www.larsstanley.com
Hours: By appointment only

Mr. Stanley's firm designs and fabricates custom garden elements, which are hand-crafted from forged steel, copper, brass and other metals. His work includes elegant entry gates, gazebos, lighting, furniture and sculpture. It has been featured in leading magazines, and each piece is unique. Staff architects help homeowners and designers elaborate their own ideas into well-detailed reality.

Miguel's Imports
5209 Burnet Rd
Austin, Texas 78756
512.323.5563
Hours: Mon–Sat 10–6, Sun 12–5

Miguel and Laura Martin recently bought this large site on Burnet Rd, which they've made quite wonderful with a new iron fence and classic entry portal. Their wares include both Mexican and Asian containers, Latin folk art, furniture, fountains, carved stone columns, and lighting. It's a fun place to browse, and the owners are most gracious.

Music of the Spheres
4909B East Cesar Chavez
Austin, Texas 78702
512 385 0340 or 888.324.4637
www.musicofspheres.com
Hours: Mon–Fri 8:30–5:30

In business since 1989, Music of the Spheres® has become one of the country's leading manufacturers of tuned wind chimes. In fact, its slogan is "the Stradivarius of windchimes®." Designed by the late Larry Roark, who held a degree in music theory from the University of North Texas, the chimes are tuned to standard orchestral pitch and come in seven voices/sizes

(LISTING CONTINUED ON THE NEXT PAGE)

(CONTINUED)

ranging from soprano to basso profundo. They also come in a variety of musical scales. You can actually listen to the choices on-line and choose the one most pleasing to you! Once you have settled on your favorite musical scale, you can start collecting all the voices for an ensemble in your own backyard. Created from tempered aluminum alloy, the matte black electrostatic powder-coat finish protects the tubes from environmental issues like salt air and even acid rain. Activity level is controlled by the detachable wind-catcher and by sliding the clapper up the central cord to turn off the music. The company also designs one-of-a-kind acoustic sculptures. You may buy the chimes at the East Austin workshop, online or at the Texas Renaissance Festival north of Houston in the fall. The chimes are likely to be in a garden center near you.

Wild Ideas: The Store
4801 La Crosse Ave
Austin, Texas 78739
512.292.4300

While you are at the Lady Bird Johnson Wildflower Center, be sure to visit the gift shop, Wild Ideas. Here you will find a wide variety of books, including the largest collection of books on native plants in the country. Wild Ideas also carries seeds, "state fact packets," pots, tools, gloves, gardening apparel and accessories. This is a great place to buy a gift, especially one for yourself! For the Wildflower Center's complete listing, see page 199.

Bandera / Medina (Bandera County)

Specialty Nurseries

The Apple Store
14024 Hwy 16 N (Main St)
Medina, Texas 78055
830.589.2202 or 800.449.0882
Hours: Mon–Sun 9:30–5

Bryan Hutzler operates a small nursery here that is supplied by Love Creek Orchards, which is only about a mile down the road. (See next listing.) There's a charming bakery that specializes in "everything apple" — pies, cakes, jams, jellies and ice cream. The Patio Cafe, open 11–3, is a fun place for lunch, and the gift shop in front sells all kinds of Texas products, including apple strudel coffee, salsas and decorative gift items with an apple theme.

Love Creek Orchards
13558 Hwy 16 N
Medina, Texas 78055
830.589.2588
www.lovecreekorchards.com
Hours: Mon–Fri 9–5

Baxter and Carol Adams sold the store listed above to concentrate their efforts on the large orchard where they grow many varieties of apple, dwarf apple and other fruit trees and berries. People can visit the nursery to pick their own fruits and berries in season: blackberries (May and June), peaches (June and July), apples and figs (July and August) and persimmons (late-September and October.) The company also grows big-tooth maple, black escarpment cherry, bald cypress and Texas ash and Monterrey, lacey and chinquapin oaks from the Texas Hill Country, and it ships seedlings during the dormant season. Call for a catalog.

Medina Gardens
13417 Hwy 16 N
Medina, Texas 78055
830.589.2771
Hours: Tues–Sun 9–5

Ernest Curino opened Medina Gardens in 2002, and two short years later this five-acre nursery was featured in *Texas Highways* magazine. He now hosts Master Gardeners and Native Plant Society groups and, in season, allows visitors to view his private garden. (Not all areas of the gardens are wheelchair/stroller accessible. Most of the stock is grown on site, and there are hundreds and hundreds of species. An absolute fount of knowledge, Ernest is constantly experimenting to determine "which plant works where." We were particularly impressed with the scores of perennials, rare Texas styrax, huge rusty blackhaw viburnums and the butterfly/hummingbird display garden. Ernest uses lots of compost and no pest management products. Medina Gardens is indeed a valuable source for the serious native plant gardener.

Garden Furnishings

Cedar Crafted Creations
14150 Hwy 16 N
Medina, Texas 78055
830.589.7261 or 877.558.0618
www.craftedcedar.com
Hours: Mon–Fri 8–5, Sat 9–5, Sun by appointment

Porch swings, benches, sofas, chairs and tables are all shown in this little company's catalog. They can be as rustic or refined as you wish because every piece is custom built to your specifications with satisfaction guaranteed. "If at first we don't succeed, we'll try again until it's just right for you," says Chris Sheridan. "We have been in business for 18 years and are learning more everyday — we can make about anything anybody can think up!" There are stock items available in his shop, but he gets a kick out of making something to exactly fit the dimensions of the person who will be enjoying the piece.

Country Accents
8312 State Hwy 16 S
Bandera, Texas 78063
830.535.4979
www.countryaccentsantiques.com
Hours: Fri–Mon 10–6

Eva Lee's Country Accents is a fun and funky place to visit! Although this is a serious antique business (she shows at the Round Top Antique Fair), the decorative architectural fragments really spark a gardener's imagination. You will find an abundance of old cast iron fencing, gates, cupolas, double arbors, plants stands, statues, lawn chairs, willow furniture and custom bird houses. There are demonstration butterfly and herb gardens as well as antique roses and deer-resistant Texas natives. As Eva Lee says, "There is always something new." *Directions: Country Accents is 6.0 miles out of Bandera towards Pipe Creek.*

Blanco (Blanco County)

Garden Centers

Blanco Gardens
500 Main St
Blanco, Texas 78606
830.833.2433 or 888.494.2433
Hours: Tues–Sat 9–5:30

As Cheryl Foegelle told us, "Pete and I pretty much started from scratch. We opened Blanco Gardens in 1998, read a lot and asked a lot of questions. We learned what our customers needed and which growers sold the healthiest plants." The aviary with ringneck doves that we had enjoyed on our last visit to the nursery is still situated under old native pecan trees. Blanco Gardens carries lots of herbs, native trees, annuals and perennials As Cheryl says, "A little of everything." The plant material is most reasonably priced, and there is always a selection of glazed terra cotta pots from Italy and Viet Nam.

Boerne/Comfort (Kendall County)

Garden Centers

Maldonado Scenic Landscaping & Nursery
136 Adler Rd
Boerne, Texas 78006
830.249.4694
Hours: Mon–Sat 8–5

Maldonado's, owned and operated by Jesse Maldonado, Sr., opened 10 years ago and boasts depth in landscaping plants. There are two acres of trees from which to choose, and delivery and planting are available. At this all-organic nursery, you will find five greenhouses with a lot of natives, shade plants and deer-resistant plants. Bulk material is plentiful, and irrigation services are offered.
Directions: From Hwy 46, take a right on Main. Turn right again at Adler Rd.

R & A Nursery
6859 Hwy 27
Comfort, Texas 78013
830.995.3087
Hours: Mon–Fri 8–5; Sat 9–5 (10–5 in winter)

The first things that caught our eye as we turned into this small garden center were the display of large cacti and the vast array of stone, mulch, gravel, compost and statuary. The tidy greenhouse was filled with vegetables, perennials, hanging baskets, tropicals and more cacti and succulents...at least ten varieties of aloe. Having opened R & A Nursery only three years ago, Alfredo Avalos has become fascinated with growing cacti and succulents. His sister, Abby, is the design half of the team, and her colorful plant combinations, displayed both in pots and hanging baskets, are artistic delights. The nursery's own potting soil is available, as are four inch containers of annuals and perennials. Alfredo told us that they are planning to expand and that his wife is working on opening a gift shop. We say, "They're off to a great start!"

Specialty Nurseries

Hill Country African Violets
32005 I-10 W
Boerne, Texas 78006
830.249.2614
Hours: Daily 8–6

Explains owner Ken Froboese, "We began with just African violets 38 years ago and started the plant nursery about 28 years ago. From one small greenhouse, we have expanded to 11 greenhouses. Our goal is to offer the best quality blooming plants, foliage plants and hanging baskets available, and I am known for being 'particularly picky' with the growers. We normally keep over 150 varieties of herbs on hand year-round. If you're looking for African violets, our selection is one of the largest in the state." Not only does the nursery carry hundreds of the best varieties (both old and new), but also all types — miniatures, semi-miniatures, trailers and standards. In addition, there are quite a few gesneriads (violet related plants) and a full line of violet supplies. We loved the pleasant, shady atmosphere and were blown away by the gorgeous begonias, bougainvilleas, hydrangeas, hibiscus and fabulous fern baskets. "Visitors are always welcome!" says Ken. "At Hill Country, the staff is happy to offer advice on everything we sell."

Directions: Take Exit 543 off I-10. The nursery is on the west (two-way) access road 13.0 miles north of San Antonio's Outer Loop 1604 and 2.0 miles south of Boerne.

Garden Furnishings

El Artesanos
32127 I-10 W
Boerne, Texas 78006
830.249.9994
Hours: Mon–Sat 9–6, Sun 10–5

Zooming down I-10, we just happened upon this purveyor of "all things Mexican." El Artesanos is a treasure trove of Talavera pottery...all sizes, shapes and colors. You will also find equispales furniture, appealing tile insets for walls, fountains, statuary, benches and iron work. There are bins of gate hardware, lanterns, wind chimes and wall ornaments. This is a fun place to browse.

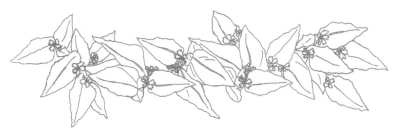

Fredericksburg (Gillespie County)

Garden Centers

Dodds Family Tree Nursery
515 West Main
Fredericksburg, Texas 78624
830.997.9571
Hours: Mon–Sat 8–6, Sun 12–5

John Dodds describes his nursery as "a very whimsical destination — a must to see in Fredericksburg." What we found was an ever-expanding test garden display area, a fascinating assortment of native plants and perennials that bloom and grow under the 200 feet tall canopy of a spreading live oak. We really enjoyed our stroll through the place and could have stayed all day. Dodds carries lots of interesting garden items, both hardscape and plant materials. Sales are in late May, and garden advice is always available. The company offers a full-service landscape department and floral division.

Wildseed Farms, Ltd.
425 Wildflower Hills
Fredericksburg, Texas 78624
830.990.8080 or 800.848.0078
www.wildseedfarms.com
Hours: Daily 9:30–6

Wildseed Farms, the largest working wildflower farm in the United States, now offers a lovely, complete garden center. It's stocked with every kind of drought-tolerant plant and good garden supplies. You'll find a large cacti display garden, a butterfly house and an array of pots and fountains that covers a full half-acre. There's something for everyone here. A quick stop may yield lunch and a packet of seeds or you may decide to make a whole day of it. There are fields where some of the 90 varieties of wildflowers and grasses are grown. The Market Center features the Bluebonnet Café, where the peach ice cream (in season) is a special treat, and an extensive gift shop offering all things Texan...wines, jellies, pickles, relishes, honey, salsas, barbeque sauces and much more. Check the calendar online for seasonal events.

Directions: The store is located on Hwy 290, 7.0 miles east of Fredericksburg.

Georgetown / Cedar Park / Leander / Liberty Hill / Round Rock (Williamson County)

Garden Centers

Forever Gardens
6770 Williams Dr (RR 2338)
Georgetown, Texas 78633
512.868.3373
www.forevergardens.net
Hours: Mon–Sat 8–5:30, Sun 10–4 (spring–fall); winter hours vary, so call ahead

Tricia and Jon Martin have always loved gardening, and their charming six-year-old garden center displays an ambience that comes from a love of plants (her passion) coupled with a sense of design (his bailiwick). Jon does a lot of landscape design and installation. Located just a mile and a half west of Sun City, this artful nursery is brimming with low-maintenance trees, shrubs, herbs and perennials — mostly things the local deer tend to shun! Their website features a hand-drawn map of the garden layout. "This garden is all-organic except for one rose fungicide," Tricia explains. The couple hosts seminars on the benefits of growing organically. Don't miss their Fall Fest in October.

McIntire's Garden Center
303 Leander Rd
Georgetown, Texas 78626
512.863.8243
www.mcintiresgarden.com
Hours: Mon–Sat 8–6, Sun 11–5

When first we visited McIntire's, Ruby McIntire was on hand to show us around. More recently, Ruby's son Mark Ney, a Certified Nursery Professional, shared his time with us. This nursery, which has been family-operated since 1976, specializes in native and hardy plants. In addition to a large selection of trees and shrubs, you will find cacti, tropicals, vines, seasonal color and pond and bog plants. They also carry fountains, birdbaths and Christmas trees in all sizes. The company provides landscape consultation and design, as well as an annual program of lawn care fertilization. You will find lots of organic products, including Back to Earth and liquid seaweed. As Mark says, "We offer our customers an organic product first." The staff is friendly and professional, and there is a fall sale in October and a spring sale in May. Be sure to check out their website for ideas, information and directions.

Round Rock Gardens
901 Sam Bass Rd
Round Rock, Texas 78681
512.255.3353
www.roundrockgardens.com
Hours: Mon–Sat 9–6, Sun 10–5

(LISTING CONTINUED ON THE NEXT PAGE)

(CONTINUED)

Owned by Jeff Ramert since 2002, this nursery now focuses on natives and hardy species adapted to the Central Texas environment. Do-it-yourself gardeners are catered-to here, and the designer on staff specializes in refurbishing old gardens. The staff has years of horticulture experience. There's an array of fruit trees that have been recommended by the Williamson County Extension Service and a lot of houseplants, too. You'll find bedding plants year-round and over 20 varieties of crepe myrtles, plus basic shrubs and trees. We were happy to discover an impressive display of organic products, including the entire Lady Bug line. There was also a big selection of pots and tools when we visited. We found it an especially pleasant place to shop because so many of the plants are displayed under the shade of large old trees.

Specialty Nurseries

Hill Country Water Gardens and Nursery
1407 North Bell Blvd.
Cedar Park, Texas 78613
512.260.5050
www.hillcountrywatergardens.com
Hours: Mon–Sat 9–6, Sun 11–5 (summer); call for winter hours

With water spilling from at least 50 to 75 sources, this destination nursery provides a multi-sensory experience. You'll find an abundance of pots. There are glazed Chinese vessels of varying sizes, shapes and colors and Big Bend stone planters, including patterned and textured ones. There are tanks filled with koi and goldfish of all kinds and a great selection of water plants. There are Japanese lanterns, tufa rock for rock gardens, pumps and filters, and books on ponds and pond building. Over the years, owner Steve Kainer has added nursery stock (lots of natives and unusual tropicals) to enhance the water features that are set under a canopy of huge, old live oaks. In other words, you'll find it all at Hill Country Water Gardens and Nursery, including inspiration and friendly, knowledgeable service. Seminars are held often, and sales are coordinated with these events. Be sure and check their website and treat yourself to a visit!
Directions: Follow old Hwy 183 (not the toll road) through Cedar Park almost to Leander.

Garden Furnishings

Georgetown Fireplace & Patio
8 Sierra Way
Georgetown, Texas 78626
512.863.8574
Hours: Mon–Fri 9:30–6, Sat 9:30–5

With its large inventory, Georgetown Fireplace & Patio offers a variety of outdoor furnishings. The lines carried are Tropitone, Mallin and Lloyd Flanders, which come in a wide selection of wrought iron, cast aluminum and outdoor wicker. You will also find wooden swings and rockers, hammocks, umbrellas, replacement cushions and patio heaters and fireplaces. A helpful staff is always ready to assist you, and there are numerous newspaper, TV and radio ads to alert you to special sales.

Mind Over Metal
4050 North Hwy 183
Liberty Hill, Texas 78642
512.258.7000 or 800.320.1076
www.mindovermetal.com

As Richard Schultz told us, "Mind Over Metal has been in business since 1976 making heirloom-quality metal furnishings and architectural appointments. The pieces are produced by a small, tight-knit group of Texas artisans who pride themselves on dedication to their craft and attention to detail." They've produced handsome chairs, rockers and tables, plus garden gates, fountains, figurative and abstract sculpture, gazebo spires, railings and trellises. They work in bronze, copper, wrought iron and stainless steel, and they supply fossilized limestone tops for tables. Call Richard for an appointment if you are interested in the work. They can custom-make almost anything to meet your special needs. The website shows a multitude of creative items and 12 different metal finishes. We were especially impressed by the Squash Blossom fountain and the intricate railings for stairways and balconies.

Kerrville (Kerr County)

Garden Centers

Alltex Nursery & Landscape
1302 Bandera Hwy
Kerrville, Texas 78028
830.895.5242
www.alltexlandscapes.com
Hours: Mon–Sat 8–5:30

Having been in the landscape design and installation business for 18 years, Danny and Wendy Massey opened Alltex Nursery four years ago. The landscaping services include every-thing from patios and ponds to gazebos and irrigation systems. When we visited, this tidy nursery was filled with color! They also offer native perennials, shrubs, ground covers, hanging baskets, cacti, deer-resistant plants and seeds. We found a nice selection of fountains, statuary, birdbaths, pots and Mexican wrought iron. This all-organic nursery carries Medina, Hastagro, Gardenville, Greensand and GarlicGP products. Alltex employs two Texas Certified Nursery Professionals, and, as Manager Mitzi McCollum told us, "We are still growing."

Maldonado Nursery Landscape
3603 Memorial Blvd
Kerrville, Texas 78028
830.896.6869

(LISTING CONTINUED ON THE NEXT PAGE)

CH 9

(CONTINUED)

Hours: Mon–Sat 8–5

Maldonado Nursery Landscape was opened by Ed Maldonado in 1976. The first thing we noticed when we arrived at the nursery was the quantity of hardscape materials — stones, gravel, sand and more. As we found out, this company does a great deal of landscape design and installation with a Texas-registered landscape architect, Hector Lozano, on staff. We also were impressed with the huge selection of trees and shrubs, many of which are grown on site. A rainy day allowed us only a glimpse of the extensive inventory, but we did visit the greenhouse. This large space was attractively arranged and brimming with seasonal color and tropicals.

Directions: This nursery is on the southeast side of town, across from the VA Hospital on Hwy 27 (Memorial Blvd)

The Plant Haus 2
528 Jefferson St
Kerrville, Texas 78028
830.792.4444

Hours: Mon–Sat 8–6, Sun 10–4 (Mar–Oct); Mon–Sat 8–5 (Nov–Feb); Sun 8–5 (Nov & Dec)

Despite a very windy day, Manager Karen Smith bravely gave us a guided tour of the Plant Haus 2, which opened in 1989. This predominately organic nursery carries many plants native to the Texas Hill Country, as well as trees, shrubs, annuals, perennials, hanging baskets, tropicals, bulbs and vegetable seeds. You will find accessories and gifts, and we were most impressed with the gorgeous display of Talavera pots. According to one friend who has a beautifully landscaped property, "I buy everything at the Plant Haus. The plants do well, and the service is always friendly."

Directions: Take Hwy 27 west of the town center and turn right on Clay and left on Jefferson.

Specialty Nurseries

Natives of Texas
4256 Medina Hwy
Kerrville, Texas 78028
830.896.2169
www.nativesoftexas.com

Hours: Mon–Sat 9–4, Sun 11–4

The late Betty Winningham began this wonderful native plant nursery. She was a retired math teacher who "fell in love" with the Texas madrone, and began growing them from seed, two the first year, then ten, then 100..."I killed a few in the learning process," she admitted to us when we visited the nursery twelve years ago. We're so happy that her husband, David, is continuing to run this place. People come from all over the Hill Country to see the native demonstration garden Betty and David established on their beautiful ranch and buy the plants they so lovingly propagated. This nursery grows a wide range of plants that includes trees, shrubs, vines, cacti, grasses and lots of native perennials. The website is a delight; its online catalog lists every plant. Make an appointment with Mr. Winningham, who can tell you which plants are not favored by deer and will be happy to share all he knows about the cultural requirements of the plants he sells. Accessibility is difficult.

Directions: It is located 11.0 miles south of Kerrville along a winding, scenic section of Hwy 16. Look for the sign on the right side of the road.

Killeen (western Bell County)

Garden Centers

Oma's Garten Pflanzen
2301 Old FM 440 Rd
Killeen, Texas 76549
254.526.8792
www.omasgartenpflanzen.com
Hours: Mon–Fri 9–6, Sun 11–5

This nursery, owned by Walter and Randa Daude, is all-organic and stocks locally-grown plants that are proven to be well adapted to the area. Oma's carries natives as well as low-maintenance plants in a wide variety of trees, shrubs, grasses, perennials, annuals, bulbs, herbs and certified-organic seeds. There is also a good selection of deer-resistant plant material! Seminars with an impressive roster of speakers are held at 10:00 a.m. on Saturdays. Check the website for further information about them as well as a number of other topics, and be sure to pick up your free gardening calendar with any purchase. Even on a busy day, we enjoyed our chat with Randa and found the staff helpful at this tidy nursery. "We can assist you with plant information and advice on 'smartscaping' your yard."

Marble Falls / Briggs / Spicewood (Burnet County)

Garden Centers

Backbone Valley Nursery
4201 FM 1980
Marble Falls, Texas 78654
830.693.9348
www.backbonevalleynursery.com
Hours: Mon–Sat 8–5, Sun 1–5

Finding a nursery new to us is always a special treat, and Backbone Valley Nursery certainly filled the bill. Owners Ben and Dale Robertson and David Martin grow all of the numerous trees, which vary in size from 15 to 300 gallons. Biologist Jessica Burg (soon to be Robertson) gave us the guided tour, and we were amazed to see such huge old segos and agaves. This nursery offers many native plants as well as seasonal color, and the large array of orchids is sure to please. They blend their own soils and provide beneficial insects, organic products and compost tea. Backbone Valley offers full landscape design and installation, and the owners work with Master Gardeners and garden clubs. Their good looking pots are from China and Thailand. And one more plus...buy four trees and get the fifth one free.
Directions: From downtown Marble Falls, take 1431 W about 4.0 miles. At the light, turn right on FM 1980. The nursery is 3.2 miles on the right.

Specialty Nurseries

Spicewood Spines Cactus Nursery
9900 Hwy 71
Spicewood, Texas 78669
830.693.5466
www.spicewoodspines.com
Hours: Wed–Fri 9–5, Sat & Sun 9–6

Mark and Kathryn Rehfield describe their cactus nursery and art gallery as "the best kept secret in Spicewood." They carry a wide variety of cold-hardy cactus and succulents from around the world. Although not cold-hardy, the large selection of succulents native to Madagascar and South Africa was impressive. There were lots of containers, and we were particularly taken with the handsome, hand-carved limestone planters for displaying your cacti collection. Check their informative website for ordering information.

Wright's Nursery
6040 FM 2657
Briggs, Texas 78608
512.489.2239
www.wrightsnursery.net
Hours: Mon–Sat 9–6

This four-acre rural nursery in northeast Burnet County has been in business for only six years, but both Bobby and Barbara Briggs were born into gardening families who "grew vegetables to live and flowers to enjoy." As Barbara, a Brit by birth, explains, "We like trying out new plants and really enjoy finding uncommon native plants. We try to teach our customers about natives and alternatives to overused landscape plantings. What we sell (with few exceptions) is grown here, so we know it will grow under the Texas sun." Among the many hard-to-find perennials we discovered were big red sage *(Salvia penstemonoides)* Texas betony *(Stachys coccinea)*, white and pink turk's cap *(Malvaviscus spp.)* and wild foxglove *(Penstemon cobaea)*. You'll also find heirloom and heat tolerant tomatoes and other veggie starts. Although Wright's is only partially wheelchair/stroller accessible, it is definitely a "find" for the serious gardener who loves what grows best in this region. Its business is both wholesale and retail. An availability list online will keep you informed. Call for directions from your area.

Garden Furnishings

Pottery Ranch
6000 Hwy 281 N
Marble Falls, Texas 78654
830.693.0100
www.hillcountryteak.com
Hours: Daily 10–6

Put Pottery Ranch on your list of places to visit if you are looking for outdoor furniture and accessories for a rustic Texas ranch house. It is known as "Hwy 281's Must Stop Mega Shop." Owner Scott Kilpatrick's inventory includes chimeneas (especially made for the company), a good selection of pots, teak and wrought iron furniture, fountains, outdoor light poles and barbecue pits. In addition, the large and well-stocked gift shop/interior store offers "even more things Texan."

Woodscaping Company
2409 Commerce St
Marble Falls, Texas 78654
830.693.6377
http://woodscaping.com
Hours: By appointment only

This collection is handcrafted for those who enjoy the relaxation and comfort of the outdoor environment. The basic structure of each piece of the company's furniture is specifically designed to follow the natural curvature of the body, hence "ergonomically designed." Non-corrosive screws, quality heart- and clear-grades of redwood, plus the addition of glue joints make each piece durable and weather resistant. As Rod Oberhaus told us, "They are made one-at-a-time for a lifetime of pleasure."

Directions: From Hwy 281 on the north side of Marble Falls, Commerce St is 1 block east of the highway across from Walmart.

San Marcos / Wimberley (Hays County)

Garden Centers

Garden-Ville of San Marcos
2212 Ranch Rd 12
San Marcos, Texas 78666
512.754.0060
www.garden-ville.com
Hours: Mon–Sat 8:30–5:30; Sun 12–4; Closed week between Christmas and New Year's Day; closed Sundays in January

Garden-Ville of San Marcos sells and promotes only environmentally sound gardening supplies and products. The plants you'll find here are either native or well adapted to this part of Texas. Says manager Juanita Vale, "Our goal is to turn people on to the joys of gardening ...naturally!" This charming little garden center specializes in hard-to-find plants. It carries an eclectic mix of garden accessories and gift items and takes pride in personalized services such as repotting plants and diagnosing plant problems. There's a very good supply of rock, which is sold by the pound for small projects. The bulk soils, soil amendments and mulches are

(LISTING CONTINUED ON THE NEXT PAGE)

(CONTINUED)

awesome, and what is unusual is that the company will let you buy just a bucketful if that's all you need. (Bring your own bucket.) Delivery of bulk products is also available. The staff provides expert advice, and you'll find fact sheets on many gardening topics.

Directions: Travel west from downtown San Marcos on RR 12. The nursery is on the north side in a red log cabin.

King Feed and Hardware
14210 RR 12
Wimberley, Texas 78676
512.847.2618
Hours: Mon–Fri 8–7, Sat 8–6, Sun 10–4

The name might suggest your typical farm store, but the garden center here is everything a good hometown nursery should be. The plants are selectively chosen and carefully tended, and the "hard goods" in every department are top-quality. Its success can be credited to Tim Thompson, who started the garden branch of this 75-year-old feed store in the parking lot in 1988. By '99 he had expanded it into a shady, pleasant area on the north side of the property. The cache of colorful containers, visible from the road, is sufficient to attract gardeners. What they find inside the gate is a surprising array of native and hardy adapted trees, shrubs, perennials, ground covers, tropical plants and shade plants, with good signage to lead the way. Tim writes a monthly newsletter that's available at the checkout desk and a monthly column for the *Wimberley Valley News and Views*. He observes, "We have a very good staff of experienced gardeners, and we are working hard to meet the needs of this changing and growing community."

Specialty Nurseries

Ellie's Greenhouse
5013 Airport Hwy 21
San Marcos, Texas 78666
512.392.0507
Hours: Mon–Sat 9–5:30, Sun 11–5

This is the place to go for big, beautiful houseplants at very, very reasonable prices. Owner Elida De Leon also keeps her several greenhouses brimming with hanging baskets, seasonal color and even a good selection of deer-resistant perennials. She has some trees, shrubs and herbs as well.

Directions: Go east of I-35 on Hwy 80. Turn north on Hwy 21 and proceed 3.5 miles. It's on the left.

Jade Gardens Bonsai Nursery
12404 RR 12
Wimberley, Texas 78676
512.847.2514
www.wimberley-tx.com/~bonsaijg
Hours: Vary with the season; call ahead.

"All art reflects the personality of the artist, the environment and the culture in which he or she works," says Chuck Ware. In patiently sculpting trees, he seeks to create an image that brings peace and serenity to a hectic world. He particularly enjoys working with trees native to Central and South Texas (trees with which Texans can identify) to demonstrate that the ancient art of bonsai is "not something foreign or exotic." Drawing on his own background as a high school science teacher and his interest in art and philosophy, Ware began his collection in the early '80s. He and his wife Pat later developed The Central Texas Bonsai Exhibit beside their home. There is no admission charge to view this extraordinary display of mature living sculpture. For sale here are over 100 species of trees from 1 gallon to specimen-size, both finished or ready to be planted, and all the pottery, slabs, tools and books you could want for taking up this art form. It's a joy to see the plants and visit with this charming couple.

Wimberley Herbs
818 Mountain Crest
Wimberley, Texas 78676
512.847.3335
Hours: By appointment

Sara Holland's home garden features displays of Mediterranean, Mexican and Asian culinary herbs. She grows everything she sells, and keeps a large stock of 75 to 100 varieties in her greenhouse throughout most of the year. She has a nature trail and desert garden, which lead to The Herb Shed, a gardening and herb gift shop where you'll find bird houses, bird feeders, dried herbs for cooking, herbal soaps and books about herbs. She also teaches classes on her favorite subject!

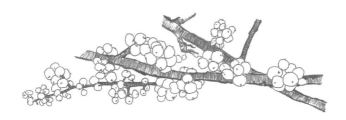

Garden Furnishings

Star Antiques
301 River Rd
Wimberley, Texas 78676
512.847.9970
Hours: Wed–Sat 10–5 or by appointment

You never know what treasure you may find here! Star Antiques usually has a huge cache of trellises, topiaries, gates, arbors, plant stands, benches, birdbaths and urns sitting in front of the little house that Lisa Kiefer converted to a shop. "I've specialized in vintage lighting for 25 years," said Lisa. "I love having an outdoor area to display lights, architectural embellishments and garden accessories. Check out our new, and very popular tree light fixtures."

Una Tierra Distante
110 Old Kyle Rd
Wimberley, Texas 78676
512.847.2618
Hours: Mon, Wed–Sat 9:30–5:30, Sun 12–5

Kim Hunt's collection of pottery, accessories and folk art is indeed drawn from distant lands — Bulgaria, Morocco, India, Greece, Italy and several Asian and Latin American countries. Each piece is "handpicked." There is always a most unusual selection of large ceramic pots and urns; most are high-fired glazed ceramics, but a few are raku-style wares made of Vietnamese blue clay. You'll also find birdbaths, sculpture and pedestals here. She receives new shipments every couple of weeks, and her inventory sells quickly. Una Tierra Distante's shady, spacious setting provides a very pleasant setting to shop or browse.

10
Red Rolling Plains

Red Rolling Plains

Abilene, San Angelo and Wichita Falls serve as the major markets within this vast region that spans West Texas from the Red River to a line some 50 miles south of San Angelo. The stark and rugged landscape of this part of Texas may be an acquired taste, but there is great beauty to be discovered here. It's especially lovely in late spring and early fall when rains green the grasses and bring on bursts of wildflowers. The undulating mid-grass prairies alternate with lacy mesquite groves that may include small junipers and shinnery oaks. As you travel west, the land gradually becomes more rough and broken.

Red soils are usually visible between the plants that naturally grow throughout most of this region. Islands of sandy soil appear irregularly, usually on high ground, and soils adjacent to streams tend to be gravelly. Regional gardeners will find that the sandy loams and clayey soils support a variety of native flora. Because limestone-based soils exist alongside red sand or clay, gardeners are well advised to have their soils tested before deciding on the plant materials that will best grow on their properties.

Rainfall varies from about 20 to 27 inches per year. Although the entire region falls within Zone 7, winter temperatures occasionally drop below zero. Summers are extremely hot and dry. For this reason, more and more gardeners here are learning to appreciate such native plants as the lacy mesquite trees, flowering yuccas and beautiful blue-green sand sagebrush.

Between Abilene and San Angelo, white hills (a northern extension of the limestone of the Edwards Plateau) called the Callahan Divide stand in sharp contrast to the overall reddish color of the landscape. **Abilene State Park** is located in this semi-arid region of short prairie grass. (16 miles southwest of Abilene, through Buffalo Gap, on FM 89, then on Park Rd 32 to the entrance). You'll also discover brushland, and wooded stream valleys filled with juniper, cedar, native pecan, elm, live oaks, hackberry, Texas red oak, red bud and wildflowers. For thousands of years, Buffalo Gap (now a town with a population of 469), provided passage through the divide for the migrating herds. Later it served as a route for cattle trails and wagon trains headed for California.

The City of Abilene has done a particularly good job of introducing native plants into its public parks and **Abilene Zoological Gardens**. San Angelo's approach has been quite different; it's city parks focus on the surprisingly verdant Concho River and a series of "plant collections." The **San Angelo Nature Center** takes visitors through three different native ecosystems and a large wetland that resulted from an accidental 25-year leak in a dam!

Many of the region's place names refer to striking natural features in the landscape. Big Spring was named for a natural spring that served as the only watering place for herds of bison, antelope and wild horses within a 60-mile radius. Mesquite, shin oak, skunkbush sumac, redberry juniper and various cacti cling to the rocky slopes at **Big Spring State Park**, which is located off I-20 on FM 700. In 1936 the CCC used limestone quarried on the site to build a 3-mile drive that loops around the mountain following the ledge of limestone rimrock that caps the bluff. From here the views are spectacular. Three ecological regions merge in the area around the park. To the north and east is Rolling Plains; to the south is the Edwards Plateau; to the west is the High Plains. The mixing of ecological regions results in a variety of plant and animal life.

The naming of Wichita Falls was easy, but for most of the 20th century there were no falls to be found! Today a wooded walkway provides access to the Wichita River where a manmade waterfall recalls natural falls that washed out in a flood in the late 19th century. Nearby, the new **River Bend Nature Center** in Wichita Falls offers 15 acres of trails, wetlands and ponds to explore. Here you'll discover the Ruby N. Priddy Butterfly Conservatory where plants and butterflies from five different Texas native plant habitats are exhibited under a soaring glass roof.

In the northwestern reaches of the Red Rolling Plains at **Copper Breaks State Park** between Quanah and Crowell, visitors enjoy the rugged, scenic beauty of red mesas covered with grasses, mesquite and thick juniper breaks, plus abundant wildlife. The Juniper Ridge Nature Trail includes 24 information points. Prior to the arrival of early settlers, this region was the realm of the Comanche and Kiowa tribes, and part of the official Texas longhorn herd resides here now. Nearby, on State Hwy 6 between Quanah and the park, observe the prominent hills to the east that make up Medicine Mound, a ceremonial and religious site of the Comanches.

Public Gardens and Nature Preserves to Visit

Abilene (Taylor County)

Abilene Zoological Gardens
2050 Zoo Ln
Abilene, Texas 79602
325.676.6085
www.abilenetx.com/zoo/
Hours: Daily 9–5 (front gate closes at 4:30); Thurs 9–9 (Memorial Day–Labor Day). Closed Thanksgiving, Christmas Day and New Year's Day.
Admission: $4 (ages 13–59), $3 (60+), $2 (ages 3–12), free (children under 3)

This zoo garden offers inspiration to gardeners looking for alternatives to standard annual bedding plants and imported trees and shrubs. Rather than landscape with water-guzzling exotic plants, the city's landscape architects have chosen to focus on plants indigenous to Abilene. Especially interesting is its wetland habitat exhibit, which features native riparian plants. The wildflower/butterfly exhibit is filled with native cold-hardy perennials, including a fine collection of salvias.
Directions: The Gardens are near the intersection of Hwy 36 and Loop 322 in Nelson Park.

San Angelo (Tom Green County)

International Lily Pond
Civic League Park
Harris Ave at Park St
San Angelo, Texas
325.657.4279
Hours: Daily dawn to dusk
Admission: free

This noteworthy collection of water lilies in Civic League Park includes the world's largest cultivar, 'Victoria', which grows up to eight feet in diameter with fragrant flowers 18-inches wide. The newly expanded ponds include many old favorites along with some rare and endangered varieties. Special lighting allows you to view the night-blooming species. Kenneth Landon, director and chief horticulturist for the collection, is available to conduct tours. Nearby (in the same park) is the San Angelo Municipal Rose Garden at Park St and West Beauregard. The Sunken Garden Park at Avenue D and Abe St features a fabulous canna collection. *Directions: Civic League park is 3 blocks west of Hwy 87 in the downtown area. From the rose garden to the canna collection, go back to Hwy 87 on Beauregard and go south about a mile to Avenue D.*

San Angelo Nature Center
7409 Knickerbocker Rd
San Angelo Texas 76904
325.942.0121
Hours: Tues–Sat 12–5; Trails: Daily dawn to dusk; closed all major holidays.
Admission: $2 (4–adult)

The Nature Center here is a regional museum located at Lake Nasworthy in Mary Lee Park. It features a Xeriscape Garden that displays native shrubs, trees and flowers and trails that include a walk through nearby Spring Creek Wetland, an astonishing 260-acre wetland in the midst of semi-desert which resulted from a serendipitous leak in the dam! Another trail at Spillway Rd takes visitors through three different ecosystems found in the immediate area. Twenty-two markers along the trail correspond to a guide that is available at the Nature Center. This guide identifies animal tracks and provides information and pictures of some of the grasses, shrubs and trees that form this preserve. Interpreted tours, conducted by Nature Center naturalists, are available on a limited basis. Call to make reservations.
Directions: Take Hwy 87 south from the city. Turn right on Knickerbocker Rd to the south shore of Lake Nasworthy.

Wichita Falls (Wichita County)

River Bend Nature Center
2200 Third St
Wichita Falls, Texas 76301
940.767.0843
www.riverbendnaturecenter.org
Hours: Fri & Sat 10–4, Sun 12–4
Admission: $5 (adults), $4 (seniors/students/military), $3 (children 4–12)

We were thrilled to visit the stunning new Ruby N. Priddy Butterfly Conservatory right after it opened in 2007! It is unique among facilities of its kind in the United States because five different Texas native plant habitats are growing here under the glass roof, and only the butterflies that normally rely on the plants of those regions inhabit this building. (Most butterfly exhibits feature tropical species.) There is a fascinating cross-section of the plants, insects, reptiles, fish, hummingbirds, quail and other animals to be discovered here. The J.S. Bridwell Terrace also displays native shrubs and grasses in planting beds. It connects the Conservatory to a big new stone structure pavilion with soaring ceilings and comfortable table seating for up to 300 people, accessible restrooms and drinking fountains. A new Prairie Pathway leads down to 15 acres of trails, wetlands and ponds to walk and enjoy, as well. Nearby in Lucy Park you'll also find a 0.25-mile walking trail to Wichita Falls Waterfall (reminiscent of falls on the Wichita River that washed away in the flood of 1886). The water cascades down 54 feet of massive red sandstone blocks.

Directions: Take Hwy 277 (Seymour Hwy) west from I-44. Turn right on Sunset Dr, and left on 3rd.

Red Rolling Plains Resources

Abilene (Taylor County)

Garden Centers

Baack's Landscaping & Nursery
1842 Matador
Abilene, Texas 79605
325.692.7763
Hours: Mon–Sat 8–5:30, Sun 1–5 (spring)

Over the years Baack's has established its reputation as a garden center for "the serious gardener," offering hard-to-find selections and wide varieties of well-adapted perennials, herbs and shrubs. It was the first in the area to carry antique roses and David Austin English roses, and it's known throughout the area for zonal geraniums and bougainvilleas. Baack's has full landscaping design and services available, and the nursery staff will also deliver merchandise upon request. Sales are held Mother's Day and Memorial Day weekends. Staff members offer seminars on organic gardening, roses, planting container gardens and other areas of interest. Not all areas of the nursery are wheelchair/stroller accessible.

Garden Place
4002 North First St
Abilene, Texas 79603
325.676.0086
Hours: Mon–Sat 9–6; Sun 12–5 (spring and Christmas only)

This complete garden center specializes in perennials and herbs. Trees here range from small to large container-grown stock. Garden Place also offers water plants, pond supplies and disappearing fountains as well as tropicals, hanging baskets and container plants. Soil, soil amendments, organic supplies and a large selection of terra cotta pots are also available. Indoors, there are houseplants, pottery and fountains, books, tools and garden accessories. Two landscape designers, one floral designer and two licensed irrigators are on staff to help with your gardening needs. Tim McCloskey, the nursery's floral designer, maintains a beautiful garden with three ponds and hundreds of plants at 2902 S. Willis, where Garden Place customers are welcome. Color starts in early April and continues until frost, and Tim invites you to "wander and enjoy."

Garden World
2850 South Clack St
Abilene, Texas 79606
325.698.2401
Hours: Mon–Sat 9–6, Sun 1–6

Three Certified Texas Nursery Professionals are on duty at this complete garden center to help do-it-yourself gardeners. The company takes pride in the quantity and quality of its plant materials, which include trees and shrubs as well as natives, tropicals, hanging baskets and cacti. You'll find soils, mulches, tools and organic supplies as well as pottery, statuary, fountains and gardening gifts.

Specialty Nurseries

The Gardens of the Southwest
5250 South 14th St (US Hwy 277 S.)
Abilene, Texas 79605
325.692.1457
Hours: Mon–Sat 8–5

Our first impression of The Gardens of the Southwest was a lovely surprise in its residential setting. It is set back from the street among beautiful, large trees and raised stone planters. Although this firm carries a good selection of garden furniture, building materials and pots, The Gardens of the Southwest specializes in trees and shrubs. The trees come in all sizes (both container and ball and burlap) and include native, ornamental and fruit trees. The shrubs are hearty for the area and include several conifers. Rodney Fulcher, who is the owner and a Texas registered landscape architect, told us, "I've been in business since 1971 and have done a lot of repeat business...three, four, even five residences for some people. We're good 'problem solvers' and this firm is quality and customer-oriented."

The firm carries an array of large, very handsome terra cotta containers, Italian urns and other planters made of brass, copper, ceramic and stone. There is statuary by Austin productions, metal fountains and furniture (mostly Brown Jordan) from which to choose. The prices at The Gardens of the Southwest are competitive, and Mr. Fulcher has years of experience to offer and is a most welcome speaker at area garden clubs.

Garden Furnishings

Extreme Exteriors
1800 Industrial
Abilene, Texas 79602
325.698.2410
Hours: Mon–Fri 9–6, Sat 9–4

Extreme Exteriors, which has been open for two years, is an outdoor living store with very attractive displays to fire your imagination. The company carries Hanamint furniture and Design Décor slate table tops. You will also find accessories such as umbrellas, outdoor tableware, custom and replacement cushions and more. There is a landscape and maintenance division, which has been in business for 12 years and provides lawn and tree care, as well design advice.

Fire Escape
501 Hickory
Abilene, Texas 79601
323.672.3473
www.myhearthandpatio.com
Hours: Mon–Fri 9:30–5:30, Sat 10–3

Fire Escape is a merchandiser of garden related products, and the company's outdoor displays provide great ideas for furnishing your own garden area. There is wrought iron furniture by Meadowcraft and Tropitone, and the outdoor fireplaces are made by Majestic and Vanguard. You will also find complete outdoor kitchens and fire pits as well as fireplace and barbecue accessories.

S & S Ornamental Iron
1314 FM 89
Abilene, Texas 79606
325.698.3601
Hours: Mon–Fri 8–5:30

S & S Iron Works fabricates wrought iron tables, benches, arbors and gazebos in addition to custom garden gates and fences and decorative iron stairways and handrails. Visitors are welcome although the business is not wheelchair/stroller accessible.

Mertzon (Irion County)

Specialty Nurseries

Native Ornamentals
P.O: Box 997
Mertzon, Texas 76941
325.835.2021
Hours: Times vary, call ahead

Native Ornamentals is a small nursery that grows plants native to the Chihuahuan Desert and Hill Country regions of Texas. Steve Lewis told us, "Our goal is to provide plant materials that are low maintenance and resistant to pest and weather extremes." About 95% of the species are unknown in the nursery trade — such plants as paper-shell piñon, seven-leaf creeper and unusual strains of desert willow, to mention a few. The plants are small (generally 1 gallon containers), but truly rare. Valorie Lewis added, "We grow a lot of perennial wild-flowers, shrubs of various shapes and sizes and larger trees, such as burr oak and chinquapin. We also try to find plants that are fragrant as well as those that bloom at different times of the year." Programs are available to interested groups statewide. Native Ornamentals is situated on several levels, making wheelchair/stroller accessibility difficult.

Directions: The nursery is located off Hwy 67. Turn west onto Main St. Go approximately 6 blocks and turn at the sign.

San Angelo (Tom Green County)

Garden Centers

Brannan Nursery & Landscape
4044 South Bryant
San Angelo, Texas 76903
325.653.7723
Hours: Mon–Fri 9–5:30, Sat 9–5

This complete garden center offers landscape services as well as a varied selection of plant material. What really caught our attention were the wonderful custom hanging baskets and the beautiful, tall bougainvilleas. Brannan's carries soil, soil amendments and organic supplies along with wrought iron furniture, concrete benches and garden tools and accessories.

M & R Nursery
1601 W. Beauregard
San Angelo, Texas 76901
325.653.3341
Hours: Mon–Sat 8–6, Sun 12–5

M & R Nursery is a very tidy garden center with healthy plants, including cacti and tropical houseplants. You will also find soil, soil amendments, organic supplies and garden tools as well as garden accessories and wrought iron and concrete furniture.

Olive's Nursery
3402 Sherwood Way
San Angelo, Texas 76901
325.949.3756
Hours: Mon–Sat 9–6 (9–5 in summer)

W.E. Olive, grandfather of present owner Tommy Olive, opened Olive Seed Store in 1942 in downtown San Angelo. In 1951 Tommy's father, John, moved the store and started carrying quality nursery stock. "When my mother, Mary, came on board, she brought a flair for color and garden accessories. We try to maintain a setting that's beautiful and comfortable, not a lot of steel and concrete." This complete garden center is also dedicated to keeping the nursery business local. Having started the move towards organics 20 years ago, Tommy formulated his own bio-stimulant, (Olive Oil) which has revived the soil for many clients' gardens. Olive's not only has a very knowledgeable staff but also is competitive in price, even with the chain stores. "Just bring in their ad," he challenges. Long-time customers eagerly await the annual Christmas half-price sale on December 26th and the gift clearance sale on July 5th.

When you visit San Angelo's international water lily display, you will be motivated to visit Olive's Nursery. As Debbie Olive told us, "We have been in the water gardening business for 30 years, long before it became so fashionable! We've had lots of experience selling, building and installing water features." This nursery carries not only water plants, but also materials, equipment, goldfish and koi, supplies and books. There are also many free informative pamphlets and a water garden display, complete with a waterfall and some "wild life." But Tommy warns, "Please don't bring your boat. The Coast Guard patrols our pond for speeders!"

Scherz Landscape Co.
2225 Knickerbocker
San Angelo, Texas 76904
325.944.0511
www.scherzlandscape.com
Hours: Mon–Fri 9–6, Sat 9–5; Sun 1–5 (March–June, Nov–Dec)

This company, established in 1927 by Phillip Scherz, is "as well-rooted in the West Texas soil as the nursery stock we grow and sell." The firm grows 85–90% of its plant materials, which assures the customer of stock that's acclimated to West Texas growing conditions. Scherz is both a retail and wholesale nursery, and it offers landscape design and construction. There are two designers, a licensed irrigator and a professional staff to assist you. The maintenance department provides TLC (Total Landscape Care) with a variety of services. The patio and display areas ensure a pleasant shopping experience and are a source of inspiration. You'll be pleased to find such a large diversity of plant materials and sizes. The stock ranges from trees to seeds, with lots of seasonal color and native plants. Incredible bougainvilleas! Says

(LISTING CONTINUED ON THE NEXT PAGE)

(CONTINUED)

Kyle Conway, "We have specific interest in growing specimen and unique items that do well in West Texas. We are producers of the "Concho Valley Live Oak" and "Scherz Green-Up Fertilizer." Look for bargains in September and October. Delivery is provided in the San Angelo area.

Specialty Nurseries

Magic Farm Greenhouses
7678 Country Club Rd
San Angelo, Texas 76904
325.944.0617
Hours: Daily 7–7; 7–6 (winter)

Magic Farm Greenhouses has been serving the San Angelo area for 25 years. The company offers greenhouse construction as well as a huge selection of bedding plants, hanging baskets, some tropicals and bagged compost and fertilizer. Magic Farm holds end-of-the-season sales, and the prices are exceptionally good. It is also great to know that the nursery will store your plants as well as deliver locally and to nearby towns.

Directions: From San Angelo, take Hwy 87 to the El Dorado exit and take the first right. Go 3.0 miles, take a sharp left on Country Club Rd and go 0.25 miles. You will see the five greenhouses.

Wichita Falls (Wichita County)

Garden Centers

Holt Nursery & Landscape
3913 Kell Blvd W
Wichita Falls, Texas 76308
940.691.4757
Hours: Mon–Fri 9–5, Sat 9–12

"Serving the Wichita Falls area since 1974," Holt Nursery & Landscape does mostly landscape construction and irrigation. However, the company carries ornamental trees and shrubs, annuals, perennials and bulbs, fruit trees, vegetable starts, hanging baskets and cacti as well. Holt's also provides landscape design, irrigation systems, sodding and hydromulching. Charles Astwood, who received a degree in horticulture from Texas Tech, is there to help with your landscape and irrigation needs.

Smith's Garden Town Farms
4940 Seymour Hwy
Wichita Falls, Texas 76310
940.692.7100
www.smithgardentown.com
Hours: Mon–Fri 8:30–5:30, Sat 9–5; Sun is seasonal, call ahead

Our first impression of Smith's Garden Town Farms was the bucolic scene in front with a lovely pond surrounded by a mass of Texas Star Hibiscus. Imagine our additional delight when we entered the very large state-of-the-art, computerized, climate controlled reception area and greenhouses. A welcome sight on a hot Texas day! And, a first-rate establishment by any standard! This wholesale/retail nursery has been in business for 60 years. Steve Smith and Katherine Smith, who is a Texas Certified Nursery Professional, are part of the third generation carrying on this family tradition. They grow all of their bedding plants and seasonal color (11,000 poinsettias, for example), and over 75 varieties of herbs. They stock Earth Kind roses, as well as beautiful bonsai and water plants. You will find everything from a large selection of furniture to books, bagged goods and Nature's Guide organics products. Smith's Garden Town holds seminars and publishes a newsletter every three to four months.

Wichita Valley Landscape
5314 Southwest Pkwy
Wichita Falls, Texas 76310
940.696.3082
Hours: Mon–Fri 8–6, Sat 9–6, Sun 12–6 (Sundays during spring and fall only)

"What makes Wichita Valley Landscape different from other nurseries in Wichita Falls is that this company specializes in native plants and organic products," says Paul Dowlearn. "It was the first nursery of its kind in North Texas and continues to stay a step ahead." He's convinced that today's consumer wants a low-maintenance landscape and safe pesticides. "We are constantly bringing in new plant material to experiment with in our area. This makes the business exciting for us and for our customers," he says. "We tend to have what can't be found elsewhere in our town. We're definitely not just another sales-oriented nursery!" The company offers handmade items (as opposed to mass-produced merchandise) and creates its own bonsai, water features and plant arrangements. It has a good collection of garden books and reference materials. He adds, "We especially enjoy working with people who want to develop more natural, easier-to-maintain properties. There are new horizons opening up in this part of the state, and we are proud to be a part of it." Wichita Valley actively supports garden clubs, municipal projects, a chapter of the native plant society and the River Bend Nature Works. At the River Bend Nature Center, Dowlearn designed the native gardens as well as interior gardens at the Ruby N. Priddy Butterfly Conservatory. Sales are random because everyday prices are competitive.

Specialty Nurseries

Shade Tree Nursery & Landscaping
3122 Old Iowa Park Rd
Wichita Falls, Texas 76305
940.322.9833

Hours: Mon–Sat 8–5:30; Sun 10–4 (March–May and Aug–Oct)

Red oaks, live oaks, cedar elms and red buds are among the native trees this company grows alongside such hardy non-natives as Austrian, black and slash pines, Chinese pistache, Bradford pears and purple plums, ranging in size from 5 gallon to sizable 6–7-inch caliper specimen trees. Shade Tree Nursery also carries a good selection of shrubs suitable for North Texas landscapes. With its 36-acre growing yard, this company can offer a good selection of topiaries and abundant fruit trees, as well. It sells topsoil by the truckload and will install anything from a single tree to a complete landscape. The site is partially accessible.

11

High Plains

High Plains

L ubbock and Amarillo are the major market cities of the northern portion of the High Plains, which is commonly called "The Panhandle." Throughout the mid-20th century, this area was the state's most prosperous farming region, producing up to a quarter of the world's cotton. At the southern edge of the High Plains are the cities of Midland and Odessa, a.k.a. "The Petroplex." These towns came to prominence as the hub of the most productive oil and gas-drilling area in the vast Permian Basin, so named because it has one of the world's thickest deposits of rocks from the Permian geologic period. Ranching always balanced the boom or bust oil economy of the Permian Basin. Outside of the Midland/Odessa, the population has always been sparse in this vast portion of the High Plains. Midland was so named because it is the halfway point of a rail line between the 600 miles that separated Fort Worth from El Paso.

The region's future hinges on water; its annual rainfall averages a scant 15 to 20 inches. Because no rivers drain the High Plains, rainwater collects in thousands of shallow playa lakes and filters down into underground aquifers that provided irrigation water for acres and acres of cotton and wheat in the Panhandle from the 1930s until the '80s. By that time, the water table of the aquifers had dropped radically as demand outstripped inflow.

According to the Texas Water Development Board, the Ogallala Aquifer, which principally underlies the western portions of Texas, Oklahoma, Kansas and Nebraska, had more than 281.7 million acre-feet of recoverable groundwater in Texas in 1974. It will have been reduced to 76.1 million acre-feet here by 2031. If the trend continues, the area will someday revert to the short grasses that once covered this high, dry region of Texas. The Panhandle's numerous farming communities are already losing population.

Adding to the limitations of water, gardening is made more difficult by temperatures that regularly plunge below zero. A wide range of cold-hardy native wildflowers bloom on the High Plains, but gardeners can forget about incorporating native trees into local landscapes. There aren't any. Supplied with sufficient water, however, the rich loamy soil that is so hospitable to agricultural crops in the northernmost reaches of the High Plains supports a surprising variety of hardy adapted trees and shrubs. While the **Ranching Heritage Center** in Lubbock is a testament to the difficulties pioneers faced in an area devoid of materials for building homes, much less gardens, the **Lubbock Memorial Arboretum** introduces gardeners to a rich variety of drought-tolerant ornamental plants from similar warm summer/cold winter regions of the world.

The Panhandle includes areas of exquisite beauty in its colorful canyons (actually fingers of the Red Rolling Plains) that punctuate this seemingly featureless landscape. South of Lubbock on FM 669 between Post and Gail, you'll encounter some of the state's most dramatic cliff and canyon vistas. Hwy 207 between Silverton and Claude dips down into **Palo Duro Canyon**, and about 100 miles southeast of Amarillo off Hwy 86 is the entrance to **Caprock Canyons State Park**. Opened in 1982, this 15,313.6-acre preserve includes rocky canyons that were home to Native Americans of several cultures dating back more than 10,000 years. Here, badlands dotted with mesquite, cacti and junipers give way to bottom-lands filled with tall grasses, cottonwoods, plum thickets and hackberries where gardeners may find design inspiration. The **Amarillo Botanical Garden** is setting a wonderful example in the High Plains by displaying species adapted to this high, dry environment and promoting sustainable gardening practices.

The southern area of the High Plains is mostly flatland, broken only by draws. Midland and Odessa (with a combined population of about 250,000) have secured a "long-term water supply," met by both underground and surface water sources from reservoirs that contain 65.9 square miles of surface water. Although groundwater is a renewable resource, its reserves replenish relatively slowly. Ecologists and conservation-minded citizens are diligently urging the practice of water conservation throughout the region. One important governmental goal is to attain true sustainability for the region's aquifers, with average groundwater withdrawals not exceeding a rate that can be replenished through recharge. On the private level, Midland's **Sibley Nature Center** is totally dedicated to working in harmony with southwestern ecology, introducing gardeners to a wide range of native shrubs, as well as wildflowers suitable for landscaping. You'll find detailed descriptions of the High Plains' public gardens and nature centers in Chapter Two of *Texas Gardening for the 21st Century*.

Public Gardens and Nature Preserves to Visit

Amarillo (Potter County)

Amarillo Botanical Garden
1400 Streit Dr
Amarillo, Texas 79106
806.352.6513
www.amarillobotanicalgardens.com
Hours: Tues–Fri 9–5, Sat & Sun 10–2 (spring, summer and fall). Closed weekends after Thanksgiving; closed on major holidays.
Admission: $4 (adults), $3 (seniors 60+), $2 (children 2–12), free (children under 2)

Organized in 1954 by the Council of Garden Clubs, this organization is rapidly advancing with a facility master plan for its 3.3 acres in the Harrington Regional Medical Center. The Harrington Fragrance Garden, Butterfly Demonstration Garden and Children's Garden are among the brilliant attractions here. A leader in horticultural therapy, the garden also offers a horticulture library and Lattice Gift Shop. Exhibitions and educational programs are geared to both horticulture and environmental issues.

Directions: From I-40 (west of downtown) take the Coulter St exit north to Wallace. Turn right on Wallace before High Plains Hospital, right on Hagy Dr, then left on Streit.

Hale Center (Hale County)

Bell Park Cacti Garden
FM 1424 at FM 1914
Hale Center, Texas
806.839.2642
Hours: Daily dawn to dark
Admission: free

The late Hershall Bell began this half-acre labor-of-love in the early '60s. More than 350 cacti representing 40 species are on display for all to enjoy.

Directions: The two roads intersect just west of the Hale Center exit off Hwy 27 between Lubbock and Amarillo.

Lubbock (Lubbock County)

Lubbock Memorial Arboretum
4111 University Ave
Lubbock, Texas 79413
806.797.4520
www.lubbockarboretum.org
Hours: Daily dawn to dusk; Interpretative Center: Sat 10–1, Sun 1–4
Admission: free

Designed for both pleasure and education, this arboretum in Clapp Park is a pocket of tranquil beauty with paths, vistas and resting sites. In a region that has no native trees or shrubs, it serves as exhibit space for the ornamental plants that can be grown in the area and a laboratory for studying existing plants and testing and evaluating new plants. The 55-acre site is managed by a private foundation and supported by gifts and memberships. Volunteers staff the Arboretum Interpretive Center. It houses a horticulture library, gift shop and meeting spaces where experts regularly present programs on gardening topics. Guided tours are available.

Directions: From the east side of the Texas Tech campus, take University south to 41st St.

Ranching Heritage Center
Texas Tech University
Lubbock, Texas 79401
806.742.2498
Hours: Tues–Sat 10–5, Sun 1–5
Admission: free

Here, it's not the vegetation that surrounds this fascinating collection of old homes and ranch buildings that's memorable, but rather its scarcity. The 1904 Picket and Sotol House was built with the only materials the people had at hand — stalks of sotol and small cedar pickets. It's held together with mud chinking and roofed with grass. The entire 14-acre site provides a poignant reminder of how difficult it might have been to feed a family on the prairies of the High Plains before the discovery of underground water supplies in the early 1900s. The Center's buildings and windmills, which are drawn from numerous locations on the High Plains, speak not only of the early pioneers' isolation and hardships, but also of our present-day dependency on water resources. It's a history lesson every Texan should appreciate.

Directions: The Center is located next the Texas Tech campus, at the corner of Indiana and 4th St.

Midland (Midland County)

Sibley Environmental Learning Center
1307 East Wadley
Midland, Texas 79705
432.684.6827
www.sibleynaturecenter.org
Hours: Mon–Fri 8–5 or by appointment
Admission: free

"The Llano Estacado boasts an abundance of natural resources," says naturalist Burr Williams. "Unfortunately, rainfall is not one of them." Believing that the conservation of water is of utmost importance to southwestern ecology, this learning center, under the direction of the very knowledgeable Mr. Williams, strongly advocates xeriscaping. And, it provides valuable resources to help residents learn more about this important practice. There are two miles of trails, a pond and a demonstration garden with 80-90 species here. He notes that indicator species from four different regions appear in and around the Midland area, and he is undertaking a capital campaign to enlarge the garden's holdings as well as group plants according to habitat. The building and 0.75 mile trail are completely wheelchair/stroller accessible. In 2008 the Center was the recipient of a large challenge grant from Texas Parks and Wildlife, which will allow the organization to expand the facility and multiply its educational mission in coming years.
Directions: From downtown, go north on Hwy 349, turn east on Wadley.

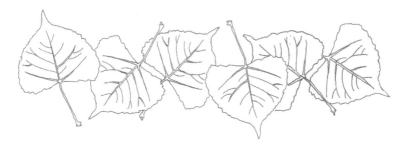

High Plains Resources

Amarillo (Potter County)

Garden Centers

Coulter Gardens and Nursery
4200 South Coulter
Amarillo, Texas 79109
806.359.7432
Hours: Mon–Sat 9:30–5:30

When you enter the "big red barn," you have the feeling that it goes on and on! Everything you could want can be found in this tidy, cheery place. There's a large greenhouse with bedding and container plants, and you'll find a big selection of trees and shrubs drawn from sources throughout the country. We inquired about everything from natives and grasses to water plants and seeds — Coulter's has it! The nursery also carries materials for walks and

(LISTING CONTINUED ON THE NEXT PAGE)

patios, soil and soil amendments, pest management supplies, tools, books, gifts and accessories. Having been in business for 30 years, owners Jim and Warren Reid feel that their clientele is loyal because of the quality of the materials and the helpful customer service." We think we have the most knowledgeable staff in the Panhandle. This claim is supported by the large number of Texas Certified Nursery Professionals who work here!" Sales are seasonal. Coulter's is a rewarding place to shop for your garden or patio.

Love & Son, Inc.
7525 Soncy Rd
Amarillo, Texas 79119
806.352.4667
Hours: Mon–Fri 9–5:30, Sat 9–4; Sun 1–4 (early spring through Mother's Day)

In business since 1945, this nursery is presently being run by third and fourth-generation family members. Love's is not only one of the most complete garden centers in the Panhandle area, but also it provides garden design and installation services. The friendly staff includes a graduate horticulturist, a licensed landscape architect and three licensed irrigators to provide advice as needed. The nursery carries a good selection of large, hardy Texas native trees, such as cedar elms and hackberries. As they say at Love's, "We have the largest selection of trees between Dallas and Denver." The staff will special-order almost any plant to meet customers' needs.

Pete's Greenhouse
7300 Canyon Dr
Amarillo, Texas 79109
806.352.1664
Hours: Mon–Sat 9–6, Sun 1–5

When we arrived at The Gardens at Pete's Greenhouse, we thought we had "died and gone to heaven"...or maybe to Europe! The atmosphere here is warm and welcoming with honeysuckle vines and an arborvitae arch through which you pass to the ponds and a charming selection of gifts, furniture and antiques. According to owner Darren Ruthardt, "We go to market every year to find the best selection of indoor and outdoor garden accessories. Our plants are second to none; we're known as the "plant specialist." Every year, the two greenhouses at Pete's are brimming with 20–30 thousand geraniums as well as other annuals. An addition since our last visit, is the extensive collection of Summer Classics patio furniture. Inside, there are tools and books, as well as friendly service and advice. What a lovely place to shop!

Sutherlands Lumber & Home Center
4717 South Washington
Amarillo, Texas 79110
806.373.3057
Hours: Mon–Sat 7:30–8pm

The garden center at Sutherlands is known for plants that require little water and are well adapted to the area, as well as for very reasonable prices. In addition, there are hardy trees and shrubs, tropicals, ornamental grasses and a lot of vines. You will find annuals and a vast array of perennials, some of which are quite unusual. And, the geraniums are real stars! Soil amendments, pest control supplies and compost are also available. Since much of Sutherlands' inventory is supplied by a local grower, you can be assured of healthy, hardy plants.

Garden Furnishings

Patio & Fireplace Shop
6018 Canyon Expressway
Amarillo, Texas 79109
806.352.2031
Hours: Mon–Sat 9–5:30

The Patio Shop offers a very attractive display of patio furniture and much more, including friendly and knowledgeable service. Homecrest, Brown Jordan, Winston, O.W. Lee, Meadowcraft, Woodard and Kingsley-Bate are just some of the furniture lines represented. You will also find statuary, fountains, planters, barbecue equipment (wood and gas), bird feeders, cushions, umbrellas, baker's racks and other outdoor or garden room accessories. As the name suggests, this company is into year-round comfort.

Canyon (Randall County)

Specialty Nurseries

Canyon's Edge Plants
11691 West Country Club Rd
Canyon, Texas 79015
806.670.5736
www.canyonsedgeplants.com
Hours: Fri & Sat 9–5 (April and May only)

For 11 years, Neal Hinders has been growing a wide array of native and other xeric plants. You can't go wrong with his hardy stock! His website allows you to print a complete plant list, which includes several varieties of columbine, prairie clover, butterfly bush, penstemon, salvia, veronica and much more. These are perennial species suitably tough for the Panhandle's tough climate. Although open only two months of the year, you can also find him at the Amarillo Botanical Gardenfest for the annual Plant Sale the first weekend in May. *Directions: Take Buffalo Stadium exit from I-27, from overpass go 3.0 miles west on West Country Club Rd to intersection of Hope Rd. Neal is 0.125 miles south on a private dirt road.*

CH 11

Lubbock (Lubbock County)

Garden Centers

Little Red Riding Hood
4006 34th St
Lubbock, Texas 79410
806.795.4834
www.littlerednursery.com
Hours: Mon–Sat 9–6 (open later in spring and during Christmas)

Anna Johnson, who assumed ownership of Little Red Riding Hood with husband Aric four years ago, is a real boon to Lubbock gardeners. She knows exactly which plants will grow beautifully in the harsh West Texas climate without depleting the water supply. The nursery, which started out in an old gas station, now occupies almost a city block in downtown Lubbock and carries native and well-adapted plants as well as tropical houseplants and orchids. As one writer reported, "Walking through the nursery during spring and summer resembles a stroll through a rainbow. Vibrant colors tempt you at every turn." Organic products can be found here along with tools and garden accessories, most notably a fabulous collection of containers from China, England and Italy. Anna conducts free gardening seminars, and the website is an absolute wealth of information and gardening tips.

Mary Lee Gardens
6702 82nd St
Lubbock, Texas 79424
806.798.1444
Hours: Mon–Sat 9–6

Mary Lee, the original owner of Little Red Riding Hood, left that business in the capable hands of daughter and son-in-law and moved out of midtown to a more spacious location. Here, she and son Mark Lee have three greenhouses and nine wonderful display gardens to spark the imagination. There is a good selection of trees, shrubs, annuals and hanging baskets, but the real stars of the show are the perennials. You will also find sod, pest control supplies and tools. Friendly service and artistically arranged plants guarantee a very pleasant shopping experience at Mary Lee's.

Sparkman's Nursery
11109 Slide Rd
Lubbock, Texas 79424
806.794.3614
www.sparkmansnursery.com
Hours: Mon–Sat 9–6

Sparkman's is an immaculate, easy and relaxing place to shop. According to the Sparkmans, "We are the only nursery in this area where a retail customer can find such a large inventory of green goods. Our inventory turns quickly, and this enables us to keep fresh stock on hand at all times." There are 18 acres of trees (many of them very large), an excellent stock of shrubs, grasses, herbs, bulbs, seasonal color and ground covers. The company also offers a large selection of garden accessories — pots, fountains, statuary, garden benches, arbors, bird baths and garden tools. Wander through the gift shop, Serendipity Square, and you'll find everything from houseplants, books, and furniture to candles, mirrors, rock fountains and much more. Sparkman's carries soil amendments, pest control supplies, paving materials, lattice and beautiful, moss-covered landscape boulders, as well. It has, in fact, almost anything you could want.

TG Trees Nursery & Garden Center
11706 CR 1800
Lubbock, Texas 79424
806.794.6766
Hours: Mon–Sat 9–6; Sun 12–6 (spring)

With over 70,000 square feet of greenhouses, TG Trees was ablaze with colorful annuals and perennials when we visited. Started in 1984, this friendly, family-owned nursery boasts of "the most certified staff in the area." The nursery carries a wide range of plant material as well as soil, soil amendments, organic supplies and materials for walks, patios and walls. The company also builds ponds and provides water plants and pond supplies. Some of the services offered include landscape design, maintenance and installation and tree and lawn care. In addition, you will find garden tools, books, furniture and accessories. Custom potting, delivery, seminars and tours are also available. Customers are sure to find just what they need (or can't live without) at TG Trees.

Directions: TG Trees is at the intersection of 118th and South Frankfort.

Tom's Tree Place
5104 34th St
Lubbock, Texas 79410
806.799.3677
www.tomstreeplace.com
Hours: Mon–Sat 8–6

With four landscape architects on staff, Tom's Tree Place generates synergy between its nursery, design and installation services. This design-oriented company, established in 1950, is owned and operated by the Scarborough family, which includes their friendly Labradors. According to Alex Scarborough, "We promote natives, and all the plant material here is for outdoor use. With 30 acres of growing space in the Lubbock area, we have a vast selection of specimen trees (the specialty of the nursery)." You'll also find a full line of shrubs and ground covers, as well as seasonal color, seeds and vegetables. There are also lots of tools, garden supplies and soils on hand. Customers are encouraged to help themselves to a "prescribed care guide schedule," which contains month-by-month tips. And don't miss the season for Tom's fresh, homegrown pecans!

Specialty Nurseries

Ivey Gardens
1318 East Municipal Dr
Lubbock, Texas 79423
806.744.4839
Hours: Mon–Sat 9–5

   This is a jewel! Upon entering Ivey Gardens, one is overwhelmed with seasonal color in flats and hanging baskets. It seems to go on and on! They do indeed sell 40,000 flats of bedding plants yearly and 10,000 hanging baskets. They also carry ground covers, shrubs, tropicals, vegetable starts, herbs and natives among others. Says Mark Ivey, "We carry plants that are homegrown and, therefore, acclimatized. We don't carry plants shipped in trucks, so they don't go through shock. People come back year after year because our plants do well for them." Texas Tech horticultural classes come by to look and learn, and advice is freely given to all customers.

Directions: Ivey Gardens is near the airport off Loop 289 on Municipal Dr where it intersects Martin Luther King (formerly Quirt.)

Garden Furnishings

Spears Furniture
7004 Salem
Lubbock, Texas 79405
806.747.3401
www.spearsfurniture.com
Hours: Mon–Fri 10–8, Sat 10–6, Sun 1–5

   Spears Furniture has been in business since 1950, and the main showroom occupies 32,000 square feet. During the spring and summer months, an additional 15,000-square-foot building houses the outdoor furniture display. You'll find Woodward wrought iron, Martin Smith teak, Lexington outdoor wicker, as well as furnishings from Carolina Forge (a less expensive division of Woodward), Kessler, Uwharrie Adirondack and Atlantic Beach & Leisure. David Spears says, "We have very well-trained staff members who really know their furniture and are of great assistance to every customer. We are happy to special order pieces at no additional charge. 'Adding to the quality of life' is the way we like to think of Spears." Look for sales advertised in the local paper and on TV.

Midland (Midland County)

Garden Centers

Alldredge Gardens
3300 North Fairgrounds Rd
Midland, Texas 79710
432.682.4500
www.alldredgegardens.com
Hours: Mon–Sat 9–6, Sun 10–5

   Alldredge Gardens is just as wonderful as we remembered it...only more so! The Permian Basin's largest complete garden center (in business for 30 years) occupies over 100 acres with 14 greenhouses in which most of the plants are grown. There are 11 acres of full-grown balled and burlapped trees, and Alldredge carries perennials, herbs, tropicals, cacti, hanging baskets, as well as water plants, pond supplies and fish. With a landscape architect on staff, the company provides landscape design, renovation and installation and stocks paving and retaining wall materials. It also has residential and commercial accounts for spraying, feeding and pruning. You will find a large selection of garden furniture by such fine manufacturers as O. W. Lee, Brown Jordan, Lane Venture, Castelle, Kellsler, Tropitone and Hanamint and an outstanding array of accessories. Since our last visit, owner David Alldredge has added the Café at the Gardens, which is open for lunch Monday–Saturday from 11–2. A waterfall, koi pond and lush tropical plantings provide an exotic backdrop for a delicious meal. Alldredge's is a most impressive operation and a treat to visit!

La Casa Verde Nursery, Inc.
2615 North Midland Dr
Midland, Texas 79707
432.520.2144
Hours: Mon–Sat 9–6, Sun 11–5; closed Christmas Eve–Jan 1.

   "We hope to serve you!" is the motto here. Says manager Rick French, "We focus on quality, neatness and service. Since we grow many of our bedding plants, we are able to provide quality care. Our greenhouses are greatly enjoyed by our customers during the growing season. Every customer can be a good friend, and that's the way we treat them! If we don't have the answer to your question, we'll do our best to get it for you." He added that La Casa Verde acclimatizes its plants, ensuring a better success rate for the gardener. It also offers complete landscaping services. You can find almost any plant that performs well in the area, plus all the soils, pest management supplies and books needed to improve your garden. There's a good selection of furniture, fountains, statuary and a large supply of clay and concrete pottery. To make a visit to this beautiful nursery even more fun, there's always something on sale!

Manning's Garden Center
2820 West Golf Course Rd
Midland, Texas 79701
432.682.8533
Hours: Mon–Sat 8:30–5:30

   Some of the descriptive comments you'll hear about Manning's Garden Center are, "peaceful, restful atmosphere," "nooks and crannies of interest" and "charming and appealing." We agreed with all of the above! Also offering a full service florist, this nursery

(LISTING CONTINUED ON THE NEXT PAGE)

(CONTINUED)

has been family-owned since the early '40s. Although Manning's is not a large nursery and only partially wheelchair/stroller accessible, you'll find a great variety of healthy trees, shrubs, wonderful tropicals and other plants from which to choose. As Tom Manning told us, "We provide an especially good selection of bedding plants, and we assist our customers with a 'color plan' for beds or containers." You will also find the unusual — bromeliads and orchids not found elsewhere, a wonderful selection of baskets (including the larger, moss-lined ones,) and a very creative assortment of gifts and accessories as well as books and Alan Simpson cast aluminum tools. An annual July clearance sale is advertised in the local paper, and Tom often speaks to garden clubs.

Specialty Nurseries

Garden View
7112 West Hwy 80
Midland, Texas 79706
432.563.2684

Hours: Mon–Sat 9–7 (spring), 9–5 (fall), Sun 12–5 (all year)

Jorge and Silvia Hernandez have owned this specialty nursery for 20 years. They specialize in bougainvilleas, hanging baskets, bedding plants (80% of which are grown on site) and tropical houseplants. Christmas is really ablaze at Garden View with the 10,000 poinsettias they grow each year. A very special feature offered at this nursery is winter boarding for your plants.

Sandy's Nursery
302 South Weatherford
Midland, Texas 79701
432.687.7097

Hours: Mon–Sat 8–7

Sandy's is a small nursery that stocks oak trees, shrubs, annuals, perennials, cacti tropicals and hanging baskets. Owner Homero Galindo grows his own fan palms, and the nursery carries a large variety of palm trees. You will also find soil and soil amendments, garden accessories, plus wrought iron and concrete furniture.

Odessa (Ector County)

Garden Centers

La Casa Verde Nursery, Inc.
3600 Andrews Hwy
Odessa, Texas 79762
432.550.7000

Hours: Mon–Sat 9–6, Sun 11–5; closed Christmas Eve–Jan 1

The really good news for Odessa is that La Casa Verde opened a second store here in April of 2008. As manager Rick French told us, "It is still a work in progress, but we have twice the display and parking space. We carry the same quality plants, offer the same services and uphold the same high standards as the Midland store."

Specialty Nurseries

Down to Earth Home & Garden Store
622 Dale St
Odessa, Texas 79761
432.582.2555
Hours: Mon–Sat 10–5:30

Jeff and Darlene Wells specialize in natives bought from growers in Austin and Phoenix. As Jeff explains, "We carry a variety of natives, but they all grow really well in this area." At Down to Earth, you will also find tropical houseplants, cacti, container plants and hanging baskets. When asked about organics, Jeff said, "We have always been organic, although I will admit to Roundup® when all else fails." In addition, there are garden tools and apparel as well as gardening books and accessories. Down to Earth offers landscape design and installation, and assistance is provided for wheelchairs in less accessible areas.

12
Trans-Pecos

Trans-Pecos

The Pecos River Valley more or less forms the eastern boundary of this region of desert and mountains. El Paso is its major market area, but the towns of Alpine, Fort Stockton, Pecos and Monahans also serve farmers and ranchers who live in this most sparsely populated part of the state. There are thirty named mountain ranges in the Trans-Pecos. Between the mountains, the terrain is mostly sandy basins and salty playas, which are shallow lakes created when rain leaches salts and other minerals from the mountain walls. After the water evaporates, the playas become salt flats. The dry, hot basins support desert plants and the tough shrubs that are called chaparral. Only a few halophytes (salt-growers) can survive in the playas.

Most of the region falls within the Chihuahuan Desert, but this landscape bears no resemblance to the Sahara. Plant life in the Trans-Pecos is diverse, amazingly abundant and uniformly tough. Average annual rainfall ranges from only 12.2 inches in Pecos County to a mere 7.8 inches in El Paso County. The "rainy season" is July, August and September. The scant rainfall comes in sudden cloudbursts that cause flash floods and quickly runs off. Nature trails, desert gardens and scenic highways at or near several of the region's National and State Parks offer easy access to the natural wonders of the Trans-Pecos.

Big Bend National Park at the region's southern tip draws visitors from all over the world to enjoy the spectacular scenery of the Rio Grande and the Chisos Mountains' diverse flora and fauna. Five separate life zones exist in Big Bend alone. Willows and cottonwoods hug the river. Desert vegetation inhabits the flats, and grasslands cover the foothills. Woodlands beginning above the 4,500-feet level consist mostly of piñon pines, junipers and oaks. On the high, cool north sides of the Chisos mountains, you'll find trees more typical of the Rocky Mountains. Altogether it is a fragile environment, easily damaged.

Some of the most remote and rugged terrain in the Southwest can be found in **Big Bend Ranch State Park** between Presidio and Lajitas. This park encompasses two mountain ranges with ancient extinct volcanoes, steep canyons, waterfalls and thousands of acres of Chihuahuan Desert wilderness. It's home to diverse and rare species. The scenic drive along The River Rd (Texas FM 170), which follows the meanders of the Rio Grande, is among the most beautiful in the nation. Thirty miles of hiking and backpacking trails are accessible at trailheads along highway. This park can be accessed through **Barton Warnock Environmental Education Center**, where you'll discover a world-renowned desert garden.

In the northern reaches of the Trans-Pecos, moist canyons and dry, rocky mountains draw numerous nature-loving travelers to the **Guadalupe Mountains National Park**. The Guadalupe Mountains are the limestone remains of a Permian sea fossil reef. Within the park, you'll not only discover four of the highest peaks in the state, but also plant life that includes ponderosa pine, Douglas fir, ferns and abundant spring wildflowers. A stream that flows through McKittrick Canyon nurtures plants from several habitats. There are conifers from the mountains above, desert plants from below and several plant species that grow nowhere else in the world, including Texas madrone, an endangered tree that does not thrive outside its present range. Walnuts and big-tooth maples are remnants of faraway forests. The park is not developed as a recreation area, but for serious hikers, it is a joy to behold. Autumn colors are spectacular!

Between the Chisos and Guadalupe Mountains lie the Davis Mountains. These mountains were formed by volcanic activity around 65 million years ago. Their fertile soils support vegetation different from rest of the Trans-Pecos area. Winters are often below freezing in this mile-high landscape, and visitors may be treated to an occasional snowfall. Summer days are hot and dry, but the nights are cool. A scenic loop west of Fort Davis (Hwys 118 and 166) takes you to McDonald Observatory, Madera Canyon and **Davis Mountains State Park**. Scattered stands of ponderosa and the more common piñon pine, mixed with oak and juniper, cover the higher elevations. During wet years, the park abounds in wildflowers. Emory oak is predominant along Keesey Creek. Scarlet bouvardia, little-leaf leadtree, evergreen and fragrant sumac, Apache plum, little walnut, tree cholla, Torrey yucca, catclaw acacia, and agarito are among the several flowering shrubs. Four miles south of Fort Davis on Hwy 118 is the **Chihuahuan Desert Nature Center and Botanical Gardens**, which also offers hiking and nature study.

In El Paso, **Franklin Mountains State Park** takes you into the largest urban wilderness park in the nation! The largest sustained mountain range in Texas rises here to an elevation of 7192 feet, some 3000 feet above the City of El Paso. For thousands of years, native peoples, soldiers, priests, traders, gold-seekers and adventurers passed through the gap known as Paso del Norte in an endless procession of expansion, settlement, raiding, and conquest. Early native groups left colorful pictographs and deep mortar pits (used to grind seeds) in rock outcrops near scattered water sources. When developers began carving roads into these almost pristine mountains in the 1970s, it became obvious that its scenic, ecological and historic features should be protected. To the satisfaction of conservationists across the nation, the Texas legislature acquired the Franklin Mountains as a state park.

Year-round running water from natural springs attracts abundant wildlife here. Observant visitors may even catch a glimpse of a cougar. The skies are home to golden eagles, a variety of hawks, the occasional falcon, and at night, bats and owls. Existing vegetation is typical of the Chihuahuan Desert, with lechuguilla, sotol, ocotillo, several yuccas, and numerous cacti. This is the only known location in Texas for a number of plant species, including the Southwest barrel cactus.

The Monahans Sandhills, unlike true desert dunes, are the remains of a Permian sea. **Monahans Sandhills State Park** contains one of the largest oak forests in the United States. However, its trees seldom grow more than waist-high! Shinoak (*Quercus havardii*) is not a stunted form of a larger tree, but rather a plant that normally stands less than four feet at full maturity and bears an abundance of large acorns. This park is only a small portion of a dune field that extends from south of Monahans into New Mexico. Fresh water occurs at shallow depths within the dune field, and most of the dunes are stabilized by vegetation, although many are still active, growing and changing shape in response to seasonal, prevailing winds. Some reach up to 70 feet in height.

The Stockton Plateau, which is south of the dunes between the Chisos Mountains and the Pecos River, is technically the westernmost section of the Edwards Plateau and therefore not actually part of the Trans-Pecos. In this area, it's not just the lack of rainfall that limits vegetation to cacti and chaparral, but also the absence of soil. Where the Pecos and the Rio Grande come together in Val Verde County, cave-dwelling people lived for thousands of years, harvesting wild plants and game, and leaving a record of their lives in cave paintings. Strategic stops for early travelers included Comanche Springs near Fort Stockton, Balmorhea Springs between Pecos and Alpine and Hueco Tanks (now **Hueco Tanks State Park**) near El Paso where natural rock basins store precious water. The muddy mineral-laden Pecos River does not offer particularly good drinking water. Even today, I-10 follows the route of reliable water sources west to El Paso (The Pass).

Lack of moisture and extreme summer heat combine to severely limit agricultural pursuits in the Trans-Pecos. Some counties produce no crops at all, but most of the region is suitable for raising cattle, sheep and goats. Where irrigation water is available, apples, pecans, grapes and onions thrive, especially in the sandy loam soils of the Pecos Valley and along the Rio Grande. Pecos is renowned for its cantaloupes. Deep volcanic soils around Marfa and Alpine allow profitable ranching. Spanish mission lands within the city limits of El Paso have been in constant cultivation since 1682. However, rapidly growing El Paso and Juarez, which have a combined population of 1,800,000, are now consuming water much faster than nature can replenish it.

Although it boasts a mild winter climate, gardening is especially complex in this region. Most of the area's soils are extremely alkaline and high in salts due to the scarcity of rainfall, (7.2-inches per year, on average.) Soil types within the Trans-Pecos region range from the sandy, alkaline soils of the basins to the acidic soils of the Davis Mountain area, which weathered from volcanic rock.

The wide range of soil types supports a surprisingly wide variety of native plant life. All of it is, by necessity, drought resistant — creosote bush, yucca, cenizo, sand sagebrush, ocotillo and several species of short, sparse grasses. Unfortunately, right yellow-blooming broomweed and several other poisonous plants have invaded depleted rangeland. The occasional rains bring out colorful desert marigolds, blackfoot daisies, ocotillo, mountain laurel, a variety of blooming cacti and big, beautiful Chisos bluebonnets. The mountainous areas are clothed in piñon pine, juniper and other vegetation not found elsewhere in the state.

You'll find detailed descriptions of the region's public gardens and nature centers in Chapter Two of *Texas Gardening for the 21st Century*. With the combined resources of The University of Texas at El Paso's **Centennial Museum and Chihuahuan Desert Gardens**, **Texas AgriLife Research Center** at El Paso and the new **El Paso Desert Botanical Gardens** local gardeners are being exposed to the region's botanical treasures. There's no lack of inspiration and information here!

Public Gardens and Nature Preserves to Visit

El Paso (El Paso County)

Centennial Museum and Chihuahuan Desert Gardens
University of Texas at El Paso
500 West University
El Paso, Texas 79902
915.747.5565
www.museum.utep.edu
Hours: Daily dawn to dusk
Admission: free

This botanical garden is dedicated to the flora of the Chihuahuan Desert and adjacent regions in the United States and Mexico. Opened in 1999, it currently contains over 625 different species of plants, one of the largest displays of Chihuahuan flora in the world. It is cultivated as a series of "theme" gardens with water features and designed to show the attractiveness of native desert plants for landscaping. The gardens are the result of the vision and hard work of Wynn Anderson, the Centennial Museum Botanical Curator. The Museum and Gardens sponsor a number of educational activities for both children and adults. The FloraFest takes place every year on the last weekend in April, with a presentation on native plants on Friday night, followed by a sale of native plants on Saturday and Sunday. Volunteers support these and other Museum and Gardens activities. The gardens serve as a resource for informal and formal botanical and environmental education. The organization has an extensive database of plant images and associated information.

Directions: From I-10, take the UT El Paso/Shuster exit. The Centennial Museum building is located at the corner of University and Wiggins on the campus of the University.

El Paso Desert Botanical Gardens
4200 Doniphan Rd
El Paso, Texas 79922
[ph] 915.584.0563
www.elpasobotanicalgardens.org
Hours: 10-2 Sat and Sun only, year-round
Admission: $2 (adults), $1 (children 2-12, seniors and military)

New to Keystone Heritage Park (an archeological site that dates back about 4,500 years) is this extremely environmentally friendly series of gardens. Massive native rock walls enclose the gardens, providing shelter from the wind, and rock retaining walls of varied heights separate the walkways from planting areas that feature colorful flower displays, a butterfly garden, culinary garden and koi pond. Heavy overhead beams throughout suggest Old World pergolas. This astoundingly sophisticated two-acre garden can be credited to a huge cadre of volunteers and generous funding by The Junior League of El Paso and the Rotary Club.

The entrance opens into a plaza with a square pool and central fountain. The Cactus and Succulent Garden showcases desert plants, demonstrating how this diverse group can be adapted to a variety of garden styles. The Formal Gardens prove that native and hardy adapted plants can be used to create a traditional garden. A Healing Garden displays plants historically used for medicinal purposes. In the Sensory Garden, soft and fragrant plants, beautiful mosaics and a water feature stimulate the senses. A pit house maze and an archeological dig site are

(LISTING CONTINUED ON THE NEXT PAGE)

CH 12

(CONTINUED)

favorites in the Children's Garden. Beyond a gate on the north side of the garden is The Keystone Wetlands, one of the last remaining wetland sites that once lined the Rio Grande. The Audubon Society has observed more than 200 bird species there, including five species considered rare.

Texas AgriLife Research Center at El Paso
1380 A & M Cir
El Paso, Texas 79927
915.859.9111
Hours: Center: Mon–Fri 8–5; Gardens: Daily dawn to dusk
Admission: free

You'll find a broad spectrum of native and adapted plants (about 140 species) suitable for El Paso landscapes in the demonstration gardens here. The organization has seven different turf plots going, and its gardens exhibit walkways and other hardscapes, as well as good mulching techniques. Scientists at the El Paso Center are developing technologies and methods to improve water-use efficiency, increase water supplies and protect water quality, and the Center has received international recognition for its research. The small garden provides a model for xeriscaping with plants native to the Chihuahua desert and adapted plants from different regions. Many colorful flowers, shrubs and trees thrive here, demonstrating that with a correct landscape plan, regional gardens can be "watertight" and beautiful, unlike a traditional landscape, which can account for 40–60% of homeowners' summer water use.
Directions: From I-10, take Exit 34. A & M Cir is on the SE quadrant of the intersection. Look for the green sign that says Texas A & M Research Center. It's in a brown building.

Fort Davis (Jeff Davis County)

Chihuahuan Desert Nature Center & Botanical Gardens
SR 118
Fort Davis, Texas 79734
432.364.2499
www.cdri.org
Hours: Mon–Sat 9–5; closed on major holidays.
Admission: $5 (adults), $4 (seniors 65 and over), free (children under 12)

The diverse flora of the desert is well served by the nature trails and cactus garden at this facility of the Chihuahuan Desert Research Institute. The organization sponsors field trips and seminars to help researchers and naturalists better understand the fragile desert ecology. The Nature Center offers an intimate setting to experience the diversity of the desert region. Visitors will find canyon springs, stately madrones, Montezuma quail and many other hidden treasures. Also included are a cactus and succulent greenhouse, a 20-acre botanical garden, indoor and outdoor interpretive exhibits and easy to moderately strenuous hiking. Seeing such an array of drought-resistant, cold-tolerant plants should provide inspiration to gardeners in the area and awaken Texans who garden in less difficult climes to the inherent beauty and untapped usefulness of native desert plants. The Institute's annual Native Plant Sale and pre-sale seminars attract enthusiastic crowds each April. A bookstore/gift shop dispenses information as well as garden-related merchandise. The Institute invites membership and publishes a semiannual magazine, Chihuahuan Desert Discovery.
Directions: The facility is located off State Rd 118, 4.0 miles south of Fort Davis.

Langtry (Val Verde County)

Judge Roy Bean Visitor Center
Hwy 90 W/Loop 25 (Torres Ave)
Langtry, Texas 78871
432.291.3340
Hours: Daily 8–5; 8–6 (summer)
Admission: free

Commemorating Judge Roy Bean's court, which established "Law West of the Pecos" in 1882, the combined saloon, billiard parlor and courthouse has been embellished with a colorful cactus and native shrub garden, complete with an Eclipse windmill. TxDOT supplies a plant list complete with medicinal and other practical uses. From the fishhook cactus that Indians used to catch fish to the creosote bush used for deodorizing skunk traps and treating arthritis, the plant descriptions are as fascinating as the historical lore that surrounds this place, which is billed as, "The Ghost Town with a Visitor's Center."
Directions: Langtry is off Hwy 90, about 60.0 miles northwest of Del Rio. If you find your way to Langtry (population: 30), you can't miss it.

Terlingua (Brewster County)

Barton Warnock Environmental Education Center
FM 170
Terlingua, Texas 79852
432.424.3327
www.tpwd.state.tx.us/spdest/findadest/parks/barton_warnock
Hours: Daily 8–4:30
Admission: $3 (13 and older), free (children under 13); free to holders of Texas State Parks Pass and Texas Parklands Passport (Bluebonnet Pass)

Built in 1982 as the Lajitas Museum Desert Gardens, this 99-acre facility was purchased by Texas Parks and Wildlife in October 1990. It was renamed to honor Dr. Barton Warnock, former chairman of the biology department at Sul Ross State University, whose *Wildflowers of the Big Bend Country* remains the definitive guidebook. The Center, which serves as the eastern entrance station to Big Bend Ranch State Park, presents an archeological, historical, and natural history profile of the Big Bend region. The sales area contains a wide assortment of books and other informational material. There's a research library and over two acres of Chihuahuan Desert plants in a self-guided botanical garden. Group tours can be arranged.
Directions: The Center is located on Hwy 170, on the eastern edge of Big Bend Ranch State Park, 1.0 mile east of Lajitas.

Trans-Pecos Resources

Alpine (Brewster County)

Garden Centers

Morrison True Value Hardware
301 North 5th St
Alpine, Texas 79830
915.837.2061
Hours: Mon–Sat 8–7, Sun 1–5

Serving as the "shopping headquarters for the Big Bend," Morrison's stocks over 27,000 items. You will find almost anything you need in its garden center, from plants to books, tools, building materials and gifts. As Bob Ward will tell you, "Help is just around the corner!" The plant material includes container-grown trees and shrubs, and a particular favorite is the elderica pine. A 720-square-foot greenhouse holds colorful year-round bedding and container plants. The "Just Ask" rental departments carries tillers, seeder, edgers, aerators and more. Morrison's holds an annual "Start-up Sale" the 2nd Saturday in April and the bargains are terrific! There's always someone on hand to offer advice.

One Way Plant Nursery
308 West Avenue E
Alpine, Texas 79830
432.837.1117
Hours: Mon 9–5 (closed at lunchtime), Tues–Fri 9–5:30, Sat 9–5

Surrounded by large old trees, this nursery's building has been around since the late '20s and, at some point, was even a gas station. In 2000, Alice Stevens transformed it into One Way Plant Nursery where she caters to a clientele gardening in three different zones. More than half of her stock is native or well-adapted trees, shrubs and perennials; among the plants are piñon and alligator juniper trees, agave, various cacti and much more. Drought-tolerant and deer-resistant plants are always in high demand! You will also find roses, bedding plants and hanging baskets as well as a good selection of pots and containers. The nursery fills a lot of special orders, mostly for people seeking rare natives. Alice carries only organic products including composts and soils. We couldn't resist asking about the nursery's name; One Way is on a one-way street. She is definitely a serious gardener with a great sense of humor!

El Paso (El Paso County)

Garden Centers

Casa Verde Nursery of El Paso
77 Fountain St
El Paso, Texas 79912
915.584.1149
Hours: Mon–Sat 8:30–5:30, Sun 10:30–5 (closed Sun in Jan)

This charming neighborhood nursery not only carries lots of healthy plants, but it is also crammed with a cheerful mélange of pots, tools, and garden accessories. The real star of the show is the seasonal color, with pond plants popular as well. Tree, shrubs and produce are grown at the wholesale location, and the nursery stocks a large supply of organic products. There is always something different going on at Casa Verde! You will find pumpkins in the fall and vine-ripened tomatoes from June until Halloween. And, Christmas is really special with a vast display of trees and poinsettias, as well as custom-made wreaths and roping. The nursery offers landscape design, installation and maintenance services, and holds sales in January and July.

Eastside Discount Nursery
8423 North Loop
El Paso, Texas 79907
915.591.3333

9435 Dyer St
El Paso, Texas 79924
915.755.3333
Hours: Daily 8–5:30 (both locations)

In 2000, Steve Zimmerly bought this nursery, founded in 1946 by the Black family, and he has since opened a second store. Eastside Discount Nursery stocks all of the landscape plants that do well in the El Paso area, as well as tropical houseplants. In addition to carrying Ferti-lome products, Steve packages his own brand of fertilizers. You will find a large selection of appealing glazed pots from Viet Nam in all shapes, sizes and colors. When asked about the "Discount" in the nursery's name, Steve explained, "With our acreage, we can carry more inventory than even the 'big box' stores and sell for less." There are bargains to be had here and healthy plants as well.

Nancy's Nursery, Plants & Things
11355 Pellicano Dr
El Paso, Texas 79936
915.598.3434
Hours: Mon-Sat 8-5, Sun 10-4

In business at this location for 18 years, Nancy Corbin-Tardis has developed quite a following for her numerous customer services. In addition to a complete garden center that carries "everything imaginable," she offers design, installation and maintenance services and even makes "house calls" to diagnose plant problems! Her gift shop is full of unusual pottery, fountains and garden art, and the nursery is well known for its gorgeously planted pots, so Nancy is often asked to decorate for outdoor parties.

Specialty Nurseries

Desertland Nursery & Pottery
11306 Gateway Blvd E
El Paso, Texas 79927
915.858.1130
Hours: Daily 8–5

Specializing in cacti and other dry climate plants, Desertland is both a retail nursery and a mail order company, Aztekaki (http://aztekakti.homestead.com). It carries a nice variety of natives, including several acacias and scrub sages, desert willow, Mexican bird of paradise and numerous cacti. The cacti are also available as seeds. You will also find a selection of attractive glazed Mexican pottery here in various sizes, shapes and colors.

Fort Davis (Jeff Davis County)

Garden Furnishings

Chihuahuan Desert Research Institute
Texas Hwy 118
Fort Davis, Texas 79734
432.364.2499

The gift shop at the Chihuahuan Desert Research Institute (four miles south of Fort Davis) carries wind chimes, birdfeeders, nature-related books and cacti and other native seeds. There is also an annual plant sale as well as a Cacti Festival/Sale. For the Institute's complete listing, see page 260.

Index